DRESS AND HABITS OF THE PEOPLE OF ENGLAND

VOLUME ONE

From a M.S. of the thirteenth Century.

A

COMPLETE VIEW

OF THE

DRESS AND HABITS

OF THE

PEOPLE OF ENGLAND,

FROM THE

ESTABLISHMENT OF THE SAXONS IN BRITAIN TO THE PRESENT TIME:

ILLUSTRATED BY ENGRAVINGS

TAKEN FROM THE MOST AUTHENTIC REMAINS OF ANTIQUITY.

TO WHICH IS PREFIXED

AN INTRODUCTION,

CONTAINING A GENERAL

DESCRIPTION OF THE ANCIENT HABITS IN USE AMONG MANKIND,

FROM THE

EARLIEST PERIOD OF TIME TO THE CONCLUSION OF THE SEVENTH CENTURY.

BY

JOSEPH STRUTT.

A NEW AND IMPROVED EDITION, WITH CRITICAL AND EXPLANATORY NOTES,

BY

J. R. PLANCHÉ, ESQ. F.S.A.

AUTHOR OF THE HISTORY OF BRITISH COSTUME, ETC.

VOL. I.

LONDON:
THE TABARD PRESS LIMITED
1970

First printed 1842
This reprint edition published 1970

S.B.N. 90195101 3

Reproduced and Printed by
Redwood Press Limited
Trowbridge & London

TO

HIS GRACE,

GEORGE GRANVILLE LEVESON-GOWER,

DUKE OF SUTHERLAND, K.G.

&c. &c. &c.

THESE VOLUMES

ARE,

WITH PERMISSION,

MOST RESPECTFULLY DEDICATED

BY

HIS GRACE'S

MUCH OBLIGED AND VERY OBEDIENT HUMBLE SERVANT,

J. R. PLANCHÉ.

PREFACE.

Nearly half a century has elapsed since the learned, patient, and industrious author of these valuable volumes placed them before the public, with a modest address, in which he stated the difficulties he had encountered, and named as a principal point in favour of his work, the novelty of its subject, there being at that time none such in the English language, "at least, none sufficiently extensive and regular to display the prevalent fashions of our ancestors, through every century."[1]

The same claim to the patronage of the Public, may still be made for his labours. With respect to the armour and weapons of the middle ages, the works of that distinguished antiquary, Sir Samuel Meyrick, have superseded all former speculative and imperfect essays on the subject, and "the Monumental Effigies of Great Britain," by the late Mr. Stothard, unrivalled for correctness of drawing and beauty of execution, have greatly contributed to the knowledge we previously possessed of those unquestionable authorities: but notwithstanding the great improvement in taste and the consequent increase of anxiety on the part of English Authors, Painters, Sculptors, and Actors, to acquire sufficient knowledge of costume, to avoid committing such errors as disgraced the works of many of their greatest predecessors, no publication has subsequently appeared in England so full of information on the general subject of costume, as the "Complete View of the Dress and Habits of the People of England," by the indefatigable and ingenuous Joseph Strutt. The "many errors" in it, of the existence of which he candidly expressed his conviction, were nearly all caused by the peculiar circumstances under which its pages were hurried through the press; and do not affect in any way the reputation for judgment or research of the author. Here and there Mr. Strutt has been misled by faith in the dates assigned to his authorities by others. But con-

[1] Vide original "Address to the Public."

sidering, as he remarks, that he laboured "as it were in the dark," and that he was in fact the pioneer of succeeding Antiquaries, we have only to wonder that so few errors should be discoverable. The principal were (as usual in works of this description, however carefully printed,) in the numerical references to the books, chapters, verses or lines of the host of authors quoted, and I beg to premise, that having simply undertaken to write notes for this Edition, there may be, although I have corrected all that came in my way, many still to rectify. I have now only to return my best thanks to Sir Henry Ellis and Sir Frederick Madden, of the British Museum, for the kind assistance I have received from them, as regards both accommodation and information.

J. R. PLANCHÉ.

December, 1841.

ADDRESS TO THE PUBLIC.

I SHALL not pretend to apologise for the introduction of this work to the inspection of the Public. If it possesses a sufficient portion of merit to recommend itself to notice, I am certain it will meet with a favourable reception: if it does not, undoubtedly it will be rejected with justice.

It may perhaps be unnecessary for me in favour of its novelty to premise, that there is no such work in the English language; at least, none sufficiently extensive and regular to display the prevalent fashions of our ancestors through every century.

The Engravings, which form the most material part of this publication, are taken from drawings in Manuscripts coëval with the times that they are intended to illustrate, or other monuments of antiquity equally authentic; and they are faithfully copied from the originals, without an additional fold being made to the draperies, or the least deviation from the form of the garments.

In the arrangement of the figures, a task attended with no small difficulty, it has been my study to render them interesting by grouping them as pleasingly as the nature of the subject would admit; and the ornamental embellishments of every kind are not, in any instance, the work of my own imagination, but accurate specimens of ancient art, and extracted from the same manuscript that the figures, or some of them at least, are taken.

The Introduction contains a general outline of the various dresses that have existed in the ancient world, and extended no farther than what seemed necessary for the fuller explanation of the early habits of our ancestors. The engravings, which accompany the Introduction, are few; but taken from originals, undoubtedly authentic.

I have avoided, as much as possible, the introducing any figures that have been previously engraved for other works, and in no one instance given a copy from a copy; but always referred to the original itself, as the best voucher for my accuracy.

I am convinced, that in the prosecution of this extensive work many errors will be unavoidable. In numberless instances I am necessitated to labour, as it were, in the dark: because, on the one hand, the descriptions of the dresses, derived from our early writers, are frequently so very vague and nugatory, that they afford but little or no light in the explication of the drawings and monumental effigies coëval with them; and, on the other hand, where these descriptions are more full, they often want the concordant assistance of painting and sculpture. I have, however, exerted the utmost of my ability to unite the two sources of information with each other; and, where my authority is in any point doubtful, or deficient, I have acquainted the Reader how far he has to depend upon conjectural evidence, which from necessity occurs in several instances.

THE AUTHOR.

July 1, 1796.

CONTENTS OF THE INTRODUCTION.

CONTENTS OF VOL. I.

PART I.

THE CIVIL, MILITARY, AND ECCLESIASTICAL HABITS OF THE ANGLO-SAXONS, TO THE CONCLUSION OF THE EIGHTH* CENTURY.

CHAP. I.

CHAP. II.

CHAP. III.

CHAP. IV.

* Vide note, page 1.

PART II.

THE CIVIL, MILITARY, AND ECCLESIASTICAL HABITS OF THE ANGLO-SAXONS, FROM THE COMMENCEMENT OF THE NINTH CENTURY TO THE ARRIVAL OF THE NORMANS.

CHAP. VIII.

PART III.

THE CIVIL, MILITARY, AND ECCLESIASTICAL HABITS OF THE ANGLO-NORMANS, FROM THE ACCESSION OF WILLIAM THE FIRST TO THE THRONE OF ENGLAND TO THE CONCLUSION OF THE TWELFTH CENTURY.

CHAP. I.

CHAP. II.

CHAP. III.

CHAP. IV.

CHAP. V.

THE INTRODUCTION.

SECTION I.

A GENERAL VIEW OF THE CLOTHING MATERIALS ANCIENTLY IN USE, AND THE ARTS DEPENDANT UPON DRESS.

THE first idea of clothing the body appears to have originated rather from shame than from necessity; for, so long as our first parents continued obedient to the commandment of their Creator, they were strangers to their own nakedness, and garments of every kind were totally useless; but, the moment they transgressed the divine mandate, their eyes were opened and "they saw," says the sacred historian "that they were naked." Shame then induced them to make a partial covering for their bodies, which does not seem indeed at any rate to deserve the name of a garment, and was by no means calculated to answer the claims of nature when a change of seasons required the extraneous assistance of clothing; but, before their expulsion from Eden, the benign author of their existence, who best knew the extent of their wants, provided them with such dresses as were suited to the exigences of their subsequent condition:—"Unto Adam also and unto his wife "did the Lord God make *coats of skin, and clothed them.*"[1]

Such were the habits of our primeval parents; and from so simple a beginning originated the vast variety of dresses, which were afterwards composed of materials of many kinds, and loaded with superfluous ornaments of gold, of silver, and of precious stones, agreeable to the taste or rather extravagance of the succeeding ages.

It is impossible to ascertain the period in which the manufacturing of cloth was first introduced among mankind; and it would be absurd to pretend to investigate

[1] כתנות עור וילבשם Genesis, iii. 21.

the causes to which it owed its origin: like most other useful inventions, it is probable that those of spinning and weaving might have arisen from some accidental circumstances; but, as they depended upon the complication of many different operations, we may reasonably conclude that they were not hastily brought to any great degree of perfection. The laborious productions of the loom must of course have been very expensive, and the use of them confined to persons of superior rank and opulence; which may account in some measure for the little progress made in the clothing arts among mankind in general for several generations posterior to the deluge. The ancient Greek authors, speaking of the first ages of the world, assure us, that men killed the beasts of the field for their food, and clothed themselves with their skins; which Diodorus Siculus expressly declares was the custom among the primitive Egyptians.[1]

It is abundantly evident that many useful arts, and probably those on which the manufacturing of cloth depended among the rest, were invented by the Antediluvians, and the knowledge of them preserved by Noah and his family: it may therefore appear extraordinary to us, that, when the descendants of that patriarch dispersed themselves upon the face of the earth, they should so generally have lost sight of them all, and by a retrograde disposition of the mind, have dwindled into a state of total ignorance:—such, however, undoubtedly is the fact. I am indeed inclined to believe that the clothing arts were known to the Antediluvian world; for, garments of various kinds, thread, and even the ornamental parts of dress, are particularized by Moses as being in use soon after the deluge;[2] and he speaks of them without the least indication of their novelty, or the most distant hint that the manufacturing of them was a recent invention, and first introduced after the restoration of mankind.

Linen and woollen garments were in use among the Egyptians at a very remote

[1] Diodorus Siculus, lib. I. cap. ii. and iv.

[2] A *hyke*, or mantle, is spoken of, Genesis, chap. ix. ver. 23, as used by two of the sons of Noah to cover him when he lay exposed in his tent. שמלה the Hebrew name appropriated to this garment, used in several subsequent passages in Scripture, is unequivocally expressive of a garment manufactured in the loom; so that there is little reason to conceive, that it should in this place alone be put for a vestment of leather. חט or thread, occurs, Gen. chap. xiv. ver. 23. For the various ornaments see Gen. chap. xxiv. ver. 22, &c. [The "golden earring of half a shekel weight," as it has been rendered by the old English translators, seems to have been a ring or jewel for the nose. It is so given in the Persian and Arabic Versions.—Ed.]

period. "Vestures of fine linen"[1] were worn by the superior officers of Pharaoh's court as early as the time of the patriarch Joseph. If, indeed, it be denied that the clothing arts descended from the Antediluvian world, the general testimony of ancient history will point to Egypt for their origin; for, it is certain that they appeared in much greater perfection there, and much earlier, than in any other country.[2] The linen especially, manufactured by the Egyptians, maintained its precedency in foreign nations for many succeeding generations: it was called *fine linen* by way of eminence, and formed a very material part of the exports of that country. From this source the Israelites certainly derived the skill in the clothing arts, for which they are celebrated by Moses; and with them it seems to have declined in proportion as they receded from their task-masters. In the days of Solomon, it is true, the thread, or, as it is called, linen-yarn,[3] was brought unworked from Egypt to Jerusalem, to make the decorations for the first temple; but, at the same time, it was necessary to call in a foreign artist to superintend the manufacturing of those materials; and he himself performed the most elaborate part of the workmanship. We are by no means, I apprehend, to conclude, from the thread being imported in an unwrought state, or from the circumstance of a Tyrian artist being employed to make it into cloth, that the skill of the Egyptians in the clothing arts was upon the decline at that period: the contrary will soon appear; and this circumstance might probably arise from some peculiarity respecting the form and ornaments of the linen, which required it to be made immediately under the direction of the Jewish priesthood; and the workman

[1] בגדי־שש Gen. chap. xli. ver. 42. The word שש however, may be rendered fine white *cotton cloth;* for, it signifies both *cotton* and *linen,* but cannot be interpreted by the word *silk,* as it is rendered in the margin of our Bibles.

[2] The Egyptians themselves claimed this honour; and put a shuttle into the hand of their goddess Isis, to signify that she was the inventress of weaving. Histoire du Ciel, c. 32. [I have not met with this book, but the invention of weaving is accorded by Pliny to the Egyptians, lib. vii. 56; and Athenæus positively names as the inventor, Pathymias the Egyptian. Deipn. lib. 2.—Ed.]

[3] 1 Kings, chap. x. ver. 28; and 2 Chronicles, chap. i ver. 16. ["The word קוה (Koh or Koa)" says the learned Editor of the Pictorial Bible, "bears no where else the meaning here given to it" (i. e. "linen yarn.") "The Septuagint and the Vulgate give it as a proper name." . . . . . "The authority of the Septuagint," he adds, "is important, in at least proving that linen yarn is *not* intended. The word, when translated, has no other meaning than that of a collection or gathering together, as in Gen. i. 9, and Jer. iii. 17." And Mr. Taylor, the editor of Calmet, considers it in this instance to apply to the horses mentioned in the same verse.—Ed.]

was the "son of a woman of the daughters of Dan,"[1] who, from a nearer relationship to the Jews, might be better acquainted with their customs, and of course better calculated to execute such a commission, than an Egyptian artist.

Solomon has put into the mouth of a luxurious prostitute an eulogium upon the Egyptian linens: "I have decked," says she, "my bed with carpets, and the carved works with fine linen of Egypt;"[2] and the prophet Ezekiel, who lived upwards of four hundred years after Solomon, speaking of the prosperity of Tyre, mentions the fine linen with broidered work from Egypt as forming part of her most valuable imports.[3] Neither is profane history destitute of its testimony in favour of the celebrity of the Egyptian linen manufactures: for, one of the most ancient Grecian historians informs us, that Amasis, king of Egypt, "sent to the Lacedemonians a curious pectoral,[4] made of linen, adorned with many figures of animals woven into the work, and enriched with gold and variety of colours.—The chain," continues my author, "is of admirable artifice, fine and slender, though consisting of three hundred and sixty distinct threads." He then adds, "such another is to be seen at Lindus, dedicated to Minerva by the same Amasis."[5] A pectoral of the like kind was taken among the spoils at the battle of Isus, and presented to Alexander the Great, who was so much pleased with it, that he wore it himself as part of his martial habit.[6]

The Egyptian weavers, contrary to the custom of most other nations, were men; for, Herodotus assures us, that "the women of Egypt were employed abroad in trade and business; but the men were left at home to spin and weave. Other nations," adds he, "weave the rough side[7] of the piece uppermost—the Egyptians underneath."[8]

[1] 2 Chronicles, chap. ii. ver. 14.

[2] Proverbs, chap. vii. ver. 16. The Hebrew word אטון which in this passage is translated *fine linen*, may literally be rendered *the spinnings* or *linen thread:* it also signifies *fringes* made of linen thread. However, either of these interpretations will suit the present purpose. [Other versions read—"I have decked my bed with coverings of tapestry, with carved [query, figured] works, with fine linen of Egypt." The Editor of the Pictorial Bible renders it—"I have covered my couch with variegated coverings of Egyptian tapestry;" but acknowledges that "fine linen" is the best general term to use in translating the various different words for the several tissues woven by the Egyptians.—Ed.]

[3] Ezekiel, chap. xxvii. ver. 7.

[4] ϛωρηξ.

[5] Herodotus, in Thalia, xlvii. [Pliny also speaks of the remarkably fine texture of a similar one presented by Amasis to the Minerva of Rhodes, "filis singula fila constare." ccclxv.—Ed.]

[6] Plutarch, in vitâ Alexandri. He calls it *a pectoral of linen often folded and plaited.*

[7] κροκη.

[8] Herodotus, in Euterpe, xxxv.

The linen, which was made by the Jewish artists for the habits of the priests and the decorations of the tabernacle, was of several kinds: the *linen*, simply so called; the *fine linen*;[1] the *fine-twined linen*;[2] and the *fine linen of woven work*;[3] the latter, I presume, was a species of variegated cloth, in which the colours were inserted in the weaving; and, for that reason, so particularised by the sacred historian, to distinguish it from the cloth embroidered with the needle, which also formed a considerable part of the sacred decoration. The twined linen I cannot at any rate pretend to define.[4]

It is by no means to be understood from what has been said, that the manufacturing of linen was confined to the Egyptians and the Israelites: the art was well known to the neighbouring nations, and carried by some of them to a great degree of perfection. The fine linen, manufactured by the Tyrians, is spoken of by the prophet Ezekiel, as a valuable commodity, purchased by the Syrian merchants.[5] Linen formed part of the garments of the Assyrian nobility; and, in short, was an article of dress universally esteemed and worn by all who could afford to purchase it.

Garments manufactured from wool are doubtless of very high antiquity, and may perhaps claim a just precedency to those of linen.[6] But, as linen generally constituted the inner parts of the habits, the finer and softer it was in its texture, the more comfortable it was found to be by the wearer, and in proportion produced a superior price; which may in some measure account for the greater progress that appears to have been made in the linen than in the woollen manufactures: the latter, however, were by no means neglected, though the productions are not so highly distinguished, either for their beauty, or the excellency of their workmanship. Woollen garments were made and used in every country, famous for its skill in the clothing arts. The city of Tyre is particularized by the prophet Ezekiel as

[1] בד or שש. [2] שש משזר.

[3] שש מעשה ארג Exodus, chap. xxviii. ver. 5, 6, 7, and 8; and chap. xxxix. ver. 27.

[4] [Mr. Thompson in his remarks on the mummy cloth of Egypt mentions a peculiarity of structure in some given to him by Mr. Belzoni as very striking. "The thread of the warp was *double*, consisting of two fine threads twisted together."—Might not this be a specimen of the fine *twined* linen?—Ed.]

[5] Ezekiel, chap. xxvii. ver. 16.

[6] Justin (Lib. ii.) says that the Athenians first taught the manufacturing of wool. The Egyptians, as we have already seen, claim the same honour, and, without doubt, with more propriety.

a mart anciently famous for white wool, which was held in high estimation by the merchants of Damascus.[1]

The intermixture of linen and woollen threads in the making of cloth is of very ancient date: it probably originated with the Egyptians, and its fabrication is strictly forbidden by the Mosaic law.[2]

The Thracians, according to Herodotus, anciently made their garments of a particular species of *hemp*, so nearly resembling *flax*, that it required a man to have had much experience to distinguish the one from the other.[3]

It is generally admitted, and, I presume with justice, that *cotton* was manufactured into cloth at a very early period. Cotton is not, indeed, particularly specified by the early historians; but the Hebrew word, translated *silk* in our Bibles,[4] is thought by the learned to be rather expressive of a species of fine cotton cloth.[5]

Silk was certainly unknown to the ancients for many ages after every other part of the clothing-manufactures were carried to very great perfection: it was not introduced into Europe till the conclusion of the Roman Republic, after which time, it is frequently mentioned by the classic Latin writers; Josephus, speaking particularly of the triumphal garments of Vespasian and his son Titus, says they were made of *silk*,[6] which even then was considered as a very precious article; but upon this subject there will be occasion to speak more fully hereafter.

The manufacturing of cloth from the hair of animals is an art of high antiquity: the external covering of the tabernacle is expressly said by Moses to have been made of goats' hair;[7] and the inhabitants of the Western parts of Ethiopia, according to Diodorus Siculus, anciently wore a species of drawers made with the hair from their

[1] Ezekiel, chap. xxvii. ver. 18.

[2] Leviticus, chap. xix. ver. 19; and Deuteronomy, chap. xxii. ver. 11.

[3] *καvvαβις τῳ λινῳ εμφερεστατη*. Herod. in Melpom. lxxiv. Arrian, according to the author of the notes upon Strabo, says that the people of India had a kind of linen or woollen that they gathered from the trees—λινου λαμπροτατου; *linum autem appellat lanam quæ ex arboribus colligitur*. Note to Strabo, lib. xv. p. 1036.

[4] Gen. chap. xli. ver. 42; Proverbs, chap. xxxi. ver. 22; et alibi: the word in Hebrew is משח [Aitun.—Ed.]

[5] See Parkhurst, p. 363.

[6] *εσθησεσι σηρικαις*. Bel. Jud. lib. VI. chap. 24.

[7] Exodus, chap. xxvi. ver. 7, &c. The Arabs to this day make use of tents made with hair-cloth. [Is it necessary to remind the reader of the exquisite productions of Cashmere and Persia, composed of camels' and of goats' hair?—Ed.]

heads, because, says he, such is the nature of the ground, that the sheep carry no fleeces.[1] The sackcloth, as it is commonly called in Scripture[2], used by the Jews for mourning, appears to have been manufactured from hair ; and, in some instances, if not in all, it certainly was black.[3]

The Indians, says Herodotus, who inhabit Asia, clothe themselves with garments made of *rushes*,[4] which they cut from the river, and, interlacing them together like mats,[5] work them into the form of the thorax. The Hylobii, a people of India, according to Strabo, used garments that were manufactured from the bark of trees.[6]

The first garments in use among mankind were confessedly made of the skins of animals ; and *leather* certainly constituted several parts of the dress, even after the clothing-arts were carried to the greatest degree of perfection. The ancients appear to have been well skilled in the arts of tanning and dressing of leather : the outer coverings of the tabernacle were made of rams' skins, and the skins of badgers ;[7] which, from the circumstance of the former being dyed red, as mentioned by Moses, will naturally lead one to conclude that they must have been properly prepared previous to that operation. The shoes, the girdles, and even other parts of the habits in general use, are repeatedly spoken of as being made of leather.

Many of the Scythians, says Herodotus, use skins instead of napkins, and clothe themselves with the *skins of men*, which they make into garments in the same manner as other nations make them of the skins of beasts.[8]

The art of dyeing the materials for clothing of various colours must have been carried to a great degree of perfection at a very early period : blue, purple, crimson, scarlet, and scarlet double-dyed, are colours particularized for the decoration of the tabernacle, and for the embellishment of Aaron's pontifical habit.[9] Several nations were famous for certain colours peculiar to themselves, owing often to local circumstances. The Tyrian purple was remarkable to a proverb, which is said to have been extracted from a shell-fish found upon the coasts of Tyre ; though several modern authors have denied the existence of such a fish, and imagine that the purple

1 Lib. III. cap. i.

2 שק Gen. xxxvii. 34 ; et alibi frequentèr.

3 Revelations, chap. vi. ver. 12.

4 Φλοΐνην.

5 Φορμου· *modum storeæ, tanquam thoracem.* Herod. in Thaliâ. xcviii.

6 *Vestes ex arborum corticibus habentes.* Strabon. lib. XV. Also of the *Massagetæ, qui in insulis degunt*—he says, *amiciunt se arborum corticibus.* Ibid. lib. XI.

7 Exodus, chap. xxvi. ver. 14.

8 Herod. in Melpom. lxiv.

9 Exodus, chap. xxvi. xxviii ; et alibi.

of the Tyrians was made from the cochineal only. "Dyed garments from Bozrah" are mentioned by Isaiah, which, from the passage immediately following, appear to have been red "like the garments of him who treadeth the wine-fat."[1] It is said of the Massagetes, a people dwelling beyond the river Araxes, that they had a certain tree, the leaf of which, when bruised and diluted with water, served to paint or dye the figures of animals upon their garments[2] with a colour that never faded, neither could the figures be washed out with water, but continued as if they had been woven in the cloth.

I shall not say any thing farther upon this subject at present: it will of necessity be more fully exemplified in the succeeding part of the Introduction.

The art of working upon cloth with the needle, and embroidering figures of various kinds with differently coloured threads, are of very ancient date. It was well known to the Israelites, and practised by them immediately after their emigration from Egypt; and from Egypt, without doubt, their skill in embroidery was derived; for Moses does not speak of it as an art invented in his days, or peculiar to the children of Israel, which he probably would have done if the honour of its invention could have been claimed by him or by his countrymen. If we may judge of the perfection to which the art of embroidery was carried in Egypt by the decorations of the tabernacle, and conceive the Egyptians at that remote period to have been equally skilful with the Israelites, we shall form no mean opinion of their abilities. The curtains of the tabernacle and the veil of the ark were made of the finest linen, interwoven with threads of various colours, and embroidered with cherubim.[3] The hangings also for the door of the tabernacle were composed of blue, of purple, of scarlet, and of fine twined linen wrought with needle-work.[4] The ephod also and the tunic, which formed part of the official habit belonging to Aaron, were made of the finest materials, and richly adorned with embroidery.[5]

[1] Isaiah, chap. lxiii. ver. 1 and 2. [2] *Ζωα ες την εσθητα εγγραφειν.* Herod. in Clio. cciii.

[3] רקם the Hebrew word, rendered in our translation of the Pentateuch *embroidery*, may however signify *brocade*, or any *variegated work*, whether wrought in the loom, or with the needle. מעשה חשב translated *cunning work*, from the primitive signification of the word חשב to add or super-add, may more faithfully be rendered the *work of super-adding*, and applied with greater propriety to *needle-work* only, than the former.

[4] In the twenty-sixth chapter of Exodus the reader may find a full description of these splendid performances. Josephus says, that the veil of the Holy of Holies was adorned with every kind of flowers that the earth produces. Antiq. Jud. lib. III. cap. 5.

[5] Exodus, chap. xxviii. ver. 6 and 9.

Homer praises the Sidonian ladies for their skill in the art of embroidery in a passage selected by Herodotus from the Iliad; wherein the poet, adverting to the wardrobe of Hecuba, says:—

> There vestures lay in various colours wrought,[1]
> The work of Sidon's dames, from Sidon brought
> By godlike Paris.

Yet, if it be thought by the learned, that the garments spoken of by Homer were not embroidered with the needle, but worked in brocade, or perfected by variegated threads in the loom, I shall not presume to dispute the point.

We are not, however, by any means to conclude, from the partial extracts produced upon the present occasion, that the art of embroidery was confined to the narrow boundaries of Egypt and Palestine: it certainly extended to every other part of the globe, where the clothing manufactures were carried to perfection; and particularly in Europe it may be said to have arisen to full maturity.

Having briefly taken a general survey of the materials for clothing anciently in use, and of the arts dependent upon the manufacturing of cloth, it remains to add a few words concerning the artists themselves, and those by whom they were superintended. It must be premised, that dressing of flax, carding of wool, spinning, and weaving, were not considered by the ancients as mean and despicable employments, but, on the contrary, such as added dignity and lustre even to the highest rank that birthright could confer. We shall not therefore be surprised to find the ladies of the first quality engaged in the labours of the loom, when the poets have represented the goddess of Wisdom following the same employment, and priding herself in the excellence of her productions.[2] In short, it appears from ancient history, that every mistress of a large family superintended a clothing manufactory, which was carried on under her own roof; and the garments that she wore herself, as well as those of her husband, her children, and her servitors, were the produce of it. It would be endless to quote authorities in support of this assertion: the works of the historians and the poets of the former times abound with proofs of its verity. I shall content myself with laying before my readers the character of a good housewife, as we find it drawn by Lemuel, in the last chapter of the book of Proverbs; at least, so much of it as appears to be pertinent to the present purpose:

[1] Πεπλοι παμποικιμοι—*omninò variè picti.* Iliad, lib. VI. ver. 220. [2] Ovid, Metam. lib. VI.

"She seeketh," says he, "wool and flax, and worketh willingly with her hands. She layeth her hands to the spindle, and her hands hold the distaff. She is not afraid of the snow for her household, for all her household are clothed with double garments.[1] She maketh herself coverings of tapestry: her clothing is of fine linen[2] and purple. She maketh fine linen, and selleth it; and delivereth girdles unto the merchant," &c.[3]

In the remote ages, it is certain that the manufacturing of cloth was pursued for domestic uses, and occasionally for presents for visitors of distinction, and not unfrequently for the glorious purpose of clothing the poor; but, as the productions of the loom, where many servants were constantly employed, would naturally exceed the expenditure of the family, the overplus became an article of commerce; and the manufacturing of garments in process of time gradated into a trade exceeded by none in profit or usefulness.

[1] כלביתה לבש שנים I have followed the margin translation, which is more congenial with the Hebrew.

[2] שש evidently not silk, as the word is rendered in our translation.

[3] Proverbs, chap. xxxi. ver. 13; et infra. [The word סדין *sadin* in verse 24, is another of those various expressions which our version equally renders by fine linen.—Ed.]

SECTION II.

THE CIVIL, MILITARY, AND RELIGIOUS HABITS OF THE EGYPTIANS, THE HABITS OF THE ETHIOPIANS, AND OTHER NEIGHBOURING NATIONS.

The Egyptians anciently clothed themselves with the skins of animals, if the testimony of Diodorus Siculus may be relied upon; but in the time that the patriarch Joseph resided in Egypt, the manufacturing of cloth was not only established there, but carried to some degree of perfection; for, vestures of fine linen were given by Pharaoh to him as a mark of distinction; at the same time a chain of gold was put upon his neck; the king also took his ring from his own hand and put it upon his hand.[1] Josephus, relating the same circumstance, assures us, that Pharaoh gave him authority to use his own signet, and to be clothed in purple.[2]

Cambyses sent garments of purple, together with a wreathed neck-bracelet, and bracelets for the arms of gold, as presents for the king of Ethiopia.[3] Splendid robes, and the ensigns and badges of royal authority, are said to have been put on by the king of the Egyptian empire, anciently, when he went to sacrifice to the gods:—and the president of the judges, when he appeared in his official capacity, wore a golden chain about his neck, to which was attached an emblematical figure of Truth adorned with precious stones.[4]

It is an undoubted fact, that linen constituted much of the ancient Egyptian habit. The men, according to Herodotus, wore two garments; the one a linen tunic, ornamented with a welt or fringe at the bottom, which they called *calasiris*;[5] and the other a white woollen mantle,[6] which was thrown over the former. In another place the same author, speaking generally of the habits of the Egyptians, says, they wear garments of linen[7] fresh washed, taking singular care to have them always clean; for, adds he, they esteem cleanliness more than ornament. The

1 Genesis, chap. xli. ver. 42.

2 πορφυραν. Antiq. Jud. lib. II. cap. v.

3 Herodotus in Thaliâ.

4 Diodorus Siculus, lib. I. cap. vi.

5 Κιθυνας λινεους περι τα σκελεα θυσσανωτους καλεουσι καλασιρις Herod. in Euterpe, lxxxi.

6 Ειρινεα ειματα λευκα. Ibid.

7 Ibid. in Euterpe, xxxvii.

woollen mantle, mentioned above, was not constantly worn by the Egyptians; for, no man could enter the places of worship with any garment made of wool upon him; nor permit his relatives to be buried in the same without incurring the censure of profanation.[1]

It is impossible, from the source of historical intelligence, to trace the different degrees of dress existent among the Egyptians: indubital proofs, however, may be produced that various gradations of rank were distinguished by peculiar habits; but the nature and extent of such distinctions do not appear upon record. The habit of the monarch we may easily conceive to have been rich and splendid, when we recollect that the elegant art of embroidery was carried to great perfection in Egypt, if it really did not originate in that country: it is also reasonable to suppose that the example of the sovereign would naturally be followed by the nobility, and, indeed, by every individual according to his rank and circumstances: the splendid robes, rings, and chains of gold, with other badges of high authority, though indeed but barely mentioned by the ancient historians, are sufficient to justify this opinion.

Herodotus assures us, that the Egyptian women, in his time, wore only one garment;[2] but, unfortunately, he has not left us the least hint respecting its form, or the manner in which it was put on: that it was made of linen appears from the general description he has given of the Egyptian habit; and probably it resembled the calasiris just mentioned. The rank of the women was probably distinguished by the fineness and richness of this garment, as well as by other personal ornaments which were appropriated to them; for, jewels of silver and jewels of gold were used by them at the time of the emigration of the Israelites from Egypt.[3]

Notwithstanding the effeminate character given to the Egyptians by Herodotus, we find them frequently engaged in war; and, in several instances, they exhibited by no means a despicable figure in the field. We have very little knowledge of the ancient Egyptian armour:[4] the thorax, or pectoral,[5] used by them, is indeed,

[1] See the beginning of this chapter.

[2] Herod. in Euterpe, xxxvi.

[3] Exodus, chap. xii. ver. 35; et alibi.

[4] [The deficiency of information on this head of which Mr. Strutt complained, has been amply supplied of late years by the researches of modern Egyptian travellers. Vide the works of Rosellini and Wilkinson, passim, and note to this work, page xv.—Ed.]

[5] These *pectorals* were often exceedingly magnificent. See p. 5 of the Introduction.

particularly spoken of by the author just mentioned, who informs us, that it was also adopted by the Persian warriors.

The *Egyptian pectoral*[1] was made of linen, often folded, and plaited in such a manner as to resist the point of the enemy's weapon. Herodotus mentions the arms of an Egyptian soldier, which we find to be a short sword, a buckler, and a javelin.[2] The Ionians and the Carians, according to the same author, in the time of Psammetichus, king of Egypt, wore brazen armour;[3] but, whether he meant, by the insertion of this passage in the history of Egypt, to intimate that the same kind of armour was used by the Egyptians, I shall not take upon me to determine: certain it is that Psammetichus himself wore an helmet of brass when he went to war.[4]

The principal part of the Egyptian sailors, who assisted Xerxes in his expedition against the Grecians, were equipped with helmets strongly quilted.[5] They had also convex shields, javelins proper for a sea-engagement, and large double-edged axes. The inferior order had only a pectoral, and were armed with a large sword.[6]

The Egyptian priests, Herodotus expressly declares, were clothed in linen; and their shoes were also made of the same material: neither were they permitted to dress in any other manner, nor to wear any kind of woollen garments, for nothing made of wool was admitted into the temple of their gods.[7]

Diodorus Siculus, in order to prove that the manners of the Ethiopians resembled those of the Egyptians, cites a variety of similar customs; and, among them, the following which relate to the habits of the priests of both countries: they are, says he, shaven alike, and clothed with the like stoles and attire, and carry a sceptre like a plough-share, such as their kings also bear; they likewise wear the same kind of high-crowned caps,[8] twisted at the top, and wreathed round about with the serpent which they called the *asp*. The same author also informs us, that the sacred scribes among the Egyptians wore a red cap adorned with a kite's feather.[9]

1 Αιγυπτιους θωρακας. Herod. in Clio, cxxxv.
2 Herod. in Polymniâ.
3 Οπλισθεντας χαλκῳ. Herod. in Euterpe, clii.
4 Κυνεην χαλκεην. Ibid. cli.
5 Κρανεα χηλευτα. Herod. in Polymnia, lxxxix.
6 Μεπαλας μαχαιρας. Ibid.
7 Herod. in Euterpe, xxxvii.
8 Πιλοις. Diodorus Siculus, lib. III. cap. I.
9 Diodorus Siculus, lib. I. cap. VI. [One of the reasons given by Diodorus for this head-dress is a tradition that a book wherein were written all the rites and customs of worshipping of the gods bound about with a scarlet thread was brought by a kite to the priests of Thebes.—Ed.]

The Egyptians in general were remarkable for their cleanliness; their priests especially, who shaved all the parts of their bodies once in three days, and made use of frequent bathings,[1] lest vermin or any other impurity, should be found upon them who officiated in the service of the gods; and probably it was for the same reason that their heads were shaved, contrary to the custom of most other countries.[2]

Anciently, says Diodorus Siculus, when an Egyptian king deceased, the people of Egypt cast dust upon their heads, and girded themselves with a linen girdle beneath their breasts; and in this manner both men and women went about in companies, amounting sometimes to two or three hundred, twice a day, singing mournful songs in praise of the deceased monarch, and recalling his virtues as it were from the silent tomb.[3] It was customary with most nations, according to Herodotus, in the time of mourning, for those who were the most nearly concerned, to shave their heads; but, on the contrary, adds he, when any one dies in Egypt his relations cease to shave, and suffer their hair to grow upon their heads and faces.[4] The same author assures us, that the skulls of the Egyptians were much harder than those of the Persians, owing to the national custom of shaving the heads of their children at a very early age.[5]

Shaving the eyebrows was also a mourning ceremony among the Egyptians, and performed by all the family when a cat belonging to them died of a natural death; for the death of a dog, they shaved the whole body.[6] It is also said that they cut their flesh with sharp instruments at their annual mournings for Osiris.[7]

It has already been observed, that it was accounted irreligious among the Egyptians to bury their dead in woollen garments; and certain mysterious reasons, according to Herodotus, were given by the priests in justification of this opinion: the bodies of the deceased were therefore swathed from the head to the feet in bandages of linen.

It is much to be lamented, that the two valuable authors, so frequently quoted in the preceding part of this chapter, have been so sparing in their intelligence respecting the habit of the Egyptians: the suggestions, selected above, contain all the material information that they have left behind them, and, unfortunately, the

[1] Twice constantly by day, and as often by night, in cold water. Herod. in Euterpe, xxxvii.
[2] Herod. in Euterpe, xxxvi.
[3] Diodorus Siculus, lib. I. cap. vi.
[4] Herod. in suprà.
[5] Ibid. in Thalia, xii.
[6] Ibid. in Euterpe, lxvi.
[7] Seller's Antiquities of Palmyra.

deficiency cannot be supplied; though, I trust, the figures which may be found upon the first four plates belonging to the Introduction, will, on proper examination, throw some small degree of light upon this important subject.[1]

The first part of the Egyptian habit that I shall particularize, appears upon the third figure of the first plate. It is of the most simple kind, consisting only of a covering for the lower part of the body, and the thighs: in the instance before us it reaches nearly to the knees; but, in others, it does not descend so low. Sometimes it was sloped with a curve from the front of the girdle to the bottom, as it is represented by the first figure upon the fourth plate; and then a supplementary part was added, which hung beneath the aperture, and supplied the deficiency of the garment itself: the third figure upon the same plate, which is the reverse of that last-mentioned shows the appearance of this covering on the back of the wearer.[2]

It may be questioned whether this garment, simple as it appears to be, did not consist of several parts: it is almost constantly party-coloured wherever it is represented by painting; and even those parts are often marked with stripes of different colours, falling in various directions, which bear the appearance of separate pieces; but these stripes were probably ornamental only, and either wove in the cloth by threads of several colours, or worked upon it afterwards by the needle.

This garment, in some instances, constituted the whole of the clothing; but the pectoral is generally added, as we find it is upon the figure first referred to. In the Table of Isis, a curious Egyptian monument so called, because it is supposed to represent the various religious ceremonies belonging particularly to the worship of that goddess,[3] we find several figures clothed in this garment, with the addition of two broad straps, which pass over both the shoulders, and crossing each other at the pit of the stomach, appear to be fastened to the girdle: the same kind of straps,

1 [The admirable works of Sir Gardner Wilkinson, Rosellini, Lane, and other modern travellers, have amply supplied the deficiency lamented by Mr. Strutt, and to them we must refer our reader for details which would swell out the introductory portion of these volumes to an extent uncalled for by their professed objects, viz "The dress and habits of the people of England."—Ed.]

2 The original figure whence these two are taken is bronze; and it is preserved in the British Museum.

3 An ample description of this valuable relique of antiquity, accompanied by engravings upon a large scale by Laurentius Pignorius, was published at Amsterdam, 1669. A full explanation of the same, illustrated also by engravings, is given in the second part of the second volume of *L'Antiquité Expliquée*, par Bernard de Montfaucon.

though partially obscured, indeed, by the exterior clothing, may be seen upon the second and fourth figures of the first plate. In the second figure we also meet with an appendage to the garment just described, which is joined to it at the girdle, and, rising thence, encloses the body as high as the bottom of the breasts, and ends a little above the crossing of the straps or bandages mentioned above.

It is generally supposed, that this habit belonged to the priests of Egypt; and a figure, exactly so clothed, is represented, in the Table of Isis, standing at an altar before the statue of that goddess, and sacrificing an animal like a goat, which certainly strengthens this opinion; but it does not, however, seem to have belonged to the priesthood exclusively; for, upon the same monument, we meet with two figures habited in the like kind of garment; one of which bears the appearance of a military character, and holds a barbed spear in his hand; the other is fighting with a spear against an animal resembling the rhinoceros.

The name of this part of the Egyptian habit is totally unknown: we may, however, certainly conclude, that it was not the *calasiris* mentioned by Herodotus; for, the *calasiris* is expressly said to have covered the legs, and of course must have been considerably longer. The garment, represented upon the first and fifth figures of the second plate, corresponds much better with the historian's description of the *calasiris:* in both instances, it is girded with a girdle about the loins; nor is it by any means unlike the woman's petticoat of the present day, saving only, that it appears to fold one part over another, and was rather wrapped round the body than put over the head: the bottom of the garment, appropriated to the first figure, is ornamented with a variegated *welt*, or *border*, agreeable to the express words of Herodotus.[1] To this garment is attached a single strap, or bandage, which passes over the left shoulder, and in the fifth figure resembles a scarf or sash. A garment of the same kind, but more perfect, and with short sleeves, is represented upon the sixth figure of the first plate, which is also girt about the loins with a girdle, but without the appearance of a welt or fringe at the bottom.[2]

[1] See page xi, and note 5, of the same page.

[2] I wish to observe in this place once for all, that the figures 1, 2, 3, 4, and 6, plate I, and figures 1, 2, and 3, plate II, are taken from two large painted coffins, which contained two mummies; and are preserved in the British Museum: the figures 4 and 5, plate II, from the lid of another coffin; the figure 5, plate I, and the pectoral, plate III, from the mummies themselves; figures 1 and 3, plate IV. and 1 and 2, plate III, are from bronzes; figures 2, 4, 5, and 6, plate IV, from figures manufactured with a

A kind of cloak appears upon the fourth figure of the fourth plate, which is much decayed and imperfect: on the back part of it is seen a perpendicular stripe, ornamented with hieroglyphic characters, which are nearly obliterated. The first and second figures of the third plate, representing the front and back views of the same bronze, exhibit a dress much more perfect and much more splendid than any of the preceding. The tunic, which is open in the front to the girdle, descends to the ancles; the sleeves reach to the wrists, where they terminate with ornaments; and, indeed, the whole of the garment is adorned with the appearance of rich embroidery: the part like a stripe, or gusset, which descends the whole length of the back, is elevated in the original, and appears evidently to be connected with the hair, or head covering, upon the right side of the head; but, whether it was hair curiously plaited hanging to the heels, or, whether it was part of the garment, (for, the ornaments of both resemble each other) I shall not presume to determine.

The habit of the fifth figure of the first plate occurs more than once in painting upon the body of a mummy; but I own I am at a loss to account for the appearance of the full form of the figure so powerfully expressed, and the extension of a lighter-coloured garment in the front, unless the inner clothing was of a dark colour, and fitted exactly to the body, and the external dress a thin kind of gauze, through which the under-habit might be discovered.

There was no part of the Egyptian dress more universally prevalent than the *pectoral:* it appears to have been worn by all ranks and orders of people; and it was common also to the women as well as to the men. The *pectorals,* worn by the Egyptian monarchs, by the courtiers, and by the superior order of the priests, were, without doubt, exceedingly magnificent. A linen *pectoral,* adorned with figures of animals woven in the work, and enriched with gold and variety of colours, was presented by Amasis, king of Egypt, to the Lacedæmonians; and the chain, which, according to Herodotus, was a necessary appendage, though extremely slender and delicate, consisted of no less than three hundred distinct threads.[1] The form of the *Egyptian pectoral* appears upon a multiplicity of different figures: it was semicircular,

kind of earthenware: all which are at the British Museum. The figure 3, plate III, is taken from a beautiful and well-preserved figure of Osiris, in the possession of Benjamin West, Esq.; by whose permission it has obtained a place in this work.

[1] Herodotus in Thalia, xlvii. See also page iv.

and constantly adorned with rows of ornaments one above another, in which not only the ornaments themselves, but the colours also, were often much varied. The *vectorals* appropriated to the female figures are frequently smaller in proportion than those belonging to the men; but this is by no means always the case. The first, second, third, and fourth figures of the first plate, the second and fourth figures of the second plate, and the fourth figure of the third plate, are all invested with the *pectoral;* and that belonging to the last is not only the most perfect, but apparently the most elegant: it consists of seven rows of ornamental work, whereas the others have not more than three, four, or five, at the most: there seems to have been no regular number assigned to these arrangements: some pectorals have ten, some twelve; and the splendid specimen, which was taken from the breast of a mummy, and copied upon the third plate, has no less than fourteen: the chain, by which it was attached to the breast, is not to be found; but probably it was connected with the two circular parts that appear on each side, and which were fastened upon the shoulders. The representation, here given, is nearly half the size of the original: the ornaments are finished with a prodigious degree of exactness, and the colours are placed in a regular succession: the light parts of the appendages at the top are gilt; the darker parts are blue striped upon a black ground: the narrow borders, by which they are united to the pectoral, are red, blue, black, and white, alternately. The first row of the ornamental part is light blue; the second yellow, green, and white; the third bright red and black; and the fourth is the same as the second; the fifth, sixth, seventh, and eighth, correspond exactly with the four first, and are repeated in the four succeeding rows; the thirteenth is like the first; and the ground of the fourteenth is black, with red, blue, and green stripes, alternately succeeding each other.[1]

Herodotus assures us, that, in his time, the women of Egypt wore but one garment, which, according to the representation of it given by the artists of that country, did not differ very widely from the *calasiris* above described, excepting that it was girded much higher upon the body, and does not seem to have been open at the sides. The first and fourth figures, upon the first plate, may serve as specimens of this

[1] There is an astonishing similarity, not only in the form, but also in the arrangement of the ornaments between the *Egyptian thorax*, or *pectoral*, and the *war gorget*, used by the inhabitants of the South Sea Islands. It is, therefore, with great propriety, that both of them are placed in one point of view at the British Museum, so that the conformity appears the more striking.

garment; but one of a much richer appearance constitutes the habit of the second figure upon the second plate, which is the representation of the goddess Isis:[1] the first figure, upon the first plate, has only one bandage from the shoulder attached to the tunic, if the dress she wears may properly be called by that name; and, indeed, it appears to be a part of it: in both the other instances there are two bandages, one descending from each shoulder, and both of them appear to be attached to the girdle of the tunic: this dress, with all its appendages, was insufficient to cover the upper parts of the body, and left the arms entirely naked. The goddess Isis, as we find her represented by the fifth figure of the fourth plate, is clad in a garment like those described above, but without the bandages from the shoulders, or any other appendages. The habits of the second and third figures upon the first plate, of the first and fourth figures upon the second plate, and of the first and third figures upon the fourth plate, are appropriated, by the generality of modern authors, to the priests; and this opinion is justified by the frequent appearance of such figures officiating at the altars of the deities, or employed in other acts of devotion towards them; though, as I observed above, the same kind of habits, or others greatly resembling them, are sometimes attributed to such persons as seem to have no claim to the sacerdotal office. The instruments that the Egyptian figures usually hold in their hands cannot be well accounted for; the long curved staff, with the small fork at the bottom, may be intended to represent the sceptre "*like a plough-share,*" which, according to Diodorus Siculus, was borne by the priests as well as by the kings of Egypt.[2]

The deity Osiris, represented by the third figure upon the third plate, is habited in a manner differing from any of the preceding examples; for, the greater part of his body, both his arms to the wrists, and his legs, are covered with a robe, that reaches to his feet; his pectoral is large and radiated; and the mitre upon his head bears great analogy to the high-crowned *cap* with a *knob*, or *boss*,[3] upon the top of it, which the author last mentioned assures us was worn by the priests of Egypt and of Ethiopia. He also adds, that it was wreathed about with a serpent called the asp. In the present instance, the asp, or an animal of the serpent kind, appears upon the front of the mitre, with the head elevated from the verge.[4] The scourge, which is

[1] The *variegated stole* of Isis, agreeable to the present representation of that goddess, is spoken of by Plutarch and other authors.

[2] Diodorus Siculus, lib. iii. cap i.

[3] Ομφαλον. Ibid.

[4] Ibid. [A high cap, with a knob or boss on the top of it, was the crown of Upper Egypt; when

held by this figure in his right hand, and the crooked sceptre in the left, were symbolical of some peculiar attributes belonging to the deity; but the learned are by no means agreed in the application of them. In the representation of Osiris, especially when he appears with the long robe, it is thought we may find the full dress of the high priest of the Egyptians; and this opinion will, I trust, receive additional strength, when it is proved that many parts of the splendid habit which was made for Aaron originated from the dress of this deity.[1]

It would be an herculean labour to describe all the variations to be met with in the head-dresses of the Egyptians: almost every ancient relic either of painting or of sculpture belonging to this extraordinary people, in which the representation of their habits is to be found, will rarely fail to exhibit some material difference in the coverings for the head, and especially in the appendages connected with them: they varied, I presume, according to the rank or opulence of the wearers in some instances; but in others, where different monuments are referred to, and those probably executed at different periods of time, the variations may be owing simply to the changes of the fashions, which, with them as well as with us, depended greatly upon the arbitrary caprices of fancy.

Herodotus assures us that the Egyptians constantly shaved their heads, except in the times of mourning: the head coverings of course that we meet with in the examples accompanying this part of the work, and which are oftener black than any other colour, cannot be intended to represent the hair naturally belonging to the wearer; but, in those instances where the resemblance of hair will justify the supposition, a kind of peruke,[2] especially when the hair appears to be long, as we find

the crown of Lower Egypt was joined with this, the united crowns were called the Pshent. In the representation of the Coronation of Remeses at Medeenet Haboo, that Prince is announced to have "put on the crown of the Upper and Lower Country."—Vide Wilkinson's Customs and Manners, Vol III. p. 352 and 354.—Ed]

[1] The original of this curious little figure, which is nearly of the same size as the copy, was found with four others (two of them representing the same deity, and the other two the goddess Isis with the infant Orus, or Horus, upon her lap) near St. Albans, in Hertfordshire, within the site of ancient Verulam, a city of the Romans. They were purchased by Benjamin West, Esq. historical painter to His Majesty; in whose possession they now remain. The present figure is much more perfect than any of the other four.

[2] It was customary with other nations to wear false hair, especially with the Medes, as we shall see hereafter. [No doubt need exist now upon this subject, as Egyptian wigs are to be seen in the British and Berlin Museums; and head coverings were also made in woollen or other stuffs under the deno-

it upon the fifth figure of the fourth plate; or ornamented with curls, as it is exhibited upon the fourth and sixth figures of the same plate; or braided as it is exemplified upon the first and second figures of the third plate.

In the table of Isis, spoken of in the preceding part of this chapter, there are several head-coverings, differing greatly from any of those that are here given: some of them resemble the flat helmets of the twelfth century; others again are elevated with a curve towards the hinder part of the head; and to all of them are added large appendages of feathers, or flowers, or leaves, of various kinds, with other ornaments of almost every species: the head of the goddess Isis, exclusive of the horned crescent usually given to her, is decorated with the representation of a bird, whose head extends beyond her forehead, and its wings are depressed on either side below her ears.

The figure of Osiris is rarely represented without a mitre upon his head; and it is equally as rare to meet with two of those mitres exactly resembling each other, the general form of the mitre appears upon the third figure of the third plate; but the two appendages at the bottom, which in this instance bear some slight analogy to two ears, in other examples are lengthened, and resemble two horns; and the radiated part, extending on either side from the cone, in others is sometimes enclosed by an ornamental border. The second figure of the fourth plate is altogether habited in a singular manner; and the covering of his head resembles the common night-cap of the present day.

The second, third, and fifth figures of the first plate, the third figure of the second plate, and the second figure of the fourth plate, are represented with beards, which in all these instances, the last excepted, are affixed to the bottom of the chin only, and lessens gradually to a point, which is turned up with a curve; the beard of Osiris is also braided in a very curious and singular manner. The beards, as well as the coverings for the head above-mentioned, appear to have been made of false hair, and removed when the face was shaved: innumerable examples might, indeed, be produced in which the men are represented without beards; but those I trust will be deemed sufficient that have already been produced.[1]

mination of "false wigs," for those who could not afford the more expensive quality of real hair.—Vide Wilkinson's Manners and Customs, Vol. III. p 356.—Ed.]

[1] See Fig. 5, Pl I; Figs. 1, 4, and 5, Pl. II.; Fig. 1, Pl. III.; and Figs. 1 and 4, Pl. IV.

The bodies of the dead, according to the testimony of the ancient historians, were not buried in woollen clothes, but were swathed about with bandages of linen; and the truth of this assertion is abundantly proved by the examination of the mummies, many of which are remaining to the present day; the manner in which the swathing was originally performed is depicted by an ancient Egyptian artist, and may be seen upon the second plate belonging to the Introduction.[1]

It is impossible to ascertain the æra in which the ornamental appendages to dress were first introduced among mankind: it is highly probable that they were in use anterior to the deluge; for they are spoken of by Moses as existing after that event, and without the least indication of the novelty of their intervention. *Rings*, *bracelets*, and *chains* of gold, formed the decorative part of the Egyptian habits at a very early period. Pharaoh is expressly said to have taken the *ring* from his hand,[2] and to have put it upon the hand of the patriarch Joseph, and a *chain*,[3] also of gold upon his neck, as tokens of high honour. The Egyptians not only wore bracelets upon their arms, but also upon their legs, as we may see exemplified by several of the figures that accompany this work. The Israelitish women, not long after their departure from Goshen, are said to have been possessed of various jewels; and among them ear-rings are particularly specified;[4] these, indeed, might be a part of the valuable ornaments borrowed from the women of Egypt. Josephus speaks of Pharaoh's *diadem*,[5] which seems to have been nothing more than a circle or fillet of gold.[6]

The manners and habits of the eastern Ethiopians were greatly analogous to

[1] See the third figure, which is faithfully copied from a painting upon the coffin of one of the mummies, preserved at the British Museum.

[2] את־טבעתו מעל ידו

[3] רבד חזהב The word רבד may also signify a *wreathen bracelet* for the neck. Genesis, chap. xli. ver. 42.

[4] Exodus, chap. iii. ver. 22. [There is *no* mention of ear-rings in the verse here quoted: the words are "Jewels of silver and jewels of gold and raiment." It is in the xxxii. chap. of Exodus, and the 2nd verse, that golden ear-rings are distinctly mentioned as being worn not only by the women but by the men, "Of your wives, of your *sons*, and of your daughters."—Ed.]

[5] Antiquities of the Jews, Book II. chap. v.

[6] [This is not so certain, as the diadem as well as the mitre of the ancient kings and priests, mentioned in holy writ, was a turban of fine linen, with an encircling or front ornament of gold or precious stones. Justin tells us that Alexander the Great took his diadem from his head *to bind up the wounds* of Lysimachus.—Ed.]

those of the Egyptians; but the western parts of Ethiopia were inhabited by a people much less cultivated: some of them, according to Diodorus Siculus, never wore any clothing, while others cut off the tails from their sheep and bound them about their loins for modesty-sake; and others again substituted the skins of beasts for the same purpose; but the more civilized part of them clothed themselves with *drawers*, manufactured from the hair of their heads,[1] which material they used from necessity, because, adds the historian, the nature of the ground is such, that the sheep carry no fleeces; and, by way of ornament, some of them wore a ring of brass pendent from their lips. Their shields were often made of the raw hides of oxen; but, respecting the war accoutrements of the Ethiopians, Herodotus is more explicit where he speaks of the different nations that assisted Xerxes in his expedition into Greece. Such of them, says he, as inhabited the parts of the country above Egypt, were clothed with the skins of lions and of leopards. They had bows four cubits long, with arrows proportionate to the size of the bow, pointed with sharp stones instead of iron; and the heads of their javelins were made of goat's horns sharpened. They had also truncheons armed with iron; and, previous to their engagement in battle, they daubed one half of their bodies over with a kind of white plaster,[2] and painted the other half with vermilion.[3] The women of this country also bore arms, until they arrived at a certain age.

The dress of the Asiatic Ethiopians bore some resemblance to that of the Indians, who are said to have used a species of defensive armour made of wood;[4] but, in place of an helmet, they substituted the skin of a horse's head, stripped from the carcass together with the ears and the mane, and so contrived, that the mane served for the crest, and the ears appeared erected upon the head of the wearer: their shields also, unlike those in common use, were composed with the skins of cranes.[5]

The Arabians, who accompanied Xerxes, wore a girdle over a surcoat, called

[1] *Alii* subligaculis (*περιζομασι*) *tegunt clunes è capillitio contextis.* Diodorus Siculus, lib. III. cap. i.

[2] Γυψῳ. Herodotus in Polymniâ, lxix. [3] Μιλτῳ. Ibid.

[4] The words of the historian are, *ειματα απο ξυλων πιποιημενα.* Ibid. [Beloe translates the passage thus: "The dress of the Indians was cotton."—Ed.]

[5] Δορας γεραvων. Herodotus in Polymniâ, lxx. The same author informs us, that the Oriental Ethiopians had long straight hair, but the hair of Ethiopians, inhabiting the borders of Libya, were more curled than that of any other people.

zeira;[1] but the historian has not described the form of this garment, nor the materials with which it was composed.

From the Libyans, who inhabited to the westward of the lake Tritonis, says Herodotus, the Grecians received the apparel and *ægis* of Minerva, as represented upon her images, excepting only that in Libya her habit is made of skins, and the fringes below the ægis are thongs of leather, and not serpents: in all other respects the resemblance is perfect; and even the name testifies that the stole of the Palladion[2] came from Libya, for the Libyan women wear a mantle of tanned goat's skin, dyed red, and fringed, over the rest of their garments: from these skins the Grecians gave the name of *ægis* to the pectoral of Minerva.[3] The Libyans also who assisted Xerxes, were clothed in tunics of leather, and carried round-pointed lances hardened at one end by fire.[4]

The Libyan Auses, a people who anciently inhabited the west side of the river Triton, wore their hair long on the right side of their heads, but shaved the left: they also painted their bodies with vermilion.[5]

The Adrymachides, a people inhabiting near Egypt, adopted the Libyan habit, and the women wore a bracelet of brass upon each leg.[6]

The country, continues the historian, that lies above the Nasamones, is inhabited by the Garamantes, and westward of these in the maritime places, the people shave their heads quite round, leaving only a lock of hair in the middle of the crown; and, when they make war, they wear the skins of ostriches instead of armour.[7]

It is certain, that the Egyptians not only accustomed themselves to frequent ablutions, but also that they anointed their bodies with unguents of different kinds.[8] The Ethiopians, and the inhabitants of the western parts of Libya painted their bodies; but it does not appear that the Egyptians anciently adopted that custom.

1 *Ζειρας*. Ibid. lxix.

2 *Στολη των Παλλαδιων*. Ibid. in Melpomene, clxxxix.

3 *Εκ δε των αιγεων τουτεων αιγιθας οι Ελληνες μετωνομασαν*. Ibid.

4 Ibid. in Polymniâ, lxxi.

5 Ibid. in Melpomene, cxci.

6 *Ψιλλιον χαλκεον*. Ibid. clxviii.

7 *Στρουθων καταγαιων δορας φορεουσι προβληματα*. Herodotus in Melpomene, clxxv.

8 An alabaster box of rich ointment [perfumes] was considered as a present fit for the reception of a monarch. Ibid. in Thaliâ, xx.

SECTION III.

THE CIVIL, MILITARY, AND ECCLESIASTICAL HABITS OF THE ISRAELITES. THE HABITS OF THE PHILISTINES, AND OTHER NEIGHBOURING NATIONS.

THE children of Israel, at the time of their departure from Goshen, appear to have been well instructed in all the arts and sciences cultivated in Egypt, especially such of them as related to their comfort or their convenience: we have, indeed, divine authority to prove that their conductor was "learned in all the wisdom of the Egyptians;"[1] but I shall confine my observations to such matters as relate to dress only.

A loose linen garment, of the *shift* or *shirt* kind, was anciently in use among the inhabitants of Palestine; and it seems to have been common to both sexes. This garment is called a *sheet* in one part of our Bible; but the general interpretation of the original word[2] is *fine linen;*[3] and, from the manner in which it is coupled with the changes of raiment in the Book of Judges, it may be applied, with much greater propriety, to the *shirt*, or some such interior garment, than to any external part of the clothing:[4] and it is well known that shirts of linen, cotton, or gauze, are still worn by the Turks and Moors, and by persons of condition among the wandering Arabs in Arabia Felix.[5]

The tunic,[6] which was girt about the loins with a girdle, formed a very material part of the Jewish habit. This garment is called *chethomene*[7] by Josephus, and described by him as a tunic with straight sleeves closely encompassing the body, and reaching to the ancles. The tunic formed part of the sacerdotal habit. It was then made of *fine linen;*[8] and it is probable that the tunics, belonging to

1 Acts, chap. vii, ver. 22.

2 סדון Judges, chap. xiv, ver. 12-13; et alibi.

3 The LXX render the words by *σινδονας* and *οθονια*; and the Vulgate throughout by *sindonem* and *sindonas*.

4 This opinion is greatly strengthened by the 19th verse of the same chapter, where it is expressly said, that, after Sampson had slain thirty of the Philistines, and taken their apparel, he was enabled to perform his promise; the *shirts* being, I presume, upon the backs of those that he had slain.

5 Shaw's Travels, 228, &c.

6 כתנת.

7 Χιθομενη. Ant. Jud. lib. III. chap. 7.

8 *Διπλης σινδονος βυσσινης* according to Josephus. Ibid.

persons of rank and opulence, were also made of linen; and the robe or mantle of some other valuable material, and died of a purple colour; for, purple and fine linen are said to have formed the luxurious habits of the wealthy;[1] with other Asiatic nations, purple was confined to the monarchical habits, or to the habits of the royal family, and to the superior officers of the court, to whom the permission to wear it was granted as a high honour; and even the Jews themselves, at times, were restricted in this particular.

We may easily conceive that tunics of linen, or even of woollen of the finest kind, could not be purchased by the inferior classes of the people. The price, without doubt, depended upon the excellency of the materials with which they were manufactured, and the labour bestowed upon them; both of which were suited to the rank and opulence of the wearer. Certain it is, however, that a mixture of woollen and linen in the same garments was strictly forbidden,[2] though garments of both kinds unmixed were worn; and the winter tunics of the wealthy were probably made of fine wool.

The Israelites were strictly commanded to make fringes[3] upon the borders of their garments, and put upon the fringes of the borders a lace, or ribband of blue;[4] and, as this commandment appears to have been given without any peculiar exception, the tunic of course was decorated accordingly. The tunic that Jacob caused to be made for his son Joseph, as a distinguishing mark of his love to him above his brethren, is said to have been *of many colours*;[5] and, in the later times, a tunic of the same description was appropriated to the virgin daughters of the kings of Israel.[6]

1 Luke, chap. xvi. ver. 19.

2 Leviticus, chap. xix. ver. 19; Deut. chap. xxii. ver. 11. [The reason given by Josephus in which he is supported by the Mishnah is, that dresses of this description were peculiar to the Priesthood, and were on that ground forbidden to the people.—Ed.]

3 ציצת Numbers, chap. xv. ver. 38.

4 פתילתכלת Ibid.

5 כתנת פסים literally *a coat of pieces* that is made of pieces, stripes, or threads, of various colours. Genesis, chap. xxxvii. ver. 3. [The Editor of the Pictorial Bible observes upon this text that the most remarkable illustration of it is that "given by Mr. Roberts, who states that in India it is customary to invest a beautiful or favourite child with 'a coat of many colours,' consisting of crimson, purple, and other colours, which are often tastefully *sewed together*; and adds, that a child being clothed in a garment of many colours, it is believed that neither tongues nor evil spirits will injure him because the attention is taken from the beauty of the person to that of the garment."—Ed.]

6 2 Samuel, chap. xiii. ver. 18.

The length of the tunic reaching to the ancles, and the straightness of the sleeves, are great objections to the idea of its being a garment universally adopted by the Jews, at least in that state; for to those persons, whose occupations required much exertion, it would have been exceedingly inconvenient: it is more reasonable to suppose, that a much shorter tunic, with looser sleeves, which would permit free exercise of the limbs, was worn by the common labourer, servants, and slaves.

In the Asiatic countries, where the garments were long, loose, and flowing, the girdle became a necessary appendage to the dress, especially to those who were walking, running, or engaged in any exercises that required agility. The girdle was bound about the loins, as may be proved by variety of instances; but the tunics of the priests were girt about the breasts, or immediately under the paps, I presume for distinction's sake.[1] Upon entering a house, it was usual for a man to loose his girdle, and take it from his loins; but it was also constantly replaced when he was about to depart; for which reason, in the Scripture phraseology, "to be in readiness" is metaphorically expressed by "*the loins being girded.*"

Golden girdles, girdles of fine linen, and also of fine twined linen, which were worn by the priests, are spoken of in the Scripture.[2] The prophets, by way of humility, wore girdles of leather;[3] and the same, I doubt not, were used by the inferior classes of the people. Some of the girdles, worn by the Hebrews, were of great value, as we may judge from the richness of the materials with which they were composed, as well as from the excellence of the workmanship: we read of their being curiously wrought with the needle, and embellished with gold. Joab said to the man, who informed him that Absalom was suspended by the hair, "Why didst thou not smite him there to the ground? and I would have given thee ten shekels of silver and a *girdle*:"[4] and it is to be observed, that embroidered girdles are still considered as an essential part of finery by the Asiatics of both sexes.

The super-tunic, or robe, was worn over the tunic; and, according to the description given of this part of the Jewish habit by Josephus,[5] it was not composed

[1] Josephus, Antiq. Jud. lib. III. cap. vii. See also the Revelations, chap. i. ver. 13.

[2] Antiq. Jud. lib. III. cap. 7. See also Exodus, chap. xxxix. ver. 29; Jeremiah, chap. xiii. ver. 1.

[3] 2 Kings, chap. i. ver. 8.

[4] 2 Samuel, chap. xviii. ver 11. There are several names in the Hebrew for this part of the habit: I shall mention only four, אבנט and מזח rendered by the LXX ζωνη; אזור from its encompassing the body; and חגורה from the verb חגר to gird.

[5] Antiq. Jud. lib. III. cap. vii.

of separate pieces, but was one long garment woven throughout without seams, with an aperture at the neck lengthways from the midst of the back to the breast; and the selvages were bound with a ribband to give a handsome appearance to the opening :[1] it was also parted at the sides through which the arms were extended, and to these apertures I presume the sleeves, if any belonged to it, were attached. In the passage referred to, Josephus is particularizing, it is true, the several parts of dress belonging to the priests; but the super-tunic is frequently spoken of in the Bible, and indiscriminately attributed to persons who had no claim whatever to the priesthood;[2] and, indeed, the robe of Aaron was sufficiently distinguished, not only by its richness and beauty, but also by the bells and pomegranates which hung from the bottom of the hem.[3] The same author assures us, that it reached to the ancles; but it was probably shorter than the inner tunic, that the fringes of the one might not hide the fringes upon the other. This garment, I presume, in every instance was rich and costly; for, it is never applied to any persons but such as were of superior rank.[4]

The cloak, or mantle, obtained an early place in the catalogue of the Jewish habits: a garment of this kind is spoken of, immediately after the deluge, as a part of dress well known, and probably derived from times still more remote than that event.[5] This mantle[6] covered the whole of the body; and, "it seems," according to a modern author,[7] "to have been much the same kind of garment as the *hyke*, which is still worn by the Kabyles and Arabs in Africa and the Levant. These *hykes*," says he, "or blankets, as we should call them, are of different sizes, and of different

[1] Or rather "that it should not be rent," Exodus, chap. xxxix. ver. 23.

[2] מעל or מעיל expresses an upper garment, but not a *mantle* or *cloak;* and it is used for the *robe* which Job *rent* when he heard of the death of his sons. The garments also of his friends, which they *rent*, are called by the same name. Job, chap. i. ver. 20; and chap. ii. ver. 12.

[3] Exodus, chap. xxviii. ver. 33.

[4] Josephus assures us, that Agrippa wore a splendid robe, woven entirely with silver, and of admirable workmanship; *στολην ενδυσαμενος εξ αργυρου πεποιημενην, πασαν ως θαυμασιον υφην ειναι.* Antiq. Jud. lib. XIX. cap. viii.

[5] Genesis, chap. ix. ver. 23. See also note (2) page ii.

[6] שלמה and שמלה which appears to be another name for the same garment, or for one exceedingly like it; and these encompassed the body entirely, as we may judge from the root שמל to *surround on all sides, to involve,* &c. whence the name is derived.

[7] Dr. Shaw. See his Travels, pp. 224 and 225.

qualities and fineness: the usual size of them is six yards long, and five or six feet broad, serving the Kabyle or Arab for a complete dress in the day; and as he sleeps in his raiment, as the Israelites did of old,[1] it serves him likewise for his bed and covering by night. The plaid of the Highlanders in Scotland is the very same."

This mantle appears to have been universally used by every rank of persons among the people of Israel; and was, I doubt not, the garment with four edges which they were positively enjoined to adorn with fringes, and with ribbands of a blue colour upon the fringes.[2]

There is another garment said to be of the cloak or mantle kind, frequently mentioned in Holy Writ, which derives its name from a word expressive of magnificence and glory;[3] and, therefore, with reason is supposed to have been superior in splendour to any other part of the ancient dress: it is appropriated to persons of high rank and authority; and, if not composed entirely of skins, dressed with the fur upon them, it was certainly ornamented with ermines and furs.[4] The name of this mantle is given to the hairy garment of Elijah;[5] and the prophets in general were clothed with the same, but perhaps of an inferior quality. "As the high priesthood and supreme civil authority, in the patriarchal times," (says Parkhurst,) "centered in the same person, hence skins and furs, which were worn at first in a religious view, came to be the insignia of civil authority."[6] It was also this robe, or mantle, that the King of Nineveh put from him when "he covered himself with sackcloth and ashes," to deprecate the vengeance of the Almighty;[7] which is no small argument in favour of its pompous appearance. The ancient mantle, described in the preceding article, is thought to have resembled the *hyke;* and the mantle, which we are now speaking of, the *burnoose*, a garment more showy than the hyke, and for that reason worn over it by the Moors in Barbary to this day: and, in

[1] Deut. chap. xxiv. ver. 13.

[2] Deut. chap. xxii. ver. 12; and Numbers, chap. xv. ver. 38. The word כנפי translated *quarters* in our Bibles signifies properly the *extremities, skirts or borders,* of a garment, and not the *quarters* of it.

[3] אדרת from the verb אדר to become *magnificent, pompous, glorious,* &c.

[4] And for this reason it is often called אדרת שער the *hairy mantle.*

[5] 1 Kings, chap. xix. ver. 13 and 19.

[6] Hebrew and English Lexicon, p. 5.

[7] Jonah, chap. iii. ver. 6.

favour of this opinion, it may easily be proved, from a passage in Micah, that this mantle of skins was anciently used as a covering for the hyke, or common mantle.[1]

Another kind of dress,[2] which might be a mantle of a smaller kind than the hyke, was used by the Jews; and differed little, I presume, from the veil which Moses put over his face when he came down from the mountain: its form, however, is no where specified, nor the materials with which it was manufactured.

The ancient vestments of the kings of Israel bore great affinity to those belonging to the high priest: excepting the bells and pomegranates upon the bottom of the robe, and the sacred pectoral, with the inscription upon the crown, appropriated to the latter, there does not appear to have been any material difference; and, if we may judge of Solomon's dress from the profusion of his wealth, and the pomp with which he made his appearance in his court, we shall readily conceive that it was not inferior in point of lustre and magnificence to the pontifical habit.

Exclusive of the splendour of his garments, the Jewish monarch was principally distinguished by the crown that he wore upon his turban; and also by the richness and form of the turban itself; and both of them owed their origin to the mitre, and lamina of gold bound upon the mitre, which adorned the head of the high priest. The name of the *regal turban* is the same that is given to the *mitre* of Aaron: and derived from a word[3] expressive of the circumvolutions of the linen by which it was

[1] ממול שלמה אדר תפשטין *You strip the* אדר or burnoose *from off the* borders *of the* שלמה or hyke. Micah chap. ii. ver. 8. If I might offer a conjecture of my own, I should, from the very passage before me, conclude that the distinction made between these garments is perfectly needless: and that the אדרת was, in this instance at least, an ornamental border of ermine to the שלמה or mantle, added either for the sake of warmth, or to render it more magnificent; and the verb to *strip*, or *flay*, used upon this occasion, will apply more properly to the stripping or tearing the upper from the under part of the same garment, than merely to taking one garment from another. The mantle, when ornamented with the fur covering, being called by the name given to the covering, is a phraseology common in the Hebrew language: thus the girdle of the ephod is called the ephod, and the word ephod often includes the whole pontifical habit. [This seems to me a very forced explanation of the passage which in the received translation runs simply thus, "Ye pull off the robe *with* the garment from them that pass by, &c." That is, you rob them of *all* their clothes "as an enemy" does those that "were averse from war." The common form of depredation in the East, especially among the Bedouin Arabs, &c. – Ed.]

[2] סותה rendered by the LXX *περιβολη*, and by the Vulgate *pallium*, occurs, Gen. chap. xlix. ver. 11; and מסוה which the LXX explain by the word *καλυμμα*, and the Vulgate *velamen*, Exodus, chap. xxxiv. verses 33, 34, 35.

[3] צניף from צנף *to turn, roll,* or *wrap round.*

formed. The use of the turban was not confined to the king and the priests: it was also worn by persons of rank of both sexes; but, without doubt, it differed in the fashion, size, and materials, according to the rank of the wearer. Thus we find, that "the Moors and Turks in Barbary, with some of the principal Arabs, wear upon the head a small hemispherical cap of scarlet cloth; and the *turbant*, as they call a long narrow web of linen, silk, or muslin, is folded round the bottom of these caps, and very properly distinguishes, by the number and fashion of the folds, the several orders and degrees of soldiers, and sometimes of citizens, one from another."[1] The turban, indeed, continues to be the usual head-dress of the Turks, Persians, Arabs, and other eastern nations, to the present day.

The regal crown, and the crown, or lamina of gold, affixed to the pontifical mitre, are both of them expressed in the Hebrew by the same word,[2] which signifies to *separate* or *set apart*, as the pontiff and the sovereign were separated from the rest of mankind, and appointed to their respective high and authoritative offices; from the name it appears that the crown was the sign of that separation, and the mark of distinguished dignity to both; for which reason we may easily conceive that it differed in its form from the crowns, or diadems, used by the monarchs of the Gentiles; and from those permitted to be worn by the princes and persons of high rank among the Jews.

The form of the regal crown is no where ascertained; but the name of the portion of gold, belonging to the pontifical mitre, may possibly throw some light upon this obscure subject. It is called *a flower of gold* in one place; and in another *the flower of the holy crown*;[3] and in both passages signifies the crown itself. The appellation of *the flower* is supposed to have been given to it, because it is made in a *flower-like*, or *radiated form*; and we may reasonably enough conclude, that the regal and pontifical crowns bore some resemblance to each other, when we are assured, that they were symbolical, in both instances, of the same thing. It appears from several parts of Scripture, that the kings in ancient times, did not appear

[1] Dr. Shaw's Travels, p. 226.

[2] נזר [nezer] and from this root the word *Nazarite* is also derived.

[3] ציץ זהב Exodus, chap. xxviii. ver. 36; and את ציץ נזר הקדש ibid. chap. xxxix. ver. 30: the word ציץ in both places certainly means a *flower*; and by no means a *plate*, as it is usually rendered. [It is rendered *petal* in the Septuagint, thereby supporting the idea that the ornament was of the form of a flower.—Ed.]

without their crown, unless upon such occasions as they chose to disguise themselves; and even that they wore them in the field of battle.[1]

The diadem, circle, or fillet of gold,[2] was an ornament also worn upon the turban by princes, and other personages of high rank.[3] The diadem was sometimes bestowed, as a mark of especial favour, by the eastern monarchs, upon such persons as they chose to honour in a very high degree. Ahasuerus, the king of Persia, caused Mordecai to be clothed in royal apparel; and a large diadem of gold[4] was placed upon his head. The diadem, or *crown*, as it is called in the English version, taken from the king of Rabbah, weighed a talent of gold; and it was adorned with precious stones.[5] The same kind of diadem was also worn by the Jewish bridegroom at his marriage. This custom is of high antiquity, as we may learn from the following passage in the Canticles: "Go forth, O ye daughters of Zion, and behold king Solomon with the *diadem*, wherewith his mother crowned him in the day of his espousals."[6] The ancient ceremony of crowning the contracting parties is still observed in the Greek church. "This second ceremony," says a modern author, "which is properly *the marriage*, is called the office of *matrimonial coronation*, from a singular circumstance attending it, that of crowning the parties. Formerly these *crowns* were garlands made of flowers or shrubs; but now there are generally in all the churches crowns of silver kept for that purpose."[7] So in the marriages of the Maronites in Syria: "a short service being performed, the bishop puts a *crown* first on the bridegroom's head; after which the bride, the bride's man, and the bride's maid, are crowned in the same manner."[8]

It was customary with rakes and debauchees, at the time of their carousals, to

[1] 2 Samuel, chap. i. ver. 10.

[2] עטר from the same root, signifying to *encompass*, or *surround*.

[3] Remove המצנפת *the turban*, and take off העטרה *the crown* from the head of "*the wicked prince of Israel.*" Ezekiel, chap. xxi. ver. 25, 26. See also Job, chap. xix. ver. 9. It appears from Josephus, that the diadem and the crown were both worn at one time; the corpse of Herod (says he) was apparelled in purple raiment, having a *diadem* upon his head, and above that a *crown of gold*: *Διαδηματί, υπερκειμενου στεφανου χρυσεου.* Antiq. Jud. lib. VII. cap. 9. [See also note 6, p. xxii. ante.—Ed.]

[4] עטרת זהב גדולה Esther, chap. viii. ver. 15.

[5] 2 Samuel, chap. xii. ver. 30; and 1 Chron. chap. xx. ver. 2.

[6] Solomon's Song, chap. iii. ver. 11.

[7] Dr. King's Rites, &c. of the Greek Church in Russia.

[8] Dr. Russell's Nat. Hist. of Aleppo, p. 127.

crown themselves with the buds of roses and with flowers, as we may judge from the words that Solomon has put into the mouth of a drunkard: "Let us fill ourselves," says he, "with costly wines and ornaments, and let no flower of the spring pass by us; let us crown ourselves with rose-buds before that they be withered."[1]

The tiara, or bonnet, called, in our translation of the Bible, the *head-tire*, was worn by the Jews of both sexes:[2] the Hebrew name is expressive of decoration and beauty,[3] and applied to this part of the head-dress by way of eminence; because it was an ornament held in the highest estimation by them, as it is by the modern Orientals to this day.[4] The bonnets of the priests were made of linen; and in their form are thought to have resembled a truncated tone, and thereby distinguished from those appropriated to the laity; but both of them are expressly said to have been *bound* upon the head.[5]

Phylacteries, or frontlets,[6] formed part of the Jewish head-dress: they consisted of scrolls of parchment, and were inscribed with portions of the law, which they were strictly enjoined to wear upon their hands also, as well as upon their foreheads; "and thou shalt bind them for a sign upon thine hand, and they shall be as frontlets between thine eyes."[7] A modern author, speaking of the head-dress of the Arabs in Yemen, and particularly of the external cap, which was often richly embroidered with gold, assures us, that all of them, that he had seen, had these words: *There is no God but God; Mohammed is the apostle of God:* or some other sentence from the Koran;[8] and this custom seems clearly to have been derived by the Mohammedan Arabians from the *frontlets* of the Jews.

Contrary to the usage of the Egyptians, who constantly shaved their heads, the Israelites permitted the growth of their hair; and when they used the razor, it was

[1] Wisdom, chap. ii. ver. 7, 8.

[2] Isaiah, chap. iii. ver. 20; Ezekiel, chap. xxiv. ver. 17, 23.

[3] פאר to *decorate* or *adorn*. This word is joined with the *linen bonnets* of the priests פארי המגבעת Exodus, chap. xxxix. ver. 28, where it is translated *goodly bonnets;* but I rather think it should have been rendered *conical tiara;* for, the word גבע signifies a *hill*, a *mountain*, or any thing of a *conical form;* and it is applied to the *caps*, or *bonnets*, of the priests, because they were in the shape of a *cone*.

[4] See Niebuhr, Voyage en Arabie, tom. I. p. 129.

[5] Leviticus, chap. viii. ver. 13; Ezekiel, chap. xxxiv. ver. 17, 23.

[6] מטפה or טוטפת.

[7] Deut. chap. vi. ver. 8, et alibi.

[8] *La Allâh illa Allâh Mohammed rasul Allâh.* Niebuhr, ut suprà, p. 55.

a sign of deep humiliation, or of mourning;[1] but the priests were forbidden to shave their heads in times of mourning, because, by so doing, they defiled themselves.[2]

It is not possible to ascertain how long the hair was suffered to grow upon the head before it was curtailed, nor the manner in which it was decorated. Long pendent locks were admired by the Israelitish ladies in the days of Solomon;[3] and probably it was for this very reason, that Absalom, the son of David, took such pains in the cultivation of his hair, which was so luxuriant, that, when he shortened it, as he constantly did at the conclusion of every year, because the weight of it became burdensome to him, the quantity he usually cut off weighed "two hundred shekels after the king's weight."[4] The Nazarites, upon a religious account, shaved not their heads, but permitted their hair to grow, the full time of their separation; and for this reason Samson said to Dalilah, "There hath not come a razor upon mine head, for I *have been a Nazarite* unto God from my mother's womb."[5] When the time of a Nazarite's separation was finished, he was brought to the door of the tabernacle; his head was then shaved; and the consecrated locks were burnt with the sacrifice upon the altar.[6] The apostle Paul considered long hair as exceedingly unbecoming to the men, and censured them for wearing of it with much severity; but commends it as a decorous and proper ornament, for distinction's sake, when appropriated to the fair sex.[7]

Samson's hair is said to have been divided into seven locks; but whether these divisions were merely optional, and made for the sake of ornament only, or positively necessary upon a religious account, I shall not take upon me to determine.

The usage of art to beautify the hair was practised by the Eastern nations at a very remote period; but the time of its introduction among the Israelites cannot be ascertained: we may trace it, however, as far back as the days of king Solomon; for Josephus assures us, that the horse-men, belonging to that monarch, powdered their

1 Job, chap. i. ver. 20; Isaiah, chap. xv. ver. 2; et alibi.

2 Leviticus, chap. xxi. ver. 5.

3 Canticles, chap. v. ver. 11; where the word תלתל signifies *pendulous*, or *hanging down*, rather than *bushy* or *curled*.

4 Equal to four pounds two ounces, Troy weight. 2 Samuel, chap. xiv. ver. 26.

5 Judges, chap. xvi. ver. 17.

6 Numbers, chap. vi. ver. 18.

7 First Epistle to Corinthians, chap. xi. verses 14, 15.

heads with gold dust every day, so that their locks shone, and the rays of the sun were reflected by the glittering of the gold.[1]

The Jews permitted their beards to grow; but at the same time they trimmed them with care. To shave the beard entirely, or to *mar* the corners of the beard, as it is expressed in the Scripture, were signs of mourning.[2] Hanun, the lord of the Ammonites, in derision shaved half the beards of David's messengers, which was considered by the Israelites as a shameful and most unpardonable insult. The neglecting also to trim the beards seems to have been a sign of sorrow; for, it is said of Mephibosheth, that he "*trimmed not his beard*" from the day that David departed from Jerusalem to the day that he returned again in peace.[3]

The patriarch Joseph shaved his beard previously to his appearance before Pharaoh; but this was rather done in compliance with the custom, established in the court of the monarch, than from a general usage derived from his progenitors.[4]

Shoes, or indeed more properly sandals,[5] were worn in the primeval ages: they anciently consisted of a sole with strings or bandages attached to the upper part of it to fasten it upon the foot. These appendages are called *shoe-latchets* in the English Bible; but that they were strings, or bandages, appears from the name they bear in the Hebrew.[6]

Bracelets of various kinds for the arms, rings for the fingers with or without the signet, and chains of gold for the neck, with other decorative ornaments, were used at a very early period by the men of Israel; but we shall have occasion to speak farther concerning these embellishments towards the conclusion of the chapter.

The garments, appropriated to the Jewish women of high rank, were exceedingly splendid, as we may judge from several passages in Holy Writ. I shall select a few of them only. The queen is said to "stand at the king's right hand in

1 *Ψηγμα δε χρυσιου καθ' ημεραν αυτων επεσηθον ταις κομαις, ως στιλβειν αυτων τας κεφαλας, της αυτης του χρυσιου προς τον ηλιον ανταvακλωμενης.* Antiq. Jud. lib. VIII. cap vi.

2 Leviticus, chap. xxi. ver. 5.

3 Samuel, chap. xix. ver. 24.

4 Genesis, chap. xli. ver. 14.

5 נעל which is usually rendered in the Chaldee *targums.* סנדל or סַנדלא and by the LXX *σανδαλιον* and *υποδημα*; with which the *caliga*, or *calceamentum*, of the Vulgate seems perfectly to agree.

6 שרוך from the verb שרך to *twine*, *bind*, or *roll round*.

gold of Ophir." To which is added: "the king's daughter is all glorious within; her clothing is of wrought gold;[1] she shall be brought unto the king in raiment of needle-work."[2] But Ezekiel speaks more fully upon this subject, where Jerusalem is typified by a deserted female, and reproached with ingratitude by the Almighty: "I washed thee," says he, "with water; I anointed thee with oil; I clothed thee with broidered work;"—alluding to the embroidered or party-coloured tunic which the royal virgins wore;—"I shod thee with azure *sandals*;[3] I girded thee about with *a girdle* of fine linen; and I covered thee with a *mantle* of fine cotton:[4] I decked thee also with ornaments; and I put bracelets upon thine hands, and a chain upon thy neck; and I put a jewel upon thy forehead,[5] and ear-rings in thine ears, and a beautiful diadem upon thine head."[6] And Judith, when she was preparing herself to appear before Holofernes, "pulled off the sack-cloth which she had on, and put off the garments of her widowhood, and washed her body all over with water, and anointed herself with precious ointment, and braided the hair of her head, and put a mitre, or *turban*, upon it; and put on the garments of gladness,"—which in another place are said to be "*linen*, wherewith she was clad during the life-time of Manasses, her husband; and she put sandals"—which the Assyrian chieftain is said particularly to have admired—"upon her feet; and put about her her bracelets, and her chains, and her rings, and her ear-rings, and all her ornaments; and decked herself bravely to allure the eyes of all men that should see her." And, in later times, the Evangelist Saint John, in the Apocalypse, describing the habit of the woman seated upon the beast, says, "she was arrayed in purple and in scarlet colour, and decked with gold and precious stones, and with pearls."[7]

[1] Or *brocaded* with *gold*, as the word ממשבצות certainly imports. Psalm xlv. ver. 14.

[2] Or *embroidery*. Ibid. ver. 14.

[3] תחש *Badgers' skins* in our Bibles; but this translation is without sufficient authority. The ancient versions universally agree, that the word imported not an *animal*, but a colour; the LXX render it by the words υακινθος and υακινθινος; and the Vulgate by *hyacinthus* and *hyacinthinus*, *azure* or *sky blue*.

[4] Not *silk*, as in our version. See p. iii.

[5] על אפך literally, *upon thy nose:* it was probably pendent from the head-dress, and hung over the forehead upon the top of the nose; but rings in the nose were worn by the Asiatic women, as we shall see hereafter.

[6] Ezekiel, chap. xvi. verses 9, 10, 11, 12. Judith, chap. x. verses 3 and 4. See also chap. xvi. verses 8 and 9.

[7] Revelations, chap. xvii. ver. 4.

The women were strictly forbidden by the Levitical law to wear the habits pertaining to the men;[1] and there is no doubt but a proper distinction was made between the dresses of both sexes, which, I presume, consisted principally in their shape; for, many garments, fabricated with the same materials, and bearing the same names, were worn by the men as well as by the women, and without any imputation of an infringement of the commandment.

A loose garment of linen, answering the purpose of a *shift*, was worn by the Israelitish women: it is called by the same name in the Hebrew language as the linen tunic of the shirt kind, appropriated to the men;[2] and might resemble it in the same degree that the shirt and shift of the present day resemble each other.

Among the parts of the dress and ornaments belonging to Jewish ladies, enumerated by the prophet Isaiah, there is one, which, by the Vulgate, and other versions after it, is rendered *looking-glasses*;[3] but, by the connection in which it stands, should rather mean some kind of *vestures*; and accordingly it is explained in the Septuagint by *garments that one might see through, of the Lacedemonian kind*[4]—alluding to the dress of the Lacedemonian maidens, which, according to the ancient writers, reached only to the knees, and was open on both sides, and exposed the person of the wearer in walking much more than was consistent with common decency.[5] "It is possible," says a modern author, "that the Jewish ladies might wear garments of a similar fashion; but I rather think, the present vestments were of the *cob-web* kind, and so transparent as not to hinder them from appearing almost naked.[6] Such a garment Menander, an ancient Greek poet, calls a *transparent vest*;[7] and speaks of it as the dress of a courtezan. The Latin authors call it a *glassy vestment*;[8] and one of them informs us, that it was made of Coan cloth,[9]

1 The *woman* shall not wear that which pertaineth unto a *man*; neither shall a *man* put on a *woman's garment*. Deut. chap. xxii ver. 5.

2 סרין Isaiah, chap. iii. ver. 23. See also p. xviii.

3 גליונים from גלה to *discover*, or *reveal*. Isaiah, chap. iii. ver. 23.

4 Διαφανη λακωνικα.

5 Plutarch, in Vitâ Numæ. This dress, adds the author, afforded sufficient subject to the poets for raillery: they gave to these girls the epithets of φαινομηριδας, and ανδρομανεις; and Euripides says of them, γυμνοισι μηροις και πεπλοις ανειμενοις. Ibid.

6 Parkhurst, Hebrew and English Lexicon, p. 89.

7 Διαφανες χιτωνιον.

8 *Vitreas vestes.*

9 Cois *tibi pænè videre est ut nudam*; through the *Coan vest* you almost see her naked. Horace, lib. I. Sat. 2, lines 100, 101.

probably of a thin texture like gauze, and so denominated from the island of Coos where this species of stuff was manufactured, not unlike the *shift* described by Lady Wortley Montague as part of her Turkish habit, which was made of fine white silk gauze, closed at the neck with a diamond button; but the shape and colour of the bosom was very well to be distinguished through it.[1]

The *concealed dress*, or *coverings for the thighs*, mentioned by Solomon in the Canticles, as part of the dress belonging to the bride,[2] agrees perfectly well with the *drawers*, still worn by the Moorish and Turkish women of rank;[3] and is happily illustrated by the lady mentioned in the preceding article: "the first part of my dress," says she, speaking of her Turkish habit, "is a *pair of drawers*, very full: they reach to my shoes, and conceal the legs more modestly than petticoats: they are of a thin rose-coloured damask, and *brocaded* with *silver flowers*."[4]

The tunics, appropriated to the women, bear the same name as those belonging to the men;[5] but, without doubt, they differed from each other in their form: in both cases, where they belonged to persons of rank, they were made of linen,[6] and on particular occasions, embellished with embroidery. The variegated vesture, or tunic of *many colours*,[7] was worn by the virgin daughters of the Jewish monarchs;[8] and the raiment of needle work, embroidered with gold, spoken of in the forty-fifth Psalm as belonging to them, is in my opinion precisely the same garment.[9]

The girdle appears to have been considered as an essential part of the female habit, and esteemed not only for its usefulness, but also for the sake of ornament: those belonging to the women of distinction were made of fine linen; and, in many

1 Letter to the Countess of Mar, April 1, 1717. [Such transparent garments are continually pourtrayed in the ancient Egyptian paintings. Ed.]

2 חמוקי ירכיך Song of Solomon, chap. vii. ver. 1. These words are explained by "*the joints of the thighs*," which cannot bear any distant analogy to the *engraved work*, executed by *the hands of perseverance* (as it is expressed in the original), with which they stand in comparison; but the simile is perfectly applicable to the *brocaded work* with *flowers* resembling that of the engraver. The word חמק signifies *concealment* in its primitive sense; and the *drawers*, especially that part of them belonging to the *thighs*, were concealed by the *superior garments*.

3 Dr. Shaw's Travels, p. 228.

4 Letter to Countess of Mar, April 1, 1717.

5 כתן See p. xxvi.

6 Judith, chap. xvi. ver. 8.

7 כתן פס See page xxvi.

8 2 Samuel, chap. xiii. ver. 18.

9 Psalm xlv. verses 13, 14.

instances, superbly enriched with needle work and embroidery, as they are in the Eastern countries to this day.[1]

There is an ornamental part of the female habit, called *a tablet*[2] in our version of the Old Testament, but it is thought by the lexicographers to have been of the girdle kind; to which may be added the *swathe*, or *cincture* for the breast, called a *stomacher*;[3] and how far these might differ from the girdle, usually spoken of, cannot be determined.

Changeable suits of apparel, according to the English translation, are enumerated among the garments belonging to the Jewish ladies by the prophet Isaiah; but this interpretation of the Hebrew word there used is too general: it imports a *loose robe*, or *surcoat*, which was worn only upon particular occasions.[4] The same word, in another passage of the Scripture, is applied to the *robes* of the high priest;[5] and they are called by the Septuagint *robes reaching to the feet*.[6] A *surcoat* of the like kind appears to be worn by the Turkish women to this day; and it is described by an eye-witness as a *loose robe*, thrown off, or put on, according to the weather, being of rich brocade, and lined with ermines, or with sables.[7]

A mantle, analogous to the *hyke*, (the finer sorts of which are still worn by the women of rank among the Arabs,) and also to the *peplus* of the ancient Greeks,[8] formed part of the dress appertaining to the Hebrew ladies: this mantle is particularly mentioned in the book of Ruth;[9] and the attendant circumstances prove it to have been of a considerable size, and strong enough to contain a large quantity of barley:[10] in all probability it covered the whole of the body, and was chiefly used in cold, or wet, weather.

There was also another *mantle*, or *veil*, appertaining to the Jewish women, that

1 The Hebrew name for this part of the dress is חגור and it is applied to the *girdles* of both sexes.

2 כומז This ornament is said to have been made of *gold* in the two only passages in which it occurs; namely, Exodus, chap. xxxv. ver. 22; and Numbers, chap. xxxi. ver. 50.

3 פתיגיל Isaiah, chap. iii. ver. 24.

4 מחלצות from חלץ to *loosen*. Isaiah, chap. iii. ver. 22.

5 Zechariah, chap. iii. ver. 4.

6 Ποδηρη.

7 Called a Curdee, Lady M. W. Montague's Letter to the Countess of Mar, April 1st, 1717.

8 Dr. Shaw's Travels, p. 225.

9 The Hebrew name is מטפחת from טפח to *spread out*, or *extend*; it is called a *veil* in our version; but the word *mantle* seems much more applicable to it. Ruth, chap. iii. ver. 15; Isaiah, chap. iii. ver. 22.

10 *Six measures full*. Ruth, ut suprà.

reached to the feet; and it is called by the Septuagint (but for what reason I know not) a *summer garment*:[1] it was certainly an external covering, and worn by them when they went abroad; but the materials of which it was composed are not specified.

There are several words in the Hebrew language expressive of the *veil*, or covering for the head and face; and, probably, every one of them denoted some essential difference with respect to the form and texture of this part of the female dress.

The first that I shall mention was a covering for the head and face, if not for part of the body also; and was used for the sake of modesty: when Rebecca first saw Isaac at a distance, she took a *veil*,[2] and covered herself: and it was also sufficiently opake to conceal effectually the features of the wearer; for, when Tamar had *covered herself* with this *veil*,[3] her father-in-law Judah did not discover her person, though it is expressly said, that he had carnal intercourse with her, conceiving her to be a harlot, because she sat with her face concealed by the road side. The word, by which this veil is expressed, occurs only in the early part of the Jewish history: the garment itself was probably changed in the succeeding ages for others more thin and transparent; and for them new names of course were invented.

The kerchiefs, or *close veils*,[4] were certainly ornamental coverings for the head, and became the subjects of admiration either for the richness of the materials with which they were made, or for the beauty and elegance of their form.

Thin veils of gauze, or of some transparent substance of the like kind, were in use among the Jewish ladies as early as the time of Solomon: to this ornament apparently he alludes in the Canticles, where, speaking of the bride, he says, "thine eyes *are like those* of doves behind thy *veil*:"[5] in the English translation the beauty

[1] Θεριστρον; and by the Vulgate *pallium* and *theristra*; the Hebrew word is רדיד from רדה to *descend*. Canticles, chap. v. ver. 7; Isaiah, chap. iii. ver. 23.

[2] צעיף rendered by the LXX θεριστρον; but it does not by any means appear, that the use of it was confined to the *summer*. Genesis, chap. xxiv. ver. 65.

[3] Genesis, chap. xxxviii. verses 14, 19.

[4] מספחים which the LXX translate επιβολαια, *veils*, or *coverings*. Ezek, chap. xiii. verses 18, 21.

[5] עיניך יונים מבעד לצמתך and the word בעד with the מ prefixed signifies *from behind*, and not *within* Song of Solomon, chap. iv. ver. 1; see also ver. 3; and chap. vi. ver. 7. So in Isaiah, chap. xlvii. ver. 2, גלי צמתך, *remove thy* VEIL, and not *uncover thy* LOCKS, as a token of disgrace and infamy.

of this passage is lost; it is there rendered, *thou hast dove's eyes within thy locks;* that is, the *locks* of the *hair*, which, to justify the simile, must have hung over her eyes, and would of course have given her the appearance of a savage rather than of a polished lady decorated with all the splendour of Asiatic finery. Besides, it is well known, that every woman of rank or character in the Eastern part of the world to this hour appears veiled before the men:[1] the veil here mentioned is supposed to have been so transparent, that the radiancy of the eyes might be seen through it; which perfectly explains the spirit of the compliment. We need not, indeed, have gone from our own country to elucidate this text: the English ladies of the present day sufficiently exemplify it by the thin gauzes which we so frequently see dependent from their caps and bonnets. To what has been said upon this subject I shall only add, that the veil was anciently considered as a substitutional protection to the female sex; and therefore the removing or turning it forcibly aside was conceived to be the highest affront that a man could be guilty of towards them.[2]

Mufflers[3] formed part of the female habit; and were probably of the *veil* kind. Mr. Parkhurst supposes them to have been the same as the Turkish *murlins*,[4] which are thus described by a lady, who had frequent opportunities of seeing them. "No woman, of what rank soever, is permitted to go out into the streets without two *murlins;* one that covers the face all but her eyes, and another that hides the whole dress of her head, and hangs half down her back."[5]

Braiding, curling, and plaiting of the hair was practised by the Jewish ladies of rank: it seems, indeed, to have been a necessary preparation for the proper reception of a variety of ornaments, with which they afterwards adorned their heads; and contributed not a little to the setting them out to advantage: to this custom the

[1] Thus a modern author. The most essential part of the dress of the women of the East seems to be the *veil*, with which they cover their faces when a *man* approaches. Niebuhr, Voyage de l'Arabie, p. 134.

[2] And therefore it is, says Mr. Parkhurst, the removing of *the veil of Judah*, threatened in the twenty-second chapter of Isaiah, expresses the *utmost misery* and *ignominy*. Hebrew Lexicon, page 434, under סך

[3] מעטפות literally the *hiders*, rendered *mantles* in our translation. Isaiah, chap. iii. ver. 22. [The word "mufflers" occurs in verse 19. Ed.]

[4] Hebrew and English Lexicon, page 473.

[5] Lady M. W. Montague's Letter to the Countess of Mar, April 1, O. S. 1717.

prophet Isaiah alludes, where he speaks of "well-set hair" in opposition to "baldness:" we find Judith also "braiding her hair," previous to the placing of the turban upon her head, when she was decorating herself on purpose "to allure the eyes of all men that should see her."[1] The plaiting and braiding of the hair was carried to excess in the latter ages; for, we find it censured with severity by the apostles St. Peter and St. Paul.[2] The passage, quoted a few lines back from Isaiah, literally translated, would be *stiffened work*;[3] and the ladies in the East to this day *stiffen*, that is, *braid*, or *plait*, their hair, so as to make it *stiff*, with ribbands. A modern author, speaking of the Moorish women of rank in Barbary, assures us, that they all affect to have their hair hanging down to the ground, which, after they have collected it into one lock, they bind and plait with ribbands; and, where nature has been less liberal in this ornament, there the defect is supplied by art, and foreign hair is procured to be interwoven with the natural.[4] The hair of the Turkish ladies, according to another recent writer, "hangs at its full length behind, divided into tresses, *braided* with pearl, or ribband, which is always in great quantity:"—to which is added, "I never saw in my life so many fine heads of hair; in one lady I have counted a hundred and ten of the tresses, all natural;"[5] and the head-bands, or ribbands, which are placed by Isaiah in the catalogue of the female decorations,[6] were probably the same that were used in the braiding and binding up of the hair.

Crisping pins, or rather bodkins,[7] are numbered among the ornaments appertaining to the Jewish ladies; and perhaps they might be used f.r the adornment of the hair: bodkins, ornamented with jewels, make part of the finery still worn by the Turkish ladies of rank.[8]

The kerchiefs, or cawls, mentioned by Isaiah as ornaments for the head,[9] bore some analogy, I presume, to the embroidered kerchiefs which the Turkish ladies use at present to bind on their talpocks, or caps.[10]

[1] Judith, chap. x. ver. 3.

[2] 1 Peter, chap. iii. ver. 5; and 1 Tim. chap. ii. ver. 9.

[3] מעשה מקשה Isaiah, chap. iii. ver. 24.

[4] Dr. Shaw's Travels, p. 228.

[5] Lady M. W. Montague's Letter to the Countess of Mar, April 1st, 1717.

[6] קשרים from the root קשר *to bind about.* Isaiah, chap. iii. ver. 20; see also Jeremiah, chap. ii. ver. 32.

[7] חריטים Isaiah, chap. iii. ver. 22.

[8] Lady M. W. Montague's Letter to the Countess of Mar, March 10th, 1717.

[9] שביסים rendered by the LXX κοσυμβους, and by Montanus *Reticula*, cauls of net-work, Isaiah, chap. iii. ver. 11.

[10] Lady M. W. Montague's Letter to the Countess of Mar, April 1st, 1717.

The turban, or, as it is frequently called, the mitre, formed an essential part of the head-dress belonging to the Jewish ladies; but the turban was by no means confined to the usage of the fair sex: it was equally worn by the men; but then it differed, I doubt not, materially from that which belonged to the females, not only in the form, and in the materials with which it was composed, but also in the decorative ornaments.[1]

The tiara, or *bonnet* as it is called in our translation, was a head-dress worn by the Jews of both sexes, and held by them in the highest estimation, as we have seen in a former part of this chapter.[2]

Borders or rows of gold or jewels are mentioned in the Canticles as an adornment for the cheeks of the bride;[3] and probably they were like the strings of pearls which the Turkish females of distinction place round their head-dress;[4] or rather, perhaps, resembled the two or three rows of pearls which the Persian ladies wear about the head, beginning on the forehead, and descending down the cheeks and under the chin, so that their faces seem to be set in pearls.[5]

The *shoes*, or *sandals*,[6] appertaining to the Jewish women, formed an essential part of their dress; how far they differed from those belonging to the men cannot be ascertained: it appears, however, that they were more ornamental; for, the sandals of Judith are said to have *ravished the eyes* of Holofernes.[7] The materials, with which the sandals were composed, are not specified; but light blue seems to have been the colour most admired, as may be gathered from the expression, "*I shod thee with azure*," which is applied to Jerusalem under the type of a woman sumptuously adorned.[8]

It does not appear that the Israelitish ladies made use of cosmetics for the beautifying of their skins, or that they anciently adopted the custom of painting their faces: we have, however, incontestible proof that they tinged their eye-lids for the improvement of their beauty; and probably derived this custom from Jezebel

1 See a full description of the turban, p. xxxi. 2 Page xxxiii.

3 Thy cheeks are comely with תורים *rows*, or *borders*; from the root תר to go round about. Song of Solomon, chap. i. verses 10, 11.

4 Lady M. W. Montague's Letter to the Countess of Mar, March 10th, 1717.

5 Olearius, cited by Harmer, p. 205.

6 Σανδαλια. Judith, chap. x. ver. 4. 7 Ibid. chap. xvi. ver. 9.

8 Ezekiel, chap. xvi. ver. 10. See page xxxvi, and note (3) of that page.

the Sidonian, the first upon record among them for a practice of like kind.[1] It is spoken of by the prophet Ezekiel with great disapprobation, and applied to an harlot;[2] which seems to indicate that it was not very generally adopted at that time. The Moorish ladies in Barbary, the women in Arabia Felix, and those about Aleppo, continue, to this day, the custom of tinging the inside of their eye-lids, which they perform with the powder of lead ore;[3] and Dr. Russel informs us, that it was "upon the principle of strengthening the sight, as well as for the sake of ornament, that it became a general practice among the Asiatic women to *black the inside of the eyelids*, by applying a powder called *ismed*:[4] their method of doing it is by a cylindrical piece of silver, steel, or ivory, about two inches long, made very smooth, and about the size of a common probe: this they wet with water, in order that the powder may stick to it; and, applying the middle part horizontally to the eye, they shut the eye-lids upon it; and so drawing it through between them it blacks the inside, leaving a narrow black rim all round the edge. This is sometimes practised by the men; but it is then regarded as foppish." Painting the eyes was by no means anciently confined to the Jews, nor even to the Asiatic nations as we shall see hereafter.

The ornamental parts of dress, appropriated to the Jewish ladies, exclusive of those immediately connected with their garments, were exceedingly numerous; and many of them from the obscurity of the original names of doubtful interpretation; those that follow compose the greater part of them; but how far they are justly translated, or properly applied, must be left to the reader's judgment.

The nose-jewel is an adornment of high antiquity: we find it spoken of as early as the days of Abraham; and it was one of the ornaments which the servant of that patriarch presented to Rebecca: "I put," says he, "the jewel *upon her nose*."[5]

[1] 2 Kings, chap. ix. ver. 30. See also Jeremiah, chap. iv. ver. 30. [In the English translation of the Bible, the Hebrew word for *eyes* in these two passages has been rendered "*face*." Ed.]

[2] Ezekiel, chap. xxiii. ver. 40. The word here used is כחל to *colour, paint,* or *tinge;* in the two passages, quoted in the note immediately preceding, the word is פוך which signifies the *mineral,* or *substance,* from which the *paint* itself was made.

[3] Which they call *al kahol,* according to Dr. Shaw; see his Travels, p. 229; or *kochel,* which approaches nearer to the Hebrew word כחל See Niebuhr, in his Description of Arabia, p. 58.

[4] This is made of a substance called also *Ispahany* from the place whence it is brought: it appears to be a *rich lead ore,* &c. Nat. Hist. Aleppo, p. 102.

[5] אשם הנזם על-אפה Genesis, chap. xxiv. ver. 47. This jewel was of gold, and equal in weight

The nose-jewel is also mentioned frequently enough in the succeeding parts of the Bible; and we have the testimony of a modern writer, that it is "the custom, in almost all the East, for the women to wear *rings in their noses* in the left nostril, which is bored low down in the middle. These rings," continues the author, "are of gold, and have commonly two pearls, and one ruby between them placed in the ring. I never saw a girl, or young woman in Arabia, or in all Persia, who did not wear a ring after this manner in her nostril."[1] And to this custom of wearing rings of gold in the nose, without doubt, Solomon alluded in the Proverbs, when he compared "a jewel of gold in a *swine's snout*" to "a fair woman without *discretion*."[2]

The jewel just mentioned was probably worn in the ear as well as in the nose; at least, it is certain that an ornament of like kind, and bearing the same name, occurs in several passages of Scripture, and is expressly said to have belonged to the ears. The ear-rings, worn by the Jewish women during the time of their sojourning in the wilderness, were made of gold.

Another kind of ear-rings, differing, I presume, in shape or size, and perhaps in both, from the former, are mentioned in the Bible:[3] they are called by a different name; and, probably, obtained the appellation given to them from the rotundity of their form.[4] The author cited above assures us, that two sorts of ear-rings were worn in the East, when he was there: "some of them," says he, "are so small, and go so close to the ears, that there is no vacuity between them; and others are so large, that you may put the fore-finger between, adorned with a ruby and a pearl on each side of it strung upon the ring." "I have seen," adds the author, "some of these larger ear-rings with figures upon them, and strange characters, which I believe to be talismans, or charms. The Indians say, they are preservatives against enchantments: perhaps the *ear-rings* of Jacob's family, which he buried with the strange gods, were of this class."[5]

A third kind of ear-rings, if the English translation be accurate, is mentioned by Isaiah; and the word so rendered is certainly applied by the prophet to some deco-

to half a shekel, or 109 grains Troy weight. [The passage in our translation stands, "I put the ear-ring upon her face." Ed.]

1 Sir John Chardin, cited by Harmer, vol. II. p. 390.

2 Proverbs, chap. xi. ver. 22.

3 Exodus, chap. xxxii. ver. 2.

4 עגיל which signifies *rotundity*, or *roundness*.

5 Sir John Chardin, ut suprà. See Genesis, chap. xxxv. ver. 4.

rative part of the female dress; but it seems at the same time to denote a species of ornament that yielded a low whistling or tinkling sound,[1] which, indeed, two or more drops pendent from the ring might do by striking against each other; and more particularly, if they consisted of little bells resembling those that are said to be attached to the hair of the women of pleasure at Cairo to this day.[2]

It is uncertain whether the ear-rings were anciently worn by the Jewish men as well as by the women, according to the modern practice[3] in the East; we learn, however, that the ears of the male children, equally with those of the females, were decorated with these ornaments.

Little moons, or round ornaments in form of the *moon*, are mentioned by the prophet Isaiah among the adornments used by the Israelitish women: they are called *round tires*[4] in our translation; and, from the connection in which they stand with the cauls, or kerchiefs, are thought to have belonged to the head-dress. The same kind of ornaments, or ornaments at least bearing the same name, were hung upon the necks of the camels appertaining to Zebah and Zalmuna, the Midianitish chieftains: they are spoken of in the book of Judges, and particularly distinguished from the chain which surrounded the necks of the camels, and from which, I presume, the *round ornaments* were suspended.[5]

Adornments for the neck of various sorts are mentioned in the Sacred Writings: *rows* of pearls, or something of the like kind, disposed in the form of a necklace, are said in the Canticles to have graced the neck of the royal bride;[6] and this passage of Scripture may, I think, be elucidated by an extract from a modern writer, who, describing the dress of a Turkish sultana, says, "round her *neck* she wore three *chains*, which reached to her knees; one of large pearls, at the bottom of which hung a fine coloured emerald as big as a turkey's egg; another, consisting of two hundred emeralds, close joined together, of the most lively green, perfectly matched,

[1] They are called לחשים from לחש to make a *soft hissing, whistling*, or *tinkling sound*. Isaiah, chap. iii. ver 20.

[2] Pitts, pp. 99, 100.

[3] The contrary rather appears to be the case; for, in Judges, we find the Ishmaelites particularly distinguished, because they had *ear-rings of gold in their ears*. Judges, chap. viii. ver. 24.

[4] שהרנים rendered by the LXX *μηνισκους*; and by the Vulgate *lunulas*. Isaiah, chap. iii. ver. 18.

[5] Judges, chap. viii. verses 21, 26. [Vide the interesting notes on these passages in the Pictorial Bible. Ed.]

[6] חרוזים rendered by the LXX *ορμισκοι*, *collars*, or *necklaces*. Song of Solomon, chap. i. ver. 10.

every one as large as half a crown piece, and as thick as three crown pieces ; and another of small emeralds perfectly round."[1]

Chains, or a similar kind of ornaments encompassing the neck, are also particularised, which seem to have differed from the former, being called by another name ; and it appears, that the Jewish women in Solomon's time wore several of these chains at once about their necks,[2] as the Asiatic ladies do to this day ;[3] and these, I presume, were the chains which Judith forgot not to adorn herself with when she sought to charm the heart of the Assyrian general :[4] it also appears, that they were worn by the men as well as by the women.

Chains of gold, or jewels, distinguished by an appellation different from those given to the preceding ornaments, are placed in the catalogue of female embellishments, recorded by the prophet Isaiah ; but no information is added to the name.[5]

The wreathen collar for the neck[6] was worn by both sexes ; but it seems to have been a badge of high honour when it was appropriated to them.[7]

Bracelets for the arms were in use at a very remote period : they formed part of the ornaments which the servant of Abraham presented to Rebecca : the bracelets there mentioned were made of gold, and weighed five shekels each.[8] It is probable, that the Israelitish women might derive from the Egyptians the usage of wearing bracelets upon their legs also, which is practised by the Moorish women in Barbary to this day.

The arm-bracelets were not confined to the use of the fair sex : on the contrary, they were worn (and that in ancient times) by the men also ; but they are then called by a different name, and appear to have been wreathed, or twisted.[9]

[1] Lady M. W. Montague's Letter to the Countess of Mar, March 10th, 1717.

[2] "Thou hast ravished my heart באחד ענק *with one chain* of thy neck." Canticles, chap. iv. ver. 9.

[3] Niebuhr, Voyage, tom. i. p. 242.

[4] Called in the Greek χλιδωνας. Judith, chap. x. ver. 4.

[5] They are called שרות and seem (says Parkhurst) to have derived their name from their *regular* structure : the word is rendered by the Vulgate *monilia*, necklaces. Isaiah, chap. iii. ver. 19.

[6] רביד Ezekiel, chap. xvi. ver. 11.

[7] Genesis, chap. xli. ver. 42. Daniel, chap. v. ver. 7.

[8] Equal to 1090 grains Troy-weight; see Genesis, chap. xxiv. ver. 22: they are called in the Hebrew צמידים.

[9] פתיל from פתל to *wreath*, or *twist*. Genesis, chap. xxxviii. verses 18, 25.

Chains, or bracelets, ornamented, I presume, with open work, are also spoken of in the Scripture; and were worn upon the arms of both sexes.[1]

Rings, or rather bracelets of gold, set with beryl,[2] are mentioned in the Song of Solomon; and they appear to have formed part of the dress belonging to the royal bridegroom.

Ornamental fetters, or shackels,[3] translated *tinkling ornaments*, in our version of the Bible, are placed among the decorative parts of finery appropriated to the Hebrew women by the prophet Isaiah;[4] and might possibly resemble the fetters of silver, which Pliny tells us were worn by women of the lower rank among the Romans.[5] A modern author speaks of *great rings*, which the common female dancers of Egypt wear upon their legs.[6] Another writer of the present age informs us, that the Arabian women, whom he saw in his passage down the Euphrates, "wore *rings about their legs* and hands, and sometimes a good many together, which in their stepping slipped up and down, and so made a great noise;" and, according to Sir John Chardin, in Persia and Arabia the women wear rings about their ancles, which are full of *little bells*, "Children and young women," adds he, "take a pleasure in giving them motion, and walk hastily for that very purpose."[7]

Mirrors, even in the ancient times, were worn as an ornamental part of the dress by the Hebrew women: it is evident, that they were composed of metal, and particularly of brass; for, the foot of the laver which Moses caused to be made was fabricated with the mirrors of the women who assembled in crouds at the door of the tabernacle.[8] Mirrors, or looking-glasses, are still an essential part of the dress

[1] אצעדה This ornament is expressly said to have been taken from the arm of Saul, 2 Samuel chap. i. ver. 10; but the Vulgate renders the same word in Isaiah, chap. iii. ver. 20, *periscelidas*, or *drawers*; and our translators *ornaments for the legs*.

[2] גלילי זהב ממלאים בתרשיש Canticles, chap. v. ver. 14. Mr. Parkhurst thinks the word תרשיש should be translated *topaz*, rather thau *beryl*, as it stands in our Bibles.

[3] עכסים from the verb עכס to *confine* or *fetter*.

[4] "The daughters of Zion are haughty, and walk with stretched-forth necks and wanton eyes, mincing as they go, and make a tinkling with their feet. In that day the Lord will take away הפארת *the bravery* of their העכסים *tinkling ornaments* about their feet." Isaiah, chap. iii. verses 16, 18.

[5] Nat. Hist. lib. XXXIII. cap. 12.

[6] *Les grands anneaux.* Niebuhr, Voyage en Arabie, tom. i. pp. 133, 148.

[7] Rauwolf, cited by Parkhurst, p. 474; and Sir John Chardin's Travels.

[8] ויעש—את כנו נחשת במראת Exodus, chap. xxxviii. ver. 8; see also Job, chap. xxxvii. ver. 18.

of the Moorish women in Barbary: "they hang them constantly," says a recent writer, "upon their breasts, and do not lay them aside, even in the midst of their most laborious employments."[1]

Tablets or rather *perfume-boxes*,[2] are enumerated among the ornaments worn by the Jewish women of rank; and still are in use among the Persian ladies, to whose necklaces, which fall below the bosom, is fastened a large box of *perfumes*: some of these boxes are as big as one's hand; the common ones are of gold; others are covered with jewels: they are all bored through, and filled with a black paste, very light, made of *musk* and *amber*, which emits a very strong smell.[3]

Drop-ornaments,[4] or pendent jewels in the form of drops, spangles of gold and silver,[5] and clasps, or buckles,[6] to fasten the garments, are spoken of as appertaining to the habits of the Hebrew ladies; and the latter were used by the men also, among whom the permission to wear a fibula, or clasp of gold, was esteemed a high honour.[7]

The usage of finger-rings is exceedingly ancient; and it appears to have been equally adopted by persons of rank of both sexes among the Jews. The signet-rings were marks of authority, appropriated chiefly to kings, princes, and noblemen; and, when they were conferred upon persons of inferior stations, they were considered as honorary favours of the highest kind.[8]

We do not find in the Old or New Testaments the least distant hint respecting pockets appertaining to the garments of the Jewish people. The scrip, or satchel,[9] I presume, was the succedaneum for the pockets; at least, we find it to be a necessary

[1] Shaw's Travels, p. 241.

[2] בתיהנפש *houses of the soul,* if literally translated; and properly rendered *olfactoriola* by the Vulgate. Isaiah, chap iii. ver. 20.

[3] Complete System of Geography, vol. II. p. 175.

[4] נטפית [5] רעלות [6] חח

[7] The Jews, in order to confer great honour upon Simon, their governor and high priest, among other things, ordained that he should be clothed in purple, and wear a *fibula*, or buckle of gold, πορπην χρυσην; and that no other person should be clothed in purple, or wear a *fibula of gold.* Maccabees, chap xiv. verses 43 and 44; see also chap. xi. ver. 58.

[8] The word חותם or חתמה signifies not only a *signet*; but also a jewel, with the name of a beloved person engraven upon it, and worn next the heart, or upon the arm. See Canticles, chap. viii. ver. 6; Jeremiah, chap. xxii. ver. 24; Haggai, chap. ii. ver. 23; and Ecclesiasticus, chap. xlix. ver. 11.

[9] ילקוט

appendage to the dress of travellers; and it was also used by the shepherds to carry their food and other necessaries:[1] to this we may add the purse or bag for money, and for weights to weigh the money, which persons of almost every rank had constantly about them.[2]

We have little more than mere names to assist our researches respecting the military habits of the Israelites: their knowledge of tactics was probably derived from the Egyptians; and it must be confessed, that they do not appear to have been by any means deficient in military skill at the time they resided in the wilderness. The thorax, or pectoral; the plated girdles for the body; the military *sagum*, or cloak, called an *habergeon* in our translation of the Pentateuch; together with the helmet; and the shields, which are of two kinds, the one larger than the other; formed the chief part, if not the whole, for their defensive armour:[3] their offensive arms consisted of swords, some of which had two edges; daggers, spears, javelins, bows, arrows, and slings.[4] Axes also, or perhaps the word ought rather to be rendered *clubs*, or *maces*, were used as weapons of war.[5]

Their weapons appear to have been made of brass, and of iron, or steel, for the original word admits of both interpretations:[6] we read also of shields of gold, that is, I presume, plated with gold; for, we may easily conceive, that they would have been much too heavy for common use, if they had been made entirely of gold, or of any other metal.[7]

1 1 Samuel, chap. xvi. ver. 40.

2 כים Deut. chap. xxv. ver. 13; Proverbs, chap. i. ver. 14; Isaiah, chap. xlvi. ver. 6; and Luke, chap. xxii. verses 35, and 36, in which last passage the *purse* and *scrip* are clearly distinguished from each other—*βαλαντιον και πηρα*.

3 It does not appear, that the Jews used the *greaves*, or leg-armour: they are mentioned in only one passage in Scripture, 1 Samuel, chap. xvii. ver. 6, and formed part of the armour of Goliath the Philistine giant.

4 The slingers are said to have been so expert, that, "*seven hundred*" of them in one army, "*could sling stones at a hair's breadth, and not miss.*" Judges, chap. xx. ver. 16.

5 מפץ rendered *battle-axe* in our translation, Jeremiah, chap. li. ver. 20.

6 נשק ברזב a *weapon* of *iron* or *steel*, Job, chap. xx. ver. 24; קשת נחושה *a bow of brass*, ibid. and Psalm xviii. ver. 34. [It is improperly rendered a bow of steel, in our translations. The Hebrew word is, *pechushah*, the common word for brass.—Ed.]

7 The *shields* and *targets*, which Solomon caused to be made and hung up in his palace, were of *massy gold*; but at the same time it appears that they were merely ornamental. 1 Kings, chap. x. verses 16, 17.

The thorax, or *pectoral*,[1] is a part of body-armour exceedingly ancient. If it originated in Egypt, and there is some foundation for such an opinion, it is not unlikely, that the Israelites derived its usage from that country. The pectoral is usually called, in the English translation of the Old Testament, a *coat of mail;* and probably, in remote times, it was attached to a short tunic in the same manner that the sacred breast-plate was fastened upon the ephod.[2] Beneath the pectoral were belts, plated with brass, or other metal; and the uppermost of them was bound upon the bottom of the tunic, which connected the pectoral with the belts; and all of them together formed a tolerably perfect armour for the front of the whole body.[3]

The military *sagum*, or cloak, is called, in our translation, an *habergeon ;* that is, a kind of mail, or armour, to cover the head and breast: the original word is of doubtful signification;[4] but, of whatever kind the garment may have been, it appears that it had an aperture at the upper part of it, through which the head was passed when it was put upon the body. If I might hazard a conjecture upon a subject so uncertain, I should say, that it was the tunic upon which the thorax was

[1] The Hebrew word is שרין or שריון from שרה *to be strong*; and probably the same kind of armour is meant by Jeremiah, who uses the word סרין or in the plural סרינות from the verb סר *to turn aside,* as the armour does the point of the weapon. Jeremiah, chap. xlvi. ver. 4; and chap. li. ver. 3.

[2] Resembling, I presume, the χιτων χαλκεος, or *brazen vest*, mentioned by Homer, Iliad, lib. XIII. line 439. [The English word used in both the texts of Jeremiah above quoted is "*brigandine,*" which is not a coat of mail, but a quilted tunic, with iron plates sewed up in it. Ed.]

[3] These belts, called זגות in the Hebrew, which were generally two, one above the other, are frequently met with in the ancient Grecian sculpture; and an example of them is given upon the fifth plate belonging to this Introduction; see fig. 4 and 5; but in some instances they rise higher upon the breast; and this mode of armament perfectly explains the passages in Scripture, where Ahab is said to have been smitten with an arrow בין הדבקים *between the openings*, or *joints*, that is, of the belts, ובין השרין *and between the thorax*, or *pectoral;* 1 Kings, chap. xxii. ver. 34; 2 Chron. chap. xviii. ver. 33. The pectorals of the Egyptians were made of linen; and perhaps anciently those of the Jews were the same. In after-times they seem to have been covered with plates of metal; and in the New Testament we meet with the word θωρακας σιδηρους, or *pectorals of iron;* Revelations, chap. ix. ver. 9.

[4] תחרא the word occurs only twice; "*and there shall be a hole in the top in the midst thereof;*" that is the robe of the ephod: "*it shall have a binding of woven work round about the hole of it, as it were the hole of an* habergeon, *that it be not rent.*" Exodus, chap. xxviii. ver. 32; and chap xxxix. ver. 23. [I am at a loss to know why Mr. Strutt calls this the military *sagum* or *cloak*, as it is evidently a military tunic, which furnishes the comparison as he himself conjectures immediately afterwards. Ed.]

fastened, and bore the same relation to the thorax that the ephod did to the sacred pectoral.

There were two sorts of helmets in use among the Jewish warriors; at least, the helmets are distinguished by two different names:[1] they are both of them said to have been made of brass;[2] but their form is totally unknown: the helmet belonging to the Israelitish monarch was distinguished from those of his subjects by the crown which was placed upon it.[3]

There are four sorts of shields specified in Holy Writ: their form is no where described; but it is certain, that they differed in their size.[4] From the expression of Isaiah, "arise, ye princes, and *anoint* the *shields*,"[5] some have thought, that the Israelites possessed the art of making their shields with leather, or raw hides; but the use of oil would be equally proper, if they were covered with brass, to keep them from rusting, and to make them bright.[6]

The offensive weapons, which are only mentioned by name in the Sacred Writings, have been enumerated above: it will therefore be needless to say any thing farther concerning them, as it is totally impossible to ascertain their form, which, in all probability, did not greatly differ from those in use among the other Asiatic nations. I shall only add, that the sword was usually girded upon the thigh, as we may learn from the expression frequently used in Scripture, "gird every man his sword upon his thigh;" whence also it appears, that they did not wear the swords continually, but only when the exigency of the times required the use of such weapons.

It is highly probable, that the Jews had some kind of distinctive habits appropriated to those persons who attended upon the sacred offices, previous to the dispensation of the law from Mount Sinai; and, if they resembled the religious

[1] כובע and קובע

[2] 1 Samuel, chap. xvii. verses 5. 38; et alibi.

[3] 2 Samuel, chap. i. ver. 10.

[4] *And king Solomon made two hundred* צנה targets *of beaten gold; six hundred* shekels *of gold went to one target: and three hundred* מגנים shields *of beaten gold, three pounds of gold went to one shield,* &c. 1 Kings, chap. x. verses 16 and 17. Hence it is evident, that the צנה was larger than the מגן—the שלטים in one passage seems to have been the same as the טגנים "*there hang a thousand* המגן bucklers *all* שלמי shields *of mighty men.*" Canticles, chap. iv. ver. 4. The סחרה is a *small shield, or buckler:* "*His truth* shall be thy צנה shield [translated *target* above. Ed.] and סחרה buckler." Psalm xci. ver. 4.

[5] Isaiah, chap. xxi. ver. 5.

[6] Universal History, vol. III.

habits of the Egyptians, the change then made in them will appear to have consisted rather in the form and beauty of the garments than in the introduction of such as were totally unknown before.

A tunic reaching to the feet, a pectoral, a robe of equal length with the tunic, and a mitre with an asp upon the front of it, constituted, as we have seen already, the habit of the Egyptian deity Osiris, which is supposed to have corresponded exactly with the habit of the high priest of the Egyptians; and the component parts, with some few variations and additions, formed the magnificent vestments of Aaron.[1]

The dress of the Jewish high priest included all the parts of the inferior sacerdotal habits; but such of them as belonged to him were made of richer materials, and much more splendidly decorated than those in common use.

The pontifical vestments were the *femoralia*, or drawers; the tunic; the robe of the ephod; the girdle for the robe; the ephod; the sacred pectoral; the curious girdle of the ephod; and the mitre, adorned with a lamina, or crown of gold.[2]

The femoralia, according to Josephus, was called *manachasin*,[3] because they were made fast upon the wearer: he describes them as being so constructed, that the priest might thrust his feet through them; and, when drawn up, they were fastened about the loins, and also upon the thighs, which answers well to the *drawers* now in use, saving only that they do not appear to have descended so far upon the thighs. The *femoralia* are expressly said to have been made of fine twined linen;[4] and they were common to all the priesthood.

The tunic, or *close coat*,[5] was so denominated, because it sat close to the body: it had also strait sleeves, according to Josephus, and descended to the ancles. "This vestment," says he, "has no loose or hollow parts, only a narrow aperture about the neck tied with certain strings,[6] hanging down from the edge over the

[1] See page xxiii; and plate III. fig. 3.

[2] Exodus, chap. xxviii. and xxxix to ver. 33.

[3] Μαναχασην. Josephus, Antiq. Jud. lib. III. cap. vii. The Hebrew name is מכנסים which is rendered *breeches* in our Bibles.

[4] ואת מכנסי הבד שש משזר Exodus, chap. xxxix. ver. 28.

[5] The literal translation of כתנת תשבץ is *a coat of inclosing*; in our version of the Pentateuch it is rendered a *broidered coat*; but the adjective *broidered* does not agree well with the word שבץ the primitive signification of which is to *close*, *inclose*, or *straiten*. Exodus, chap. xxviii. ver. 4, et alibi.

[6] This is according to Whiston's translation: the original word is αρπεδοσιν. Josephus, ut suprà.

breast and over the back, and it is fastened upon each shoulder: this they call *massabazanis*."[1] The tunic, according to Moses, was made "of fine linen of woven work," which Josephus calls "fine linen double."[2] The tunic of linen was worn by all the priesthood; and to it was appropriated "a girdle of fine twined linen, and blue, and purple, and scarlet, of needle work."[3] This girdle, according to Josephus, was about four fingers broad, and so loosely woven as to resemble the skin of a serpent: it was interwoven with flowers of scarlet, of purple, of blue, and of fine linen; but the warp consisted of linen only: it was several times bound round the tunic, the circumvolutions beginning at the breast where it was fastened, and the remaining part of it hung loosely down to the ancles; but at the time when the priest was employed in his sacred functions at the altar, it was cast over his left shoulder, lest it should be blown about by the wind, and interrupt him in his duty. The high priest had a girdle of the same kind, which he girt upon the robe of the ephod; but this girdle, adds our author, was more richly embellished with gold.[4]

The robe of the ephod[5] was made of *woven work*[6] all *of* blue; and *there was* a hole[7] in the midst of the robe, as "the hole of an habergeon," *with* a band[8] round about the hole, "that it should not be rent;" and upon the skirts at the bottom of the robe were promegranates of blue, and of purple, and of scarlet, and of twined linen, interchangeably placed between bells of pure gold, "a bell and a promegranate round about the hem of the robe."[9] Josephus assures us, that this garment, like the tunic, reached to the feet: "It is not," says he, "made of two distinct pieces sewed together at the shoulders and at the sides; but it is one entire long garment, woven throughout without a seam, so as to leave an aperture at the neck, not an oblique one, but parted along the back and breast; to which an edging, or border, was affixed, to give the opening a more elegant appearance: it was also parted where

1 Μασσαβαζανις, or *a coat open at the top*, according to Whiston. Josephus also gives the name χεθομενη, *chethomene*, to this garment, which he derives from χεθον, *chethon*, linen: lib. III. ut suprà.

2 Διπλης σινδονος βυσσινος, *duplicis syndonis byssinæ*. Ibid.

3 מעשה רקם may equally be rendered *variegated work* woven in the loom, or *brocaded*, as well as work *wrought with a needle*. Exodus, chap. xxxix. ver. 29.

4 Moses called this girdle αβανηθ *abaneth*, אבנט says Josephus; and we, by a word borrowed from the Babylonians, name it εμιαν *emian*. Antiq. Jud. lib. III. cap. 7; and Exodus, chap. xxxix. ver. 29.

5 מעיל See pages xxxii and xxxiii.

6 מעשה ארג Exodus, chap. xxxix. ver. 22.

7 פי or *mouth* in the original. Ib. ver. 23.

8 שפה an *edge*, or *border*. Ibid.

9 Ibid. verses 24, 25, 26.

the hands came out;"[1] from which circumstance, one may be led to judge that this robe had no sleeves, or, if any, that they were very large and loose. The robe, as we have seen in a former part of this chapter,[2] was a garment common to all persons of rank; but the robe, distinguished by the pontifical ornaments, belonged to the high priest alone, and was not even worn by him but upon occasions of great solemnity.

The ephod, according to Moses, was made of gold, of blue, and of purple, and of scarlet, and of fine twined linen: it had two shoulder-pieces "to couple it together; by the two edges was it coupled together;"[3] which seems perfectly to justify the opinion that it had no sleeves, but was like the tabard of an herald, consisting of two pieces, open on the sides, and joined together on the shoulders beneath the breast-plate: it was also made fast to the body by the curious girdle, which is expressly said to have been "upon the ephod," and made precisely of the same materials. Josephus differs from the sacred historian, and asserts that the ephod had sleeves, and that it resembled the *epomidis* of the Grecians:[4] he describes it as woven to the depth of a cubit with several colours intermixed with gold and embroidered. He also adds, that it was not at all different from a short tunic. Two onyx stones, on which were engraved the names of the sons of Israel, were set in "ouches," or *sockets*, of gold,[5] and placed upon the shoulders of the ephod; also upon the front of the ephod was affixed the sacred pectoral, which was four square and double; "a span was the length of it, and a span was the breadth of it:" it was made of "cunning work," like the work of the ephod, of gold, of blue, and of purple, and of scarlet, and of fine twined linen; and there were set in it, in sockets of gold, four rows of precious stones, three stones in each row; and upon them were engraved the names of the children of Israel, according to the twelve tribes: there were also four rings of pure gold affixed to the pectoral, in which were inserted four wreathen chains of gold; the two uppermost chains were attached to the sockets of gold upon the

1 Josephus, ut suprà. The same author also informs us, that the name they gave to this robe was *μεθειρ*, or *μεειρ*. Ibid.

2 Page xxxii.

3 Exodus, chap. xxxix. ver. 2, et infra. The manner in which they prepared the gold for the purpose of embellishing the sacred vestments deserves our notice: "*and they did beat the gold into thin plates, and cut* it into *wires, to work* it *in the blue, and in the purple, and in the scarlet,* with *cunning work.*" מעשה חשב Ibid. ver. 3.

4 Ελληνικ η επωμιδι, Antiq. ut suprà.

5 משבצת זהב Exodus, chap. xxxix. ver. 6.

shoulders of the ephod; and the two lower chains, beneath the pectoral, to two rings of gold, which were placed upon the lower part of the ephod, immediately above the girdle, on purpose for their reception.[1] The "curious girdle," which was also an appendage to the ephod, and sewed upon it, according to Josephus, encompassed the body, and, returning, was fastened upon the seam; and the ends, decorated with fringes fastened in hollow loops of gold, were permitted to hang downwards. The ephod, ornamented with the Sacred pectoral, and other magnificent appendages described above, was appropriated to the high priest alone; but ephods of linen, with girdles of the same material, were worn, not only by the sons of Aaron upon particular occasions, but also by persons who had not the least pretension to the priesthood.[2]

The tiara, or bonnet, used by the Jewish priests when they officiated at the altar, did not, according to Josephus, cover the head, but was made of thick ribbands, or of linen often folded and sewed together, so as to resemble a chaplet: the upper part of the bonnet was covered with fine linen, which descended over the front, and concealed the seams of the envelopement, because the appearance of them was thought to be inelegant. The same kind of tiara was also worn by the high priest; to which was added a second, adorned with wreaths of blue, and round it a crown of gold polished, consisting of three rows one above another, out of which arose a cup of gold resembling the herb called *saccharus*, or *hyoscyamus*.[3] Such is the description given by Josephus of the mitre and crown belonging to the Jewish pontiff; and,

[1] Exodus, chap. xxxix. verses 15, 16; et infra.

[2] 1 Chronicles, chap. xv. ver. 27.

[3] Σακχαρῳ, *called by the Greeks* ὑοσκυαμος. In another part of his writings Josephus thus describes the habit of the high priest when he officiated: he had breeches which reached to his thighs; he wore a linen tunic descending to his feet, and above it a blue round robe without a seam, reaching to his ancles: this robe was ornamented with fringes at the bottom, and hung full of bells and pomegranates: upon his breast he had *ζωνην*, a zone, or *girdle*, of five rows of colours; namely, gold, purple, scarlet, fine linen, that is, *white*, and blue. The ephod was composed of the same materials as the zone, but richer with gold: it resembled the tunic, and reached to the thighs; it was also fastened with two *ασπιλισκαι χρυσαι* or *fibulæ of gold*, embellished with the most precious sardonyx stones that could be procured, on which were engraved the names of the twelve tribes of Israel; on the other side did hang in four rows, three in each row, twelve more precious stones, every one of them bearing the name of one of the twelve tribes: upon his head was a tiara of fine linen surmounted with blue; and above it a crown of gold, whereon were engraved the sacred letters. These garments he used only once a year, when he went into the sanctuary alone. Bel. Jud. lib. VI. cap. vi.

without doubt, it corresponded exactly with those splendid adornments as they appeared in his day, for he was himself a priest, and could hardly be ignorant of the form of sacerdotal vestments then in use ; but, probably, all of them had undergone several material changes since the time of their first institution, which may account for the variation that appears in several instances, when his description of them is compared with that given by Moses.

The bonnets of the priests, and the *turban*, or mitre, of Aaron, certainly differed from each other ; and they are therefore called by different names in the Hebrew ;[1] but how far the variation is properly distinguished, or the real form of either justly given by Josephus, I cannot presume to determine : there is nothing, however, in the Sacred Text to justify the description of the *triple crown*, which, he tells us, was placed upon the turban ; neither is his representation of that crown perfectly conformable to a second description given of the sacred mitre and its appendages in a succeeding part of his work.[2]

The priests and Levites were prohibited the use of woollen garments at the time they officiated in their sacred offices : it does not, however, appear that the prohibition extended beyond that time ; indeed the words of the prophet Ezekiel afford a strong negative argument to the contrary ; they run thus : "and it shall come to pass, when they," *that is, the priests and Levites*, "enter in at the gates of the inner court, they shall be clothed with linen garments ; and no wool shall come upon them whilst they minister in the gates of the inner court, and within. They shall have linen bonnets upon their heads, and shall have linen breeches upon their loins ; they shall not gird *themselves* with anything that causeth sweat. And when they go forth into the utter court, *even* into the utter court to the people, they shall put off their garments wherein they ministered, and lay them in the holy chambers ; and they shall put on other garments ; and they shall not sanctify the people with their garments ;" to which is added : "Neither shall they shave their heads, nor suffer their locks to grow long ; they shall only poll their heads."[3]

Josephus speaks of a religious sect among the Jews, called Esseans, who, contrary to the usual custom of the Asiatics, considered the anointing the body with

[1] See page xxx. with the note (3) ; and page xxxiii. with the note (5).

[2] See the last note but one.

[3] Ezekiel, chap. xliv. verses 17, 18, 19, and 20.

oil as a defilement; but were by no means so careful to wipe away the moisture occasioned by perspiration: their garments were white; and they wore them, as well as their shoes, without any change, until they were perfectly unfit for farther service.[1]

I cannot conclude this section without a few short observations concerning the habits of the Philistines and other nations immediately bordering upon the country possessed by the children of Israel: the civil habits of the Philistines, indeed do not seem to have differed very materially from those of the Jews; for, when Sampson had lost "thirty shirts and thirty changes of raiment," which he had promised to the Philistines upon the explication of his riddle, he slew thirty men of Askelon, and took their shirts and their changes of garments, which he gave to the men who had expounded the riddle, without any notice being taken by them, that they were such garments as belonged to their own nation; neither was that circumstance any part of the stipulation, when the wager was first proposed, and received the consent of both parties.[2]

The religious habits appropriated to the Philistines are not specified; but, with respect to their military accoutrements, we have some little information left upon record, I mean in the description given of the arms belonging to Goliath the giant of Gath: they consisted of a helmet, a coat of mail, greaves, a small and large shield, a spear, and a sword.

The helmet was made of brass,[3] and no otherwise particularised; but the coat of mail consisted of plates of brass, laid over each other in the form of scales, which is expressed by a word in the original Hebrew[4] that is totally omitted in our translation; and its weight was five thousand shekels of brass.[5] The greaves, or literally *shining plates* of brass,[6] which belonged to the Philistine, are expressly said to have been "upon his feet;"[7] and not like the Grecian greaves, which covered the whole of the legs, and left the feet without protection.[8] The small shield (for,

[1] Bell. Jud. lib. II. cap. viii.

[2] Judges, chap. xiv. verses 12, 13, and 19.

[3] כובע נחשת 1 Samuel, chap. xvii. ver. 5.

[4] קשקשים *scales;* and with the word שדיון properly rendered by Espenius *lorica squamatum*, or *mail of scales:* in the Vulgate it is called *lorica hamata*, that is *hooked*, or *barbed*, *mail;* but the former interpretation agrees best with the original word.

[5] Or about 189 pounds Troy weight.

[6] כצחה נחשת Samuel, chap, xvii. ver. 6.

[7] על־רגליו Ibid.

[8] See plate v. fig. 2, 4, and 5; and the three figures, plate viii. of the Introduction.

it seems that Goliath was provided with two shields) is said to have been borne *between his shoulders*, that is, flung, I presume, at his back by a strap, or belt, whence he could easily take it when required in the time of action. The larger shield was carried before him by his armour-bearer.[1] His spear was headed with iron, and seems to have been remarkable only for its size; the head weighed five hundred shekels.[2] The materials, from which his sword and the sheath belonging to it were fabricated, are not specified: the sword, indeed, appears to have been of excellent workmanship; for, it is said that there was "*none like that*;"[3] but its size was hardly in proportion to the rest of his arms, because David, at a future period, made use of it instead of his own.[4]

The Midianites and the Ishmaelites were rich from traffic; and they seem especially to have prided themselves in the sumptuousness of their garments and valuable adornments annexed to them. The kings of Midian were clothed in purple: they wore also drop-ornaments of gold, with chains, and bracelets, and round jewels, of the same metal; and the Ishmaelites were particularly distinguished by the ear-rings of gold with which their ears were decorated.

The Ammonites, and the Moabites,[5] so far as any one may judge from the prodigious abundance of gold and precious jewels found upon the dead bodies, after they had been miraculously defeated in the wilderness of Tekoa,[6] were fond of pompous apparel: the crown of the king of the Ammonites, which David took from him, was made of gold, and adorned with precious stones; and Josephus assures us, that there was in it a sardonyx stone of great value.[7]

[1] I am well aware, that Mr. Parkhurst and Mr. Bate are of opinion, that the כידון was not a *shield*, according to the usual translations, nor yet a *large spear*, as others have thought, because, in this passage, it appears to be distinguished from both: they conceive it to have been a *missile weapon* of some kind, which, according to the latter, was not very short, because, says he, "Joshua stretched it out as a signal to the ambuscade." Joshua, chap. viii. ver. 18. The same word occurs also, Job, chap. xxxix, ver. 23; and chap. xli. ver. 26; but, with all due deference to these learned writers, I cannot see why the giant should not have had two shields, especially as his armour-bearer carried one of them; nor why a shield, stretched out by the Jewish general, might not have been as easily perceived by the people in ambush as a javelin. I have, therefore, retained the common translation: the shield borne before him was the צנה concerning which, see page lx. and the note (4).

[2] Or about 22 pounds Troy weight. [3] 1 Samuel, chap. xxi. ver. 9. [4] Ibid.

[5] Judges, chap. viii. ver. 26; Numbers, chap. xxxi. ver. 50.

[6] 2 Chronicles, chap. xx. ver. 25.

[7] 2 Samuel, chap. xii. ver. 30; and Josephus, Antiq. Jud. lib. VII. cap. 7.

The Sabeans, or *drunkards*, as the word is rendered in the margin of our Bibles, from the wilderness, are described with bracelets upon their hands, and beautiful crowns upon their heads; and the dress may probably refer to one or other of the nations mentioned above.[1]

The Phœnicians, and especially the Tyrians, were famous for their skill in the clothing manufactures: the fine linen which they wore was the produce of their own country; and the purple dye belonging to them, which was probably an invention of their own, was holden in universal estimation. We may judge of the excellence of their productions by the admirable workmanship of the Tyrian, who superintended the fabrication of the sumptuous ornaments and sacred habits for the use of the temple built by Solomon.[2] It is highly reasonable to suppose, that a nation, possessed of every requisite for finery, would appear in a manner corresponding to its ability; and this indeed, we may be assured, was the case, if the people at large followed the example of their sovereign; for, the prophet Ezekiel, addressing himself to the king of Tyre, says, "thy covering," that is, the garments which he wore, "is" adorned with "every precious stone; the sardius, the topaz, and the diamond, the beryl, the onyx, and the jasper, the sapphire, the emerald, and the carbuncle, and gold."[3]

The habit of the priests of Phœnicia and Syria, according to Herodian, was a tunic of linen, reaching to the feet, with long sleeves; and in the middle of the tunic there was a stripe of purple; and their shoes were made of linen.[4]

The Phœnicians, and the Syrians, who inhabited Palestina, at least such of them as went to the assistance of Xerxes by sea when he invaded Greece, had helmets upon their heads nearly resembling the helmets of the Grecians, and pectorals of quilted linen[5] upon their breasts: they were also armed with javelins, and every one of them carried a round shield without a boss or protuberance at the centre.[6]

[1] Ezekiel, chap. xxiii. ver. 42. [These crowns, judging from the context, may have been crowns of flowers, chaplets, or garlands.—Ed.]

[2] 2 Chronicles, chap. ii. ver. 14, &c. See also Josephus, Antiq. Jud. lib. VII. cap. 3.

[3] Ezekiel, chap. xxviii. ver. 13.

[4] Herodian, lib. V

[5] Θωρηκας λινεους. Herodotus in Polymniâ, lxxxix.

[6] Ibid.

SECTION IV.

THE ANCIENT HABITS OF THE ASSYRIANS, OF THE PERSIANS, OF THE MEDES, AND OF OTHER ASIATIC NATIONS.

If it be granted that the clothing arts existed anterior to the deluge, it will not be unreasonable to suppose, that the first exertion of those arts, posterior to that event was made upon the spot where the immediate descendants of Noah took up their abode; and especially in the plains of Shinar, where they were collected together in one large mass, and remained a considerable time in union with each other. Among the Assyrians we might therefore expect to find the clothing manufactures flourishing at a very early period, and carried to a great extent of excellence; but history is silent upon this subject: and the inhabitants of Egypt appear to have eclipsed the fame of all the Asiatic nations respecting their productions from the loom; and especially in the manufacturing of fine linen.

The first historical description we meet with concerning the Assyrian habits occurs in the writings of Herodotus: he informs us, that the Babylonians wore two tunics: the one was an interior garment made of linen,[1] and reached to the feet; the other was an upper vestment of woollen cloth;[2] but the form or length of it is not specified. Over these tunics they wore a white *chlandion*, or small cloak.[3] Their shoes, or perhaps we ought rather to say *sandals*,[4] the historian tells us, were made in a fashion peculiar to the country, not unlike those of the Bœotians; but unfortunately the form of both is totally unknown at present. "They wear," continues he, "long hair, and cover their heads with mitres," or *turbans*.[5] "They anoint the whole body with perfumed oils; and every man has a ring with a signet, and carries a staff, or *sceptre* curiously wrought, on the top of which is placed an apple, a rose, a lily, or an eagle, or some other image: neither is he permitted to carry a sceptre without an adornment of the like kind."

1 Ποδηνεκει λινεῳ, *ad pedes demisso lineo* Herodotus in Clio, cxcv.

2 Ηρινεον χιτωνα. Herodotus in Clio, cxcv.

3 Χλανιδιον λευκην, *penulam album*. Ibid.

4 Υποδηματα. Ibid.

5 Κεφαλας μιτρησι Ibid.

The prophet Ezekiel, who lived upwards of a century earlier than the Grecian historian, speaks of the large *tiaræ*, or *mitres of dyed cloth*, which the Babylonish princes wore about their heads.[1] In another place, he mentions the gorgeous apparel, and long robes of the Assyrian chieftains.[2]

Daniel tells us, that three men, Shadrach, Meshach, and Abed-nego, were, at the command of Nebuchadnezzar, bound in their mantles, with their turbans, their upper woollen tunics, and their under linen tunics :[3] which description well answers to that above, given by Herodotus ; and, if the interpretation of the Sacred Text be just, proves, that the habits of the Babylonians, in the time of the Grecian historian were perfectly conformable to the habits of the ancient Assyrians, and not confounded with those of the Persians. Herodotus makes no mention of the girdle ; but the prophet Ezekiel, in the passage cited above, assures us, that it formed a part of the ancient *Chaldean* dress.[4] The Assyrian soldiers, in the time of Xerxes, had helmets of brass to cover their heads ; every one of them had a short sword, a buckler, and javelin, after the manner of the Egyptians, a pectoral made of linen, and a truncheon of wood pointed with iron.[5]

History affords us no material information respecting the habits of the Assyrian ladies : it is natural, however, to conclude, that they were not inferior in point of finery and elegance to those of the men; and this opinion will appear more probable, when we recollect that ear-rings, nose-rings, bracelets, and other jewels of gold, formed part of their adornment at a very early period.[6] Semiramis, indeed, according to an ancient Greek author, adopted such a garment as rendered the distinction of her sex exceedingly doubtful.[7] The same kind of robe, called the *stole of Semiramis*, adds the historian, was holden in high estimation by the *Medes* when they became lords of Asia, and by the Persians after them.[8]

The Persian habits anciently were exceedingly simple, and the Persians them-

[1] סרוחי טבולים בראשיהם *spreading or stretching out to great extent ;* that is, of the *dyed attire about their heads.* Ezekiel, chap. xxiii. ver. 15. [2] Ibid. ver. 6, and 12.

[3] בסרבליהון פטשיהון וכרבלתהון Daniel, chap. iii ver. 21. ולבושיהון

[4] The Chaldeans "*girded with* girdles *upon their loins.*" Chap. xxiii. ver. 15.

[5] Herodotus in Polymniâ, lxiii. [6] Genesis, chap. xxiv. ver. 22 ; et alibi.

[7] This she did for political reasons, to give herself a more bold and masculine air, especially when she appeared at the head of her army. Diodorus Siculus, lib. II. cap. I.

[8] Ibid.

selves a rude and uncivilized people, if the description given of them by Sandanis the Lydian be just: "You are preparing, O king," says he, to Crœsus king of Lydia, "to make war against a people, who have no other clothing than skins,[1] who inhabit a barren country, and fare hardly." Their military dress was composed of leather, which was girt about the body with a leathern girdle; this was anterior to the reign of Cyrus;[2] that monarch, having extended his conquests through great part of Asia, introduced the Medean habit among his subjects; but, during the whole of his government, the Persian garments continued to be coarser and plainer than those belonging to the Medes.[3] After his death the Medean luxury was cherished in Persia; for, says Xenophon, speaking of his own time, "it is not enough for the Persians to have soft couches, but they must have carpets at their feet, that the floors may not by resistance make a noise, the carpets being placed to break the sound. In the winter it is not sufficient for them to clothe their heads, their bodies, and their feet, but they have coverings made of hair for their hands and fingers.[4] In the summer the shade of the trees and of the rocks cannot satisfy them; but under these, men stand near them with umbrellas;"[5] and, from this period, the dresses of the Medes and of the Persians were so blended together, that it was impossible to distinguish their forms from each other.

The Persians, according to Strabo, took their dress from the Medes, which, he tells us, consisted of the *tiara*, the *cidaris*, the *pileus*, *tunics* with sleeves, and the *anaxyrides;* to which may be added the *candys:*[6] the three first were coverings for the head; the anaxyrides were breeches bound upon the loins, and frequently reached to the ancles; the candys was an exterior part of the habit, resembling the pallium, or cloak, of the Greeks and Romans.[7] In another place, the same author describes the Persian dress in this manner: "the garments of their chiefs are the anaxyrides, with a double or triple lining; a tunic, with sleeves, lined, that reaches

[1] Οι σκυτινας μεν αναξυριδας, σκυτινην δε την αλλην εσθητα, φορεουσι; *who wear* subligacula, or *breeches of leather, and the rest of their garments are also of leather.* Herodotus in Clio, lxxi.

[2] Ibid.

[3] Xenophon, de Cyri institut. lib. I.

[4] Χειριδας δασειας και δακτυληθρας. Ibid. lib. VIII.

[5] Ibid.

[6] Τιαρα γαρ τις, και κιδαρις, και πιλος, και χειριδωτοι χιτωνες, και αναξυριδες, και κανδυες. Strabo Geographus, lib. XI.

[7] The candyes belonging to the Persian soldiers were fastened with a buckle; and their colour was a particular purple, called αλιπορφυρος; whereas other persons wore their candyes of a common purple colour.

to the knees; an *hypendites*, which is a kind of under-tunic, white in the inside, and on the outside flowered; the candys for the summer is of purple or violet colour, and that for the winter flowered; their tiaræ are like those of the magi; and their shoes close and double."[1]

The Persians, says Herodotus, wear the habit of the Medes, because they think it more becoming than their own;[2] and Xenophon tells us, that Cyrus chose to wear the Medean dress, and recommended it to his followers, alleging, that it hid the defects of the person, and made the wearer appear more tall and handsome. They had also a sort of shoes, or *sandals*, so contrived, that certain additional parts might be placed in them beneath the feet, without being seen, to give them the appearance of being taller than they really were.[3]

The dress of Cyrus, after he had adopted the Medean habit, and as he appeared at a public procession, is thus described: his tiara was raised above his head, and round the tiara was placed a wreath, or diadem;[4] his tunic was of a purple colour intermixed with white, which mixture of white was prohibited to every other person; and his hands were extended beyond the sleeves of the tunic; his breeches, which covered the whole of his legs, were yellow;[5] and his candys, or mantle, was altogether of a purple colour.[6]

Astyages, the grandfather of Cyrus, was arrayed in a purple tunic, with the mantle called candys; a wreathen collar[7] surrounded his neck; and his arms were adorned with bracelets;[8] his complexion and his eyes were painted;[9] and his head decorated with a peruke,[10] which was probably no more than a kind of supplemental hair added to his own; for, painting the face and eyes, and wearing additional hair, was a custom commonly practised by the ancient kings of the Medes;[11] and Cyrus, according to Xenophon, permitted his followers to colour their eyes, that they might appear to have finer eyes than they really had, and paint their faces to mend their complexions.[12]

1 Strabo, lib. XVI. 2 Herodotus in Clio, cxxxv. 3 Xenophon, ut supra, lib. VIII.

4 Ορθην εχων την τιαραν—και διαδημα περι τῃ τιαρᾳ. Ibid. Xenophon adds, that all the relations of Cyrus were permitted to wear a *diadem* upon the tiara.

5 Αναξυριδος υσγινοβαφεις. Ibid. 6 Κανδυν ολοπορφυρον. Ibid.

7 Στρεπτοι. Ibid. lib. I. 8 Ψελλια. Ibid.

9 Οφθαλμων υπογραφη. Ibid. 10 Κομαι προσθετοι. Ibid.

11 The Medes and Persians were fond of long hair, which they constantly clipped close to the head when they went into mourning. Quintus Curtius, lib. X. 12 Ibid. lib. VIII.

Alexander, says Diodorus Siculus, affecting the Persian manners, caused a Persian diadem to be put upon his head, and wore a white tunic and belt resembling those of the Persian monarchs, and adopted all the other parts of their dress, except the anaxyrides and the candys;[1] but Plutarch informs us, that he objected to the tiara also.[2]

There are several passages in Scripture, particularly in Esther and in Daniel, which convey a clear idea of the astonishing pomp and splendour prevalent in the courts of the Persian monarchs; but, as they are too general for my purpose, I shall content myself with the following quotation: "Then having passed through all the doors, she," *Esther*, "stood before the king, who sat upon his royal throne, and was clothed in all his robes of majesty, all glittering with gold and precious stones, and he was very dreadful:—and so he held up his golden sceptre"[3] Profane history also perfectly coincides with the Sacred writings upon this subject, as the following extracts selected from abundance of others will sufficiently prove. Quintus Curtius informs us, that, when Darius was preparing his army to oppose the Grecians, who, under the conduct of Alexander, had invaded Persia, Charidemus, a Persian statesman, told him, "that, although his soldiers were clothed in coloured garments, glittering in armour of gold, far exceeding in brilliancy and riches any pomp that had gone before, yet they would not readily affright the Macedonians, who," continued he, "are a brave and hardy people." The same author also describes the manner in which Darius appeared with his army: "First," says he, "there came three hundred and sixty-five young men, habited in scarlet, equal in number to the days of the year; these were followed by others habited in white, bearing rods of gold; then came the grand guard of the Persians called *immortal,* because as fast as one of them died, his place was filled up by another—the richness of their dress far exceeded any of the rest; they had all of them chains of gold; their tunics were embroidered with gold; and the sleeves of the tunics were adorned with pearls: at a small distance from these followed a band consisting of fifteen thousand, called *Doripherii,* reputed for the king's cousins, all habited like women, who, for the variety and splendor of their garments, were exceedingly remarkable; and those who were wont to receive the king's robes rode next before the chariot of Darius. The

[1] Diodorus Siculus, lib. XVII. cap. viii.

[2] Plutarch, in vitâ Alexandri.

[3] Rest of Esther, chap. xv. ver. 6—10.

monarch himself was apparelled in most sumptuous attire: his garments were composed of purple impaled with white, on which were falcons fighting with each other, richly embroidered with gold: he was girded with a girdle of gold; and from it hung his sword, the scabbard of which was composed of one entire pearl: upon his head he wore a diadem, called by the Persians *cydaris*, which had a roll about it of green and white."[1]

We meet with no particular description of the garments appertaining to the Persian and Median ladies: without doubt, they equalled those of the men in richness, delicacy, and elegance; those especially which belonged to the queens of Persia must have been exceedingly sumptuous; for, we learn from unquestionable authority, that the revenues of whole cities were given to them; the one to provide them with girdles; another to supply them with necklaces; a third to procure them shoes; and in this manner the whole of their dress was completely furnished.[2]

The robes belonging to the Persian ladies of high rank were long, and trailed upon the ground, as we learn from a passage in Esther: "she, being gloriously adorned," in order to appear before Artaxerxes, king of Persia, "took her two maids with her; and upon the one she leaned, as carrying herself delicately; and the other followed bearing up her train."[3]

Linen, I presume, formed great part of the dress of the fair sex; and an ancient author assures us, that there was nothing more disgusting, or held more dishonourable by the Persian women, than to put their hands to wool, or to be forced to wear woollen clothes.[4]

The Persians, according to Xenophon, had arms for a close fight, a pectoral upon the breast, and a shield in the left hand;[5] and the same author, speaking of the soldiers in the army of Cyrus, says, many of them had handsome tunics, and

[1] Quintus Curtius, Vita Alexandri, lib. III. I shall not presume to determine the difference between the *cydaris*, the *tiara*, and the *pileus*, the three coverings for the head, which Xenophon, and other ancient authors, assures us were used by the Medes and Persians: perhaps the reader may meet with the representations of all of them among the curious figures remaining upon the ruined walls of Persepolis, which are finely engraven in Le Brun's Voyage to Persia, vol. II. and copied in the ancient Universal History; to which books the reader is referred. [Vide also Sir Robert Kerr Porter's Travels in Persia, 2 vols. 4to. Ed.] I shall only add from Xenophon, that it was the prerogative of the Persian monarch to wear an upright tiara.

[2] Herodot. ut supra. Plato in Alcib. p. i.; et alibi.

[3] Rest of Esther, chap. xv. verses 2, 3, 4.

[4] Quintus Curtius, lib. V.

[5] Xenophon, ut supra, lib. I.

elegant pectorals, with helmets. The horses likewise, continues he, were armed with forehead-pieces, and breast-plates; the single horses with thigh-pieces; and those joined together in the chariots with plates upon their sides; so that the whole army glittered with the brass, and appeared beautifully decked with scarlet habits. In another passage he says, all those that were with Cyrus were armed with the same arms that he was: they had scarlet tunics,[1] a pectoral of brass, brazen helmets with white crests, and swords; and every one of them had a spear made of the cornel tree. Their horses were armed with forehead-pieces, breast-plates, and side-pieces; and the side-pieces served as thigh-pieces to the rider. The arms of Cyrus, and those of his companions, were gilt, and differed in no one particular, excepting that his were brighter and more highly polished.[2]

We have good authority to prove that the offensive as well as the defensive arms were often made of gold; for, Herodotus expressly assures us, that many golden swords were found among the spoils taken from the Persians.[3]

The Medean and Persian soldiers belonging to the army of Xerxes, according to Herodotus, had every man a tiara for his head that was impenetrable; a tunic, covered with plates of iron like the scales of a fish, and adorned with sleeves of various colours; an Egyptian pectoral; the anaxyrides, which covered the legs as well as the thighs; and a *target*[4] of cane, strongly compacted for a shield, which served also to cover the quiver: to which were added a javelin, a short bow with long arrows made of cane, and a sword suspended from a belt from the right side;[5] but the same author informs us, that some of the Persian cavalry wore helmets of brass.[6]

The Sagartians, a people of Persian extraction who accompanied Xerxes, had no weapon except a short sword, and a net made of cord,[7] which they threw over their opponents; and having entangled them with the net, they were presently slain.

Xenophon describes the military dress of Abradates, king of the Susians, in

[1] *Χιτωσι φοινικοις.* Xenophon, lib. VII. [2] *Ωσπερ κατοπτρον εξελαμπεν—shone like a mirror.* Ibid.

[3] Herodot. in Calliope, lxxx. [This is not such "good authority," as Herodotus may have only meant swords or cimeters hilted, scabbarded and highly ornamented with gold. Ed.]

[4] Γερρα. Herodot. in Polymn. lxi. [5] Ibid. [6] Ibid. lxxxiv.

[7] Σειρησι πεπλεγμενησι εξ ιμαντων. Ibid. lxxxv.

the following manner: when he was about to put on his linen pectoral, Panthea (his wife) brought him a golden helmet with *arm-pieces*,[1] and broad bracelets for his wrists, together with a purple tunic reaching to his feet, which hung in folds at the bottom, and a crest of violet colour.[2]

The religious habits of the ancient Persians are little known. In the time of Cyrus the Great, the principal lords of his court, who were called *Æquales*, usually assisted at the offerings and festivals with crowns upon their heads, because it was the general opinion, that the gods were delighted to behold the magnificence of those who made oblations to them, and received them the more favourably upon that account;[3] and here may be added the following extract from Herodotus: "when a Persian is about to sacrifice he builds no altar, kindles no fire, makes no libation, nor uses either flutes, fillets, or consecrated flowers; but, wearing a tiara, decorated chiefly with myrtle upon his head, leads the victim to a clean spot of ground, and invokes the gods."[4]

The Parthian habit consisted of a tunic with long sleeves, which was girded about the loins, and reached to the knees: above the tunic they wore a mantle, or *chlamys*, fastened upon the shoulder with a fibula; and it descended as low as the tunic; the tiara belonging to this people, rising nearly to a point, was bent forward after the fashion of the Phrygian bonnet; their shoes were close on all sides; and their breeches reached to the feet.[5] When the Parthians, says Justin, grew wealthy, they clothed themselves in the Medean apparel, which he describes as garments thin, translucent, and flowing.[6] According to Plutarch, the kings of Parthia imitated the dress of the ancient kings of the Medes; for, speaking of Surena, he informs us, that he was dressed, after the manner of the Medes, with pictures in his face, and a handsome peruke, very different in this respect from the other Parthians, who wore their hair as the Scythians did, dishevelled and neglected, which gave them a terrible kind of aspect. "And though," says Pere Montfaucon, "in this passage the historian does not speak of the king, but of him who was next to the king in the empire; yet it is not to be doubted that the kings of Parthia were habited in like manner. The ornament for the head of the Parthian kings,"

[1] Περιβραχιονια. Xenophon, lib. VI. [2] Λοφον υακινθινοβαφῆ. Ibid.

[3] Xenophon, ut supra, lib. III. [4] Herodot. in Clio, cxxxii.

[5] See Montfaucon's Antiquité Expliquée, vol. III. chap. xiv. [6] Justin, lib. XLI.

continues he, "is not always the same upon old monuments and medals: it seems to have been subject to many changes; and the king is sometimes represented with a simple diadem without any other adornment than that of his own hair."[1]

The dress of the Scythians and the Thracians was, in many respects, conformable to that of the Persians; and, like them, they wore the anaxyrides and the tiara: their habits, says Montfaucon, whose authority is derived from ancient sculptures, consisted of the tunic, which, in some instances, has sleeves that reach to the wrists; anaxyrides, or breeches, which descend as low as the ancles, and served at once for breeches and stockings; to these may be added the pallium, or *chlamys*, which sometimes also served for a head covering. Persons of distinction appear with a tunic reaching to the ancles; in one instance the tunic appears to be fringed at the bottom. Sometimes they are represented with a long mantle ornamented with fringes; and in every instance the tiara, or bonnet, is the same as that belonging to the Parthians. He then speaks of a Phrygian figure with two tunics, one upon the other; and the longest of them barely reaching to the knees; but, adds he, the most beautiful figure that I have seen, in the Phrygian dress, is Paris seated, and holding the apple of discord in his right hand. His bonnet is of the usual form; and above his tunic he wears a chlamys, or *mantle*, fastened with a round fibula upon his right shoulder; and his shoes resemble those of the Parthians.[2]

Herodotus, speaking of the Thracians who accompanied Xerxes into Greece, says, they covered their heads with a cap, or helmet, made of foxes' skins, and their bodies with a tunic and a mantle of various colours:[3] their shoes[4] were bound with thongs above the ancles; and they carried small bucklers in the form of a half moon; and every one of them had a javelin and a short dagger. Those Thracians, con-

[1] Montfaucon, ut supra.

[2] Montfaucon, ut supra, chap. xv. Many of the Scythians, according to Herodotus, clothed themselves with the skins of men, as other nations did with the skins of beasts; and with the skins of the right hands of their enemies they made coverings for their quivers: they also made cups of the skulls of those they had slain; the poorer sort, adds he, clothed themselves with leather; to which the more wealthy added ornaments of gold. The Melanchlænians, a nation bordering on Scythia, wear, says the same author, no other clothing than black; and the Gelonians, another neighbouring nation, wear garments made of otters' and beavers' skins. Herodot. in Melpomene, cvii.

[3] Ζειρας ποικιλας. Herodotus in Polymniâ, lxxv. [4] Πεδιλα. Ibid. lxxv.

tinues he, who retained their original name in Asia, came into the field with small bucklers composed of untanned hides, two Lycian javelins for each man, with an helmet of brass, having ears and horns like those of an ox of the same metal; and their legs were covered with Phœnician cloth.[1]

The Caspians, and the Pactyans, who were in the army of Xerxes, were clothed in goats' skins: the Colchians and the Saspirians had helmets of wood;[2] and the Saranges were magnificently habited in garments of various colours; and their buskins reached to the knees.[3] The Lycians had a covering of goats' skins upon their shoulders; they wore pectorals upon their breasts; and their legs were covered with greaves. They had also caps upon their heads, adorned with crests of feathers;[4] and every one of them carried a bow of cornel, with arrows of cane, and a dart, a falchion, and a short sword.[5] The Mosynæcians wore double tunics that did not reach to the knees; and helmets of leather upon their heads like those of the Paphlagonians, from the middle of which there rose a tuft of hair, braided to a point, resembling a tiara: their shields were made in the shape of an ivy leaf, composed of the hides of white oxen with the hair on.[6]

The Typyrians were an Eastern nation; and, according to Strabo, the men were clothed in black, and wore long hair; whereas the women, on the contrary, wore white garments and short hair.[7] The inhabitants of Panchæa, an island of the Arabian sea, wear, says Diodorus Siculus, soft garments, owing to the excellence of the wool produced in that country: both men and women deck themselves with ornaments of gold; they use circular neck-bracelets,[8] and bracelets about their wrists, like the Persians; their ears are adorned with ear-rings; and their shoes are decorated with various colours: the priests wear robes of white linen, and sometimes of pure soft wool; their heads are covered with mitres embroidered with gold;[9] their shoes, or rather sandals, are curiously wrought with exquisite workmanship;[10] and their ear-rings are of gold, resembling those belonging to the women.

[1] Ρακεσι φοινικεοισι. Ibid. lxxvi. [2] Ibid lxxix. [3] Πεδιλα εις γονυ αντεινοντα. Ibid. lxvii.
[4] Πιλους πτέροισι περιες εφανωμενους Ibid. xcii. [5] Ibid.
[6] Xenophon's Expedition of Cyrus the Younger, lib. V. [7] Strabo, lib. XV.
[8] Τραχηλοις στρεπτους κυκλους, Diodorus Siculus, lib. V. cap. iii. [9] Μιτρας χρυσοϋφεις. Ibid.
[10] Την δε υποδεσιν εχουσι σανδαλια φιλοτεχνως ειογασμενα. Ibid.

SECTION V.

THE HABITS APPROPRIATED TO MOURNING BY THE ASIATIC NATIONS; AND THE DISTINCTIONS MADE BY DRESS.

THE generality of mankind have agreed in setting apart some kind of clothing to express their sorrow for the loss of their friends and relatives; and this custom is not of modern invention, but as ancient, at least, as the patriarchal ages: among the Asiatic nations it consisted in throwing aside such garments as were best calculated for ease and elegance, and substituting others unpleasant to the sight and uncomfortable to the wearer.

The first token of sorrow, upon the reception of tidings of recent misfortunes, was that of rending the tunic, or the robe. Thus Jacob, when he was persuaded that his son Joseph was dead, "rent his robe."[1] Joseph's brethren rent their clothes, when they saw the cup produced from Benjamin's sack.[2] Job also "rent his robe" when he heard of the death of his sons;[3] and his three friends, at the time they first saw him in his distress, "lifted up their voices and wept, and rent every one his robe."[4] Numberless are the instances that might be produced, from sacred as well as from profane history, in proof of this circumstance; but those already cited, it is presumed, will be thought perfectly sufficient.

In cases of heavy affliction they laid aside the garments best calculated for their ease, and put on sackcloth, which, in some instances at least, was black, and made of hair,[5] and of course must have been exceedingly unpleasant to the wearer. Jacob "put sackcloth upon his loins;"[6] and the same mode of expression is frequently used, so that we may rest assured, it was usually substituted for the linen garments that were next the skin, which the following extracts will abundantly confirm: Job, speaking to his friends, says, "I have sewed sackcloth upon my

1 [Clothes] Genesis, chap. xxxvii. ver. 34.
2 Ibid. chap. xliv. ver. 13.
3 [Mantle] Job, chap. i. ver. 20.
4 [Mantle] Ibid. chap. ii. ver. 12.
5 Revelations, chap. vi. ver. 12.
6 Gen. chap. xxxvii. ver. 34.

skin."[1] Again, "and it came to pass, when Ahab heard those words, that he rent his clothes, and put sackcloth upon his flesh, and fasted, and lay in sackcloth, and went softly."[2] In another passage it is said that Joram, king of Israel, "rent his clothes, and he passed by upon the wall, and the people looked, and, behold, *he had* sackcloth within upon his flesh."[3]

Another token of deep humiliation, sorrow, and mourning, was defiling themselves with dust and ashes. The friends of Job "sprinkled dust upon their heads towards heaven:"[4] and Job himself emphatically expresses his grief by saying, "I have sewed sackcloth upon my skin, and defiled my horn in the dust." And the king of Nineveh, when he heard of the denunciations of Jonah, arose from his throne, and laid his robe from him, and covered himself with sackcloth, and sat in ashes.[5]

Shaving the head was also a customary mark of mourning: Job is expressly said to have "shaved his head" when he heard of the calamities which had befallen him; and the Almighty, threatening the Israelites, says, "I will bring sackcloth upon all loins, and baldness upon every head, and I will make it," that is, the day of his vengeance, "as the mourning for an only son."[6]

Shaving the eye-brows and cutting the flesh, by way of mourning for the dead, were anciently practised among the Asiatic nations, as we may judge from both being strictly forbidden by the Mosaic dispensation: "Ye are the children of the Lord; ye shall not cut yourselves, nor make any baldness between your eyes for the dead."[7] The prohibition extended still farther to the priests; for it is expressly said, "they shall not make baldness upon their heads; neither shall they shave the corners of their beards, nor make any cuttings in their flesh *for the dead*."[8]

The same methods of expressing their grief were common with the Asiatic

[1] Job, chap. xvi. ver. 15. [2] 1 Kings, chap. xxi. ver. 27. [3] 2 Kings, chap. vi ver. 30.

[4] Job, chap. ii. ver. 12. It was customary also among the Egyptians, upon the death of their monarch, to cover their heads with dust. Diodorus Siculus, lib. I. cap. vi.

[5] Jonah, chap. iii. ver. 6. The preceding verse is also to the purpose, it runs thus: "*So the people of Nineveh believed God, and proclaimed a fast, and put on sackcloth from the greatest of them even to the least of them.*"

[6] Amos, chap. viii. ver. 10. [7] Deuteronomy, chap. xiv. ver. 1.

[8] Leviticus, chap. xxi. ver. 5.

women; for Tamar, David's daughter, after she had been abused by Amnon, "put ashes on her head, and rent her tunic of many colours that *was* on her, and laid her hand on her head, and went on crying."[1] And Athaliah "rent her clothes, and cried, Treason! treason!"[2] Judith also, when she mourned for her husband, "put sackcloth upon her loins, and wore her widow's apparel."[3] And Esther, at the time the Jews were persecuted, "laid away her glorious apparel, and put on garments of anguish and mourning; and, instead of precious ointments, she covered her head with ashes and dung; and she humbled her body greatly; and all the places of her joy she filled with her torn hair."[4] So also it is said, that, when Heliodorus was about to pillage the temple of Jerusalem, "the women, girded with sackcloth under their breasts, abounded in the streets."[5]

There are instances in which the persons who mourned appeared abroad bare-footed: and in general they forbore the use of oil or precious unguents until the days of their mourning were completed.[6]

It is almost unnecessary to observe, that these tokens of sorrow were not confined to mourning for the dead: the foregoing quotations prove that they were practised by way of humiliation and penance, in consequence of private misfortunes, and in the time of public calamities.

There is no trait in the character of the ancient Asiatics that reflects more honour upon them than their hospitality: it was not deemed sufficient to entertain a guest, but he was obliged at parting, to accept of some favour from the munificence of his benefactor. The Sacred Writings abound with proofs of this prevalent liberality; and the same are confirmed by the whole tenor of history in general. These gifts consisted chiefly in clothes, personal ornaments, cups, arms, and the like; but sometimes, indeed, they were far more extensive.

The patriarch Joseph gave to each man of his brethren "changes of raiment; but unto Benjamin," as a mark of especial favour, "he gave three hundred pieces of silver, and five changes of raiment."[7] Gifts of this kind were not only considered as marks of esteem, but were often presented by way of reward, or to obtain a

1 2 Samuel, chap. xiii. ver. 19.
2 2 Kings, chap. xi. ver. 14.
3 Judith, chap. viii. ver. 5.
4 Rest of Esther, chap. xiv. ver. 2.
5 2 Maccabees, chap. iii. ver. 19.
6 2 Samuel, chap. xv. ver. 30. Ibid. chap. xi. ver. 2.
7 Genesis, chap. xlv. ver. 22.

particular favour: thus Naaman the Syrian, a Leper, took with him ten talents of silver, six thousand pieces of gold, and ten changes of raiment, as a present for the prophet Elisha in return for the cure of his leprosy.[1]

It was also considered as an honour of the highest kind when persons of a superior rank presented garments and personal ornaments to those of an inferior station. Pharaoh, when he advanced the patriarch Joseph, and set him over all the land of Egypt, "took his ring from his hand, and put it upon Joseph's hand, and arrayed him in vestures of fine linen, and put a golden chain about his neck."[2] When Ahasuerus, king of Persia, asked Haman what should be done to the man, "whom the king delighteth to honour," he replied, "Let the royal apparel be brought which the king useth to wear, and the horse that the king rideth upon, and the crown royal which is set upon his head; and let this apparel and horse be delivered to the hand of one of the king's most noble princes, that they may array the man withal whom the king delighteth to honour:" which was done to Mordecai the Jew; and "he went out from the presence of the king in royal apparel of blue and white, with a great crown upon his head, and with a garment of fine linen and purple;"[3] and Belshazzar, the king of Babylon, promised to the man who interpreted the hand-writing upon the wall, that "he should be clothed with scarlet, and *have* a chain of gold about his neck, and be the third ruler in the kingdom."[4] So in Esdras it is said, of the man who best answered a question proposed, that king Darius should cause him to be "clothed in purple, to drink in gold, to sleep upon gold, to have a chariot with bridles of gold, and an head-tire of fine linen, and a chain about his neck;[5] and that he should sit next to Darius because of his wisdom, and be called Darius his cousin." As an honorary reward to Judith, for the destruction of Holofernes, the Jews crowned her and her maid with garlands of olive.[6]

Particular colours, and especially purple, were restricted in different nations to the blood royal, or to such persons as were permitted to wear them by the royal

[1] 2 Kings, chap. v. ver. 5.
[2] Genesis, chap. xli. ver. 42.
[3] 2 Esther, chap. vi. verses 8 and 9; and chap. viii. ver. 15.
[4] Daniel, chap. v. ver. 7.
[5] *Κυδαριν βυσσινην και μανακην περι τον τραχηλον.* 1 Esdras, chap. iii. verses 6 and 7.
[6] Judith, chap. xv. ver. 13.

authority. Thus, Antiochus the younger, when he confirmed Jonathan in the high-priesthood of the Jews, among other great privileges, gave him leave to drink in golden vessels, to be clothed in purple, and to wear a golden fibula;[1] and in the Lamentations of Jeremiah it is emphatically said, "they that did feed delicately are desolate in the street; they that were brought up in scarlet embrace dunghills;" expressive of the sad reverse of the state of the Jews.[2]

Double garments are in Scripture opposed to garments of affliction and mourning.[3] Wedding-garments and garments of joy are placed in contradistinction to garments of widowhood and of sorrow. The wedding-garment is also mentioned as an indispensable requisite for every one who was a guest at a marriage-feast.[4] The attire of an harlot is spoken of in the Sacred Text;[5] and prison-garments, or vestments appropriated to malefactors, are said to have been in use at a very early period.[6] All these vestments differed, without doubt, materially from each other; but, as they are only mentioned by name, that difference cannot possibly be specified.

Putting the shoes from the feet was a very ancient mode of religious worship, and countenanced by the command of God himself.[7] The shoes were also used in remote times for the confirmation of contracts; for, in the book of Ruth, it is said: "Now this *was the manner* in former time in Israel concerning redeeming, and concerning changing; for, to confirm all things, a man plucked off his shoe, and gave it to his neighbour; and this was a testimony in Israel."[8]

1 Πορπην χρυσην. 1 Maccabees, chap. xi. ver. 58.

2 Lamentations, chap. iv. ver. 5.

3 Baruch, chap. v. ver. 5.

4 Matthew, chap. xxii. ver. 11.

5 שית זונה Proverbs, chap. vii. ver. 10.

6 בגדי כלאו 2 Kings, chap. xxv. ver. 29.

7 Exodus, chap. iii. ver. 5; et alibi.

8 Ruth, chap. iv. ver. 7.

SECTION VI.

A GENERAL VIEW OF THE HABITS OF THE GREEKS AND THE ROMANS.

It would be perfectly inconsistent with my present design to enter upon a full investigation of the habits of the Greeks and the Romans; neither, indeed, am I in the least inclined to make such an attempt, because the world is already in possession of many elaborate discussions upon this subject:[1] all that I shall pretend to do will be merely to trace out a general outline of the different parts of dress which were commonly used by both nations.

The principal habits of the Greeks were adopted by the Romans, with such variations only as appear to have been made for fashion's sake, rather than for real utility; and therefore a separate investigation of the garments belonging to either will not be necessary; but, on the contrary, many useless repetitions may be avoided by treating them conjointly, as I shall endeavour to do.

The Tunic was a garment common to the Greeks and to the Romans: it was of two kinds; the short tunic reaching to the knees, which was most generally used; and the long tunic descending to the heels.[2] The Grecians anciently wore only one tunic: in process of time, however, they introduced a second, and the first answered the purpose of a shirt.[3] This people were well acquainted with the use of linen; which knowledge, it is said, and with great appearance of truth, they derived from the Egyptians.[4] It is, however, very uncertain at what period they employed that article for the fabrication of their tunics, or if they ever universally adopted it for that purpose: we know, that tunics of linen were worn by some of

[1] See Bernard de Montfaucon, dans L'Antiquite Expliquée, vol. III. et IV.

[2] In the first instance, called in Greek χιτων, in Latin, *tunica;* in the second, ποδηρης χιτων, *tunica talaris.*

[3] Then called χιτωνισκος.

[4] L'Antiq. Expl. vol. III. part I. cap. i.

the Philosophers;[1] but, generally speaking, I presume that vestments of linen were much more frequently used by the women than by the men. A *soft tunic*[2] is specified by Homer as part of the dress belonging to Agamemnon; but this is no proof that it was linen, for the epithet *soft* may be equally applied to any other delicate fabric. The Grecian tunics, in their most ancient state, were certainly made of woollen cloth: the Athenians wore them of various colours; which usage is condemned by Ælian as an extravagance. The garments of the Greeks were not only variegated in the colours, but often embellished with birds, beasts, flowers, and different assemblages of imagery extending even to the representation of historical subjects, which were interwoven, at the time of their fabrication, with threads of gold, of silver, and of colours appropriated to the design;[3] and to some adornments of this kind I apprehend Homer alludes, when he calls the tunic of Telemachus a *splendid tunic.*[4]—A beautiful specimen of the Grecian tunic, ornamented with embroidery, is given upon the sixth plate appertaining to the Introduction.

The Exomis[5] was a *tunic without sleeves,* commonly worn by the Grecian Philosophers, but not confined to them: it was also used by valets and servants of all kinds. This garment occurs upon the figure dancing, at the bottom of the Plate just referred to, where the sleeves of the under-tunic sufficiently specify the difference between it and the exomis.

Among the ancient Romans, the tunic was made of white woollen cloth, and without sleeves, which were afterwards added.[6] In general, the sleeves were loose

[1] Called οθονη: but the *othone* was more properly part of the women's dress.

[2] Μαλακος χιτων, *mollis tunica;* Iliad, lib. II. line 42.

[3] These sorts of garments are distinguished by Homer with the epithet ποικιλος, *variegatus* and παμποικιλος, *variè pictus,* and the like. Speaking of Andromache at her loom, the Poet says,

Διπλακα, μαρμαρ ην, ενδε θρονα ποικιλ' επασσε.—Iliad, lib. xxii. v. 441.

Which line Clarke renders thus:

Duplicem, splendidam, inque flores varios sparsim-intexebat.

And Pope loosely translates the passage:

A growing work employ'd her secret hours,
Confus'dly gay with intermingled flowers.

[4] Χιτωνα σιγαλοεντα *tunicam splendidam;* Odyssey, lib. XV. ver. 60.

[5] Εξωμιδα, Montfaucon, vol. III. part I. chap. vi.

[6] Then called *chiridota,* or *tunica manicata.*

and short, reaching only to the elbow;[1] but their length and fashion seem to have depended on the will of the wearer:[2] and, in the times of the Emperors, they were brought to the wrists, and ornamented there with fringes.[3] The tunic which was worn by the Romans under the toga commonly hung down as low as the ankles: in other cases, it does not appear to have extended beyond the knees.

After the Romans had introduced the wearing of two tunics, they used the words *subucula* and *indusium* to distinguish the inner one,[4] which was also of woollen. Augustus in the winter season wore no less than four tunics at one time, besides the subucula, or under-tunic, and all of them of woollen.[5] Montfaucon is of opinion, that the interior garments belonging to the men were rarely, if ever, made of linen, until a late period of the Roman Empire.[6]

The Senators of Rome had a broad stripe of purple,[7] sewed to the breast of the tunic for the sake of distinction, which was called *latus clavus*;[8] but the Knights, and such as had not reached the Patrician honours, wore a narrow stripe of the same colour, and therefore denominated *angustus clavus*.[9] The Roman citizens, whose circumstances would not allow them to purchase a *toga*, wore the tunic only;[10] foreigners, it seems, when at Rome, appeared in the same manner;[11] so also the slaves and the gladiators.[12] In the country, however, persons of rank and opulence laid aside the toga, and used the tunic alone.[13]

1 Montfaucon thinks the difference between the tunics of the Greeks and those of the Romans consisted chiefly in the sleeves; those of the first being long and strait, those of the last short and loose. Ubi supra, cap. I.

2 Horat. Sat. i. Propert. lib. IV.

3 After the example of Julius Cæsar, *ad manus fimbriatæ*. Sueton. Jul. 45. [It is not quite certain that by *fimbriatus* we are to understand *fringed*. The *Tunic* which Suetonius is speaking of was the *latus clavus*, and as Cæsar chose to wear it with long sleeves, it was more probably *bordered* with purple at the wrists than fringed.—Ed.]

4 And, in the later ages, *interula* and *camisia*.

5 Sueton. Aug. 82.

6 Ubi supra, cap. I.

7 Or, rather, two stripes, *fasciæ, vel plagulæ*. Varr. de Lat. Ling. lib. VIII. cap. 47. [Mr. Strutt here dismisses in four lines a subject which has filled volumes. The controversy respecting the "*clavus*" may probably be ended one day by the discovery of some ancient Roman *painting*.—Ed.]

8 Ovid. de Trist. lib. IV. ver. 10, 29, et alibi.

9 Montfaucon, ubi supra, cap. vi.

10 Hence called *tunicatus popellus*. Horat. Ep. I. ver. 7. et 65.

11 Thus *homo tunicatus*, for a Carthaginian, Plaut. Pœn. V. 3.

12 Id. Amphit. I. 213; Senec. de Brev. Vit. C. 12; and Juvenal, II. 143.

13 Juvenal, Sat. iii. ver. 179.

Young men when they assumed the *toga virilis,* and women, when they were married, received from their parents a tunic, wrought in a particular manner, called *tunica recta,* or *regilla.*[1]

Montfaucon says, there was also a Senatorian habit called *colobium,* which was a kind of tunic; but its form is unknown to us, nor, indeed, is it often mentioned by the ancient authors. The colobium, in the middle ages,[2] was a tunic without sleeves, or with short ones reaching only to the elbow, and chiefly used by the clergy: it formed with us a part of the coronation-habit, and was in after-times a dress common with servants.[3]

The belt, or *girdle,* was a necessary appendage to the tunic. This part of the dress was fabricated from a variety of materials adapted to the rank and circumstances of the wearers. Among the Greeks, as far back as the time of Homer, the girdles of superior personages were exceedingly splendid, either with respect to their workmanship or to their colour, and frequently both these excellencies were united.

It was not customary with the Romans to wear the girdle at home, but no person appeared abroad without it; and it was even thought indecorous and effeminate to be seen in the street with the tunic loosely girded. In ancient times, the girdle answered the purpose of a purse, wherein money and other valuables were deposited.[4]

The Toga, or *gown.* A garment of this kind is said to have been used by the Greeks: it is certain, however, that it did not originate with them; neither does it appear to have been at any period universally adopted. Its ancient name was *Tebennos,* derived from Temenus the Arcadian, who first brought it to Ionia.[5]

The Romans originally had no other clothing than the toga; and, in imitation of his progenitors, Cato the censor used the like abstinence, and not only appeared in public, but sometimes sat upon the tribune,[6] when Prætor, habited in a toga,

[1] Plinius, lib. VIII. cap. 48. sect. 74.

[2] See Du Cange's Glossary, in voce *Colobium.*

[3] Fortescue de Legibus Angliæ, cap. 51.

[4] *Pro marsupio, vel crumenâ.* Aul. Gell. cap. xv. Plaut. Merc. v. 2. 84. And the Romans called this part of the dress by several names; as, *cingulum, cinctus, zona, and balteus.*

[5] De *Temenus,* says Montfaucon, on fait *Tebennon* par un legere corruption. Ubi supra, vol. III. 694.

[6] Arcon. in Cic. Val. Max. lib. III. cap. 6. 7.

without any additional garment. After the Romans had adopted the tunic, and other vestments which supplied the use of the toga, it was still retained by them, and considered as an habit of honour; and none but citizens were permitted to use it. In the remote times, the toga was worn in the field; but latterly it became a robe of peace.[1]

The learned have been much divided in opinion respecting the form of the toga; some supposing it to have been a large loose open garment; others again contending, and I think with more appearance of truth, that it was a loose long gown, round at the bottom, and open only at the top down to the girdle. It had no sleeves, that the right arm might remain at perfect liberty; but it covered the left shoulder, and was gathered up from the bottom to admit the projection of the left arm, falling nearly to the ground on either side of the arm in very ample folds. It was not girded about the middle like the tunic, but, a portion of it being twisted round the body, was bound in a kind of knot called *umbo*[2] beneath the left breast, and the return formed a protuberance, divided into many folds, which was named *sinus*, and occasionally answered the purpose of a pocket. The part of the toga which passed over the left shoulder was sometimes drawn up over the head, to protect it from the inclemency of the weather, or excessive heat of the sun.[3]

The size of the toga, and probably its form, was varied at different periods. Anciently, when the Romans wore no other garment, it was straight and close: it then covered the arms, and reached to the feet;[4] but, as it became more ample, its folds, of course, were increased; and these folds the wearer took great pains to adjust properly, not only for elegance-sake, but because it should not draggle in the dirt.[5]

The toga originally was made with white woollen cloth: but, in succession of time, more costly materials were used for that purpose, and especially silk. Upon certain occasions, the toga was embellished with embroidery: it was then called *toga picta*,[6] or *toga palmata;* and the latter was worn by the emperors and

1 Liv. Hist. Rom. lib. VII. cap. 10.

2 Perseus, Sat. V. v. 53.

3 Montfaucon, vol. III. part i. cap. 5.

4 Quinctil. xi. cap. 3.

5 Horat. Sat. xi. ver. 3. lxxvii. v. I. 3. 31; Epist. I. v. 95. Macrob. Sat. xi. ver. 9, & Quinctil. ubi supra.

6 The *toga picta*, Montfaucon says, was a Tuscan habit. Consuls and Tribunes were permitted to wear it; and Prætors, when they assisted at the sports. Ubi supra.

generals, when they triumphed.[1] *Transparent* togæ and *watered* togæ are also mentioned by the ancient writers.[2]

The toga, as observed above, was white, except when it was used in time of mourning: it was then of a dark colour, or black.[3] The *toga prætexta*, worn by young men of rank until they reached the age of seventeen, and by young women till they were married, was distinguished by a purple border:[4] this dress, however, was not confined to the Roman youth: it was sometimes used by the priests and magistrates.[5]

When a young man laid aside the *toga pretexta*, he assumed the manly gown called *toga virilis*,[6] and various ceremonies were performed with great solemnity upon the occasion; however, as a mark of modesty, during the whole of the first year, it was usual for him to keep his right arm within the folds of his gown.[7] It was customary with candidates for public offices to appear before the people clothed with the toga only, to shew their humility on the one hand, and to expose, with more freedom, such parts of their body as had been wounded in their country's service.[8] Under the Emperors, this garment was in great measure disused, except by clients when they waited upon their patrons,[9] and by orators when they pleaded at the bar.[10] The toga was usually laid aside in time of mourning,[11] and rarely, if ever, worn at home, where its place was supplied by a domestic habit provided for

[1] Liv. lib. X. cap. 7. Martial, Lib. vii. Ep. 1. Plin. lib. IX. c. 36.

[2] Varro in Nonius speaks of certain togæ being so transparent, that the tunics might be seen through them; the watered *togæ* were called by Nonius Marcellus *undulatæ togæ*, and by Pliny *undulatæ vestes*. Montfaucon, ubi supra.

[3] [Called the *toga pulla*. Persons wearing it were termed *atrati*. The toga pulla, is often confounded with the *toga sordida*: but the latter signifies only a toga black with age or dirt, and not a garment dyed or stained for an express purpose. Ed.]

[4] Liv. lib XXXIV. cap. 7. Cic. Verr. I. And hence they were called *prætextati*. Sueton. in Vit. August. cap. 44.

[5] And also by Augurs, Consuls, and Dictators; to these may be added private persons, when they exhibited in public games. Cic. Pis. IV.

[6] Called also *toga pura*, because it was *white*; and *libera*, because he became his own master. Cic. Att. V. and XX. Ovid. de Trist. lib. IV. Pers. Sat. v.

[7] Cic. Cœl. V.

[8] Plutarch, in Vitâ Coriolani.

[9] Suet. August. cap. 60 Martial, Ep. i. ii.

[10] Senec. de Constant. cap. 9. Tacit. Annal. lib. XI. cap. 7.

[11] [Or worn of a black colour. Vide ante. Ed.]

that purpose.[1] Neither was it ever used at feasts; for, the Romans had a particular garment appropriated to such occasions, which they called

The Synthesis. This peculiar habit, though honoured with a Greek name, was probably of Roman origin. It is generally thought to have been a loose dress, of the pallium or mantle kind, which might be easily put on or off; and the usage of this garment at festivals appears to have been universal, not only in the city of Rome, but throughout the whole of the Roman Empire, and by every rank of the people who could afford the purchase.[2]

The Trabea was anciently a habit of honour and distinction among the Romans, and thought to have received its name from certain stripes that were wrought upon it across the breast. According to Servius, there were three sorts of this garment; one, proper to the Gods, all of purple; another, to the kings, of purple mixed with white; and a third, to the priests, of purple and scarlet.[3] The learned are by no means agreed with respect to the form of the trabea; many are of opinion that it differed in nothing from the toga, excepting only in the quality of its materials;[4] Rubenius, however, contends that it was shorter, and bore a greater resemblance to the chlamys.[5]

The Pallium, or *mantle*,[6] with the Greeks, was a garment of distinction, the same as the toga was with the Romans. The Emperor Augustus, for political reasons, caused the Romans to assume the Grecian habit, and the Greeks the Roman habit, meaning that the former should wear the pallium, and the latter the toga; and from that period, the pallium came into common use among the Romans.[7]

The ancient Athenians wore purple mantles; which Ælian censures as an

[1] Called *vestis domestica*, in opposition to the toga and other garments usually worn abroad, which were denominated *vestitus forensis*. Cic. de Sin. II. Sueton. August. cap. 73. Plin. Epist. v.

[2] It was worn all the time of the Saturnalia, because the Romans were continually feasting. Martial, Ep. xiv.

[3] *De purpurâ et cocco.* Servius ad Æneidos, vii.

[4] Dionysius Halicarnassæus, lib. II. de Saliis.

[5] Alberti Rubeni de Re Vestiariâ, lib. I. cap. v.

[6] Called in Greek ιματιον, and φαρος, and, latterly, παλλιον.

[7] Sueton. in Vit. August. cap. 98.

extravagance.[1] The Grecian mantles were sometimes white;[2] but the colour, as well as the materials, depended usually, I presume, upon the rank and circumstances of the wearer.

The pallium was worn over the tunic, and was either double or single, according to the season it was required to suit.[3] It was fastened upon the right shoulder with a fibula, or buckle, whence descending, both before and behind, to the middle of the legs, it covered the greater part of the whole body, leaving the right arm at perfect liberty. According to Homer, the pharos, or mantle, was not always confined to one particular size; for, in several places, he mentions the *great pallium*,[4] which evidently implies the existence of a smaller one. The great mantle was used by persons of the highest rank.

The Tribon and Tribonion,[5] or, the *philosopher's mantle*, does not appear to have differed materially in its form from the common pallium, but rather, perhaps, in its colour, which was black or brown; and derived its name from being usually worn threadbare.[6] It was ostentatiously assumed by the Cynics and other philosophers, to demonstrate their poverty and contempt for temporal vanities:[7] it was not, indeed, confined to them; for, though it was considered as a habit of indigence, it was worn by many people above want; and at Athens it was adopted by the pleaders at the bar.

The Palliolum was a *short mantle*, or rather *cowl*, or *hood*, used to cover the head. It was worn by sick persons, or by such as were first venturing abroad after their recovery from sickness; and also by women of ill fame at Rome, to conceal themselves when they walked through the city.[8]

The chlamys was a species of *cloak*, or *mantle*, worn over the tunic. It was used by the Greeks; and from them it descended to the Romans. The form of

[1] Var. Hist. lib. IV. cap. 22.

[2] Aristander the Augur, at the battle of Arbela, was clad in a *white mantle*, with a crown of gold upon his head. Plutarch, in Vit. Alexandri.

[3] When double, it was called διπλοϊς.

[4] Μεγα φαρος, belonging to Agamemnon; Iliad, lib. II. ver. 43. The same epithet is given to the mantle of Telemachus, Odyssey, lib. XV. ver. 61; and elsewhere used.

[5] Τριβων & τριβωνιον.

[6] From the verb τριβω, to *rub*, or *wear away by frequent use*.

[7] And, not content with having it threadbare and dirty, they frequently wore it patched and torn.

[8] Montfaucon, ubi supra, cap. iv.

the chlamys has never been clearly investigated: some contend, that it was like the Roman toga; others reject this opinion, and assure us that it did not differ in any respect from the *sagum*, or *paludamentum*;[1] the last hypothesis is, I believe, the most generally received, and apparently approaches nearest to the truth. This garment was of two kinds; the *common chlamys*, and the *chlamys of Macedon:* the difference between them is thought to have consisted in the size alone; but this is mere conjecture. The chlamys was used by the Romans not only as a military vesture, but also as a garment for travelling.[2]

The Mandyas, the Ephestris, and the Byrrhus, are all of them expressly said by Artimedorous to have been different names for the chlamys;[3] however, the byrrhus seems rather, from the cowl, or hood, annexed, to have resembled the lacerna.[4]

The Sagum, or *Paludamentum*, was a military mantle. The name and the garment appear to have been both derived from the Gauls, and used by the Romans, as some think, before that people were subjected to the Empire. It had sleeves in its pristine state, which were taken from it when it was brought into Italy.[5] It was a large open cloak, made with wool, and fastened with clasps.[6] In dangerous times, it was worn in the city of Rome by all ranks of persons, excepting those of Consular dignity.[7] In the time of the Italic war, it continued in use for two years without intermission.[8] This garment, when it was assumed by the general, or chief officers of the army, was of scarlet colour, and bordered with purple.

The Chlæna,[9] or *læna*, as it was called in Latin, was a Grecian vesture, that served not only for a mantle, but, occasionally for a *coverlet*, or *bed-quilt*; and, the better to answer both purposes, it was made square, being either single or double,[10] as the exigences of seasons required. The chlæna anciently was a military garment, used in cold and wet weather as a *surtout*, being cast over all the other parts of the

1 Montfaucon, ubi supra. cap. iv.

2 *Vestis viatoria:* hence *chlamydatus* was used to express a traveller, or a foreigner. Plaut. Pseud. iv. 2. 8.

3 Lib. II. cap. 3.

4 See Montfaucon, vol. III. p. i. cap. 7; who says, "the ancients seem to have taken them indifferently the one for the other."

5 Ibid. cap. 9.

6 Sueton. August. cap. 26.

7 Ciceron. Philip. viii.

8 Liv. Epist. 72 and 73. Paterc. lib. II. cap. 16.

9 Χλαινα.

10 That is, *lined*, I presume.

dress. Homer frequently calls it the *rough* or *shagged chlæna;*[1] and full as often he distinguishes it by the epithet of *fair*, or *beautiful.*[2]

The Grecians had another garment, of the same species, called Chlanis, or Chlanidion, which was made of softer and lighter materials than the chlæna, and was worn by the women as well as the men.[3]

The Sisyra is also thought to have been a mantle of the same kind as the chlæna, but fabricated with a thicker and coarser stuff; and, like that garment, it was used equally for a part of dress and for a coverlet.[4]

The Lacerna of the Romans seems to have been greatly similar to the Grecian chlæna: it was a large cloak, or mantle, worn over the other clothing as a defence against the inclemency of the weather. It was open before, and fastened upon the breast with fibulæ, or buckles,[5] having a cowl, or hood,[6] attached to the hinder part, but in such a manner that it might easily be disengaged. It was made of thick and warm materials when designed for the winter, but of softer and lighter stuff when it was intended for the summer. The colours of the lacerna were also varied as well as its texture:[7] in general, they were black, or dark brown; but Senators and persons of rank, for distinction's sake, wore purple.[8] The lacerna was anciently a military garment, and used only in the army:[9] it was reckoned indecorous to appear with the lacerna in the city of Rome, where it was first worn by the common people; and even in Cicero's time, the Patricians and persons of distinction were ashamed to be seen in the streets so habited;[10] but, soon after, during the civil wars, the toga being laid aside, the lacerna was universally adopted,[11] and became so common in the days of Augustus, that he was offended, and commanded the Ædiles not to permit any person to enter the Forum, or the Circus, clothed with such a garment.[12] The lacerna was

[1] Χλαινας ουλας. Iliad, lib. III. ver. 299.

[2] Καλη χλαινα. Odyss. lib. X.

[3] Montfaucon, ubi supra, cap. ii.

[4] Ibidem.

[5] Especially when it was used at the public spectacles. Martial, Ep. xiv.

[6] *Cucullus*. Juvenal, Sat. vi.; Mart. Ep. xi.

[7] Juven. Sat. i. and ix. Mart. ii.

[8] Lampridius tells us, that the Emperor Alexander Severus used frequently to go to the public baths, and return to his palace, clothed in the common bathing-habit, over which he wore a scarlet lacerna as a mark of royalty.

[9] Paterc. lib. II. cap. 80. Propert. lib. III.

[10] Cic. Phil. II.

[11] Juven. et Mart. ubi supra.

[12] Sueton. in Vit. August. cap. 40.

generally used by those who frequented the public shows; but it was laid aside, as a mark of respect, the moment the Emperor entered the theatre.[1]

The Penula[2] is generally thought to have resembled the lacerna, saving only that it was shorter, and not so full. It was worn, like the lacerna, above the tunic; it had also a hood,[3] and was used in the army, and, by people travelling, for protection against the cold and rain.[4] It was sometimes covered with pile, or fur, for warmth-sake;[5] and sometimes, for the same reason, it was made with skins having the fur upon them.[6] This garment was not confined to any particular colour, and it was worn by the women[7] as well as the men. The Emperor Alexander Severus forbade the matrons of Rome to use the penula within the city, but allowed them to wear it in the country without any restrictions.[8]

The Byrrhus. This garment Montfaucon conjectures to have been "almost the same thing as the lacerna, insomuch that the antients seem to have taken them indifferently, the one for the other. It is also thought," continues he, "the lacerna took the name of byrrhus from a Greek word signifying something reddish,[9] it being usually made of a red colour. The byrrhus had a cowl annexed, as well as the lacerna; and hence it came to pass that the name of byrrhus was given to a cowl, or cap, that was used for a head-covering."[10]

The Caracalla was also a kind of pallium, or mantle, of Gaulish origin, and supposed to differ but little in shape from the lacerna. It was introduced among the Romans by the Emperor Antoninus, who, for that reason, obtained the cognomen Caracalla. It was a large loose garment, having sleeves[11] and a hood. In its original state, the caracalla reached only to the middle of the thighs; but the Emperor caused his to be made long enough to touch his feet.[12]

The Bracca,[13] or *Breeches*, was a species of vesture well known to the ancient

1 Sueton. in Claud. cap. vi.

2 φενολη & φαιλονη in Greek.

3 *Caputium.*

4 Cic. Att. XIII. Lucr. Sat. V. Senec. Epist. 87.

5 It was then called *gausape*, or *gausapina pænula*. Petron. cap. 28. Ovid, Ars Amandi, lib. II. Pers. Sat. vi. ver. 46.

6 *Scortea.* Mart. Ep. xiv. 130.

7 Ibid. Epig. vi.

8 Montfaucon, lib. III. cap. xi.

9 Πυρρος.

10 Montfaucon, ubi supra, cap. vii.

11 In this particular it certainly differed from the lacerna which had no sleeves.

12 Montfaucon, ut supra.

13 Βρακος, vel βρακας.

Greeks, though rarely used by them: indeed, it is mentioned as a proof of moderation in Alexander, after the conquest of Persia, that he adopted the Persian habit rather than the Median, and refused to wear the long vest, the *bracca*, and the tiara, appertaining to the latter.[1] Pythagoras wore the bracca;[2] and it is rather extraordinary that the example of so eminent a man did not bring this garment into fashion with his countrymen. The figure dancing, at the bottom of the sixth plate belonging to the Introduction, is depicted with breeches, which apparently were made of the same kind of stuff as the under-tunic: so are those worn by the figure on horseback upon the seventh plate. The Roman players used a species of breeches, as Cicero tells us, for decency-sake.[3]

There are no parts of the ancient dress more difficult to define than those appropriated to the legs and the feet. Neither the Greeks nor the Romans, generally speaking, wore any covering for the legs below the tunic, or above the ligature of the shoes, excepting in the time of war, when they used the greaves, or *military boots*;[4] and, among the Romans, we must also except those who encompassed their legs and thighs with bandages, or rollers of cloth,[5] which they wrapped about them for the sake of warmth: these bandages were probably introduced by the unhealthy; but the fashion was afterwards adopted by a few luxurious and effeminate persons:[6] I say a few, because it does not appear at any time to have been brought into general usage.

The people of ancient Latium wore shoes of unwrought leather,[7] which were called Perones;[8] and it was long before they learned the use of tanned leather, which was made of various colours.[9] The Romans, in some instances, distinguished the shoes appertaining to persons of rank from those of the plebeians by their colour, if not also by their form; for, no person, it seems, who had not served

[1] Plutarch. in Vit. Alexandri. [2] Ælian, Var. Hist. lib. II. cap. 32.

[3] *Subligaculum*, vel *subligar*, verecundiæ causâ. Cic. Off. lib. I. cap 35. Juvenal, Sat. vi. ver. 60. Martial, Epigram iii. 87.

[4] Κνημιδες, in Latin, *ocreæ*, see p. xcii. [And then shoes or sandals are rarely seen with them. Ed.]

[5] *Fasciæ*, vel *fasciolæ*; and these fillets, or rollers, were named from the parts they covered: *tibialia*, when applied to the legs, and *feminalia*, or *femoralia*, when they were placed upon the thighs. Sueton. in Vit. August. cap. 82.

[6] Such as wore mufflers, to keep the neck and throat warm, *focalia* or *focale*. Cic. Att. II. Horat. Sat. ii. Quinctil. cap. xi. Martial, Ep. xiv. 142.

[7] *Ex corio crudo.* [8] Virg. Æn. lib. VII. ver. 690. [9] Martial, Ep. ii. 29; vii. 34.

the office of an Ædile, might wear the shoes called *Mullæi* which were red. These shoes, we are told, were first used by the ancient kings of Alba; then by the kings of Rome; and, after the expulsion of Tarquin, they were worn by the chief magistrates in that city. Black shoes, however, were used by the Senators and people of rank[1] some time prior to the conclusion of the Republic; and therefore it was that the Senate took offence at Julius Cæsar, because he, being advanced in years, clothed himself in pompous apparel, like a young man, and wore red shoes with high heels, resembling those of the kings of Alba, from whom he pretended to derive his descent.[2] Another author, speaking upon this subject, says only, that he wore high-heeled shoes to make him appear the taller.[3] The Senators wore shoes reaching to the middle of their legs; they were also permitted to use four latchets to their shoes; and some of them had gold or silver crescents[4] fastened upon the tops of their feet;[5] but these ornaments, it is thought, were confined to the Patrician Senators.

The shoes of the wealthy were not only painted with various colours, but often sumptuously adorned with gold, silver, and precious stones.[6] Heliogabalus had his shoes set with diamonds, interspersed with other jewels, beautifully engraved by the first artists; which certainly was a useless extravagance, for the excellency of the workmanship, of course, was lost when the shoes were upon his feet.

The Emperor Aurelian did not approve of the painted shoes, which he thought were too effeminate for men; and therefore he prohibited the use of the mullæi, and of white, yellow, and green shoes—the last he called *shoes of the colour of ivy leaves.*[7] Sometimes the shoes were turned up with a point: they were then called *bowed shoes.*[8]

1 And, I apprehend, by the people in general. [The senators from the time of Caius Marius (668 A. U. C.) are said to have worn black *boots* or *buskins*, to which custom Horace is supposed to allude by the words,

"Nam ut quisque insanus nigris medium impediit crus
Pellibus."—*Lib. I. Sat.* 6. *v.* 27, 28. Ed.]

2 Dio. lib. XLIX. cap. 43.

3 Sueton. in Vit. Jul.

4 *Lunæ* vel *lunulæ;* Juven. Sat. vii. ver. 192. [The words are "Appositam nigræ lunam." Ed.]

5 Montfaucon thinks this ornament was worn behind the heel; lib. II. cap. 4.

6 Plaut. Bacch. Plin. Nat. Hist. lib. XXXVII. cap. 2.

7 *Calcei hederacei.*

8 *Calcei repandi.* Cicer. de Nat. Div. lib. I. cap. 30.

The shoes used by the Greeks and the Romans may probably be divided into two classes; the one, including those that covered the whole of the foot, and sometimes reached to the middle of the legs, called *ypodemata*[1] in the Greek, and in the Latin by several names, as *calceus, mulleus, pero, phæcasium;* the other comprehended such as covered the sole of the foot only, and were made fast to it with thongs of leather, or of other materials: these were denominated *pedila*[2] by the Greeks, and by the Romans *caliga, campagus, solea, crepida, sandalium, gallica, baxea,* and *sicyonia;* and sometimes the calceus is taken for a general appellation, including all the rest.

The Calceus of the Romans was probably the same as the Ypodema of the Greeks; for, both appear to have covered the foot, and were fastened with a latchet, lace, or thong.[3] The calceus was also worn, with the toga, when persons went abroad,[4] unless they were about to take a long journey; and then the solea was sometimes used as its substitute.[5]

The Mulleus resembled the calceus so far, as to cover the whole of the foot, but differed from it in colour, and perhaps in form. These shoes, as we have seen above, were not permitted to be worn by the common people; their colour commonly was scarlet,[6] but sometimes it was purple; and it is thought they had high soles made of cork, or some light material, to give an addition to the height of the wearer.

The Phæcasium was a species of shoe worn by the priests at Athens,[7] and also used by the Romans. It was commonly made with white leather, thin and light, and covered the whole of the foot. At Rome, it seems to have been adopted principally by foppish and effeminate persons.

The Pero, as observed before, was made with untanned hides, and, in the latter times, worn only by rustics and the lowest classes of the people.

The Caliga was a military shoe, or sandal, composed of a large sole, fastened

1 Υποδημα.

2 Πεδιλα.

3 *Corrigia,* vel *ligula.* Cic. de Divin.

4 Cic. Phil. ii. Plin. Epist. vii. Suet. Aug. cap. 73.

5 Cic. Mil. 10.

6 Pers. Sat. v. ver. 169, and Dio, as before.

7 Senec. de Benef. lib. VII. cap. 21.

with stronger fillets to the foot; and the foldings of the thongs were usually carried above the ankles, which, together with the top of the foot, appeared between the interstices of the bandages. The caligæ were sometimes strengthened with nails,[1] and were chiefly appropriated to the common soldiers, though the Emperor Gallienus wore the caligæ ornamented with jewels instead of the campagi.[2]

The Campagus was a shoe used by the emperors and generals of the army. It does not appear to have differed much from the caliga in its form; but the ligatures were more closely interwoven with each other, and oftener crossed over the foot and the ankles than those appertaining to the caliga, and bore a greater resemblance to net-work.

With the campagus I should be inclined to rank the *beautiful pedilæ*,[3] which Homer gives to Agamemnon and the other Grecian commanders. The word *pedila*, however, seems to have been a general denomination; for, it is applied by the Poet, with the same adjective, to the shoes, or sandals, of Juno.[4] Hesiod calls this Goddess the *golden-sandal wearer*.[5]

The Solea, the Crepida, the Sandalium, and the Gallica, were all of them species of sandals, fastened, like the caliga and the campagus, with fillets, or thongs, about the feet and ancles; but it is impossible, at this distance of time, to ascertain the peculiar points in which the difference between them consisted.

The soleæ, it is said, might not, in strict decorum, be worn with the toga;[6] and, indeed, it was reckoned effeminate to appear with them in the streets of Rome.[7] Caligula, however, was regardless of this rule, and not only wore the soleæ in public, but permitted all who pleased to follow his example, and use them in the theatre.[8] The soleæ might be worn in the country, with the penula and the tunic, or by

1 *Clavis suffixæ*. Plutarch informs us that Alexander the Great reproved Agnon the Teian for wearing silver nails in his shoes. In Vit. Alexandri.

2 Saying, the Campagi were nothing but nets; alluding to the redundant interlacing of the bandages belonging to them. Montfaucon, lib. II. cap. 4.

3 *Ποσσι δ' υπαι λιπαροισιν εδησατο καλα πεδιλα.* Iliad, lib. II. ver. 44.; et alibi. freq.

4 Iliad, lib. XIV. ver. 186; where the whole verse is precisely the same as it stands in the foregoing note, and may be translated, *Beneath her fair feet she bound the beautiful sandals.*

5 *Χρυσοπεδιλον*. Theog. ver 454.

6 Montfaucon, ubi supra.

7 Cic. Hor. Resp. cap. 21. Verr. lib. V. 1. 33. Liv. lib. XXIX. cap. 19.

8 Suet. in Vit. Calig. cap. 52.

persons on a journey;[1] and also at feasts; but, in the last instance, they were to be put from the feet when the repast began.[2]

The bandages of the crepida sometimes reached to the calf of the legs.[3]

The gallica, like the solea, might not be worn with the toga.[4]

The Baxea was also of the sandal-kind, and worn, according to Arnobius and Tertullian, by the Grecian philosophers; and it appears from the former author, that it was made of the leaves of the palm-tree. The baxeæ are noticed by Plautus; but nothing respecting their form is specified.[5]

The Sicyonia, Cicero tells us, was used in races; which gives us room to conclude, that it was a very light kind of sandal. Lucian speaks of it as adorned with white socks.[6]

To these we may add the *Sculponeæ*, worn by the country people;[7] and the shoes with *soles of wood*,[8] used by the poor: the latter, it seems, were also put upon persons condemned for parricide.[9]

The Soccus, according to Montfaucon and other learned writers, was a plain kind of shoe, and sufficiently large to receive the foot with the caliga, crepida, or any of the other shoes upon it, like the galloches of the Franciscans; and, in support of the argument, we are told that, in some countries, the galloches are called *socci* to this day. Cicero thought the soccus was a shoe derived from the Greeks: it was, however, worn by the comic players,[10] and, for that reason, the denomination is classically used to signify *Comedy;* as the word *cothurnus* is placed for *Tragedy.*[11]

The Cothurnus,[12] or *buskin*, was anciently worn by the Greeks, and became famous, after it had been introduced upon the stage by Sophocles in his tragedies.[13] The cothurni were made to fit either foot, and the soles were elevated; which gave an additional appearance of tallness to the wearer; and, for this reason, they were appropriated to the use of his heroes by the venerable Grecian Poet. They were also used for the same purpose by the Roman tragedians. The cothurnus is thus

1 Cic. Mil. cap. 10. 2 Plaut. Truc. ii. 4. Horat. Lib. ii. Sat. 8. Martial, Lib. iii. Ep. 50.

3 Montfaucon, ubi supra.

4 Montfaucon thinks it probable that the French word *galloches*, used for their wooden shoes, was derived from the Latin *gallica;* ibid. 5 Ibid.

6 Montfaucon, ubi supra. 7 Cato de Re Rusticâ, cap. 59. 8 *Soleæ ligneæ.*

9 Auct. ad Herenn. lib. I. c. 13. Cic. de Invent. lib. II. cap. 50.

10 *Soccus comicus.* Plin. lib. II. Epist. I. 11 Montfaucon, ubi supra. 12 Κοθυρνος.

13 And hence, to this day, the tragedians are with us denominated *the Heroes of the Buskin.*

described by an ancient author :—A ligature was fastened to the sole, which passed between the great toe and the toe next to it; where it was divided into two bands, which, passing through the latchets, secured the sole upon the foot: these bands were then carried high upon the legs, and crossed or platted over each other after the manner, as it is thought, of the campagi. "And probably," says Montfaucon, "the cothurni were anciently worn by the kings, princes, and magistrates of Greece."[1] It is certain, however, that they were indiscriminately used by both sexes.

The Romans used socks, or feet-coverings, made of wool or goats' hair, called *udones;* but it was thought effeminate for the men to wear them.[2]

The Knemis[3] of the Greeks called by the Romans *ocrea*, was a greave, or part of armour appropriated to the defence of the leg and the knee; and sometimes it is translated a military *boot*, or *buskin:* but the latter interpretation is certainly very improper. According to Homer, the knemis was used in the Trojan war; and, in its ancient form, it bore but small resemblance to the boots of modern times. It was calculated only to defend the fronts and sides of the leg, and therefore frequently was not clothed behind. It was usually made of metal, and did not reach below the instep, that it might be no impediment to the free use of the foot. Laërtes, the father of Ulysses, is described by Homer in a rustic habit, with greaves of leather;[4] and with us, the labourers in the country, when they are binding up bushes, or making hedges with thorns, have a greave, or *boot-leg*, as I think it is called, upon the right leg, with which they press the bushes together. It is generally made of very thick, or double, leather; reaches above the knee; descends to the instep; and is fastened, at the back part of the leg, with straps and buckles; forming, in my idea, a very exact counterpart of the ancient Grecian knemis, which, we know

1 Montfaucon, ubi supra, cap. 7. [The Cothurnus was a *boot* laced up the front of the leg, in some instances covering the toes entirely, in others a strap passed "between the great toe and the toe next to it," as described above, and connected the sole with the upper portion which met together over the instep, and were from thence laced up the front like the half-boots worn at the present day. Vide several specimens in Hope's Costume of the Ancients. They were of Asiatic origin, and are seen on the legs of the Amazons, Phrygian and Tyrian hunters, &c. Virgil thus alludes to them in the Æneid. —Lib. i. v. 336, 7.

"Virginibus Tyriis mos est gestare pharetram
Purpureoque alte suras vincire cothurno."—Ed.]

2 Mart. Lib. xiv. Ep. 140.

3 Κνημις.

4 Βοειας κνημιδας ραπτας; *bovinæ ocreæ consutæ;* Odyss. lib. XXIV. ver. 228.

from good authority, was sometimes worn upon the right leg only.[1] Homer bestows the epithet of *beautiful* upon the greaves belonging to the Grecian commanders; and tells us, they were well fastened upon the legs with clasps, or buckles, of silver;[2] and this species of leg-armour was worn in common by the soldiers; for, speaking of the army collectively, he often called them *well-greaved Greeks.*[3] I have given several specimens of the Grecian greaves; and the most ancient of them I conceive to be upon the figure at the bottom of the fifth plate belonging to the Introduction, of which two views are given; they are there represented exceedingly clumsy, and, according to the appearance, were made of the rough hides of some animals, and are fastened behind the legs with a single ligature upon the middle of the calf. In the two ancient figures standing to the right, upon the same plate, we see the indication of greaves, which seem to be of metal,[4] and of much neater fabrication; they do not, however, cover so much of the legs: and the ligatures, by which they were confined, do not appear. Upon the eighth plate we find them more perfectly represented: those upon the middle figure seem to have an ornamented border at the top; and those belonging to the other figure, which are seen both before and behind, have an indented border upon the posterior parts, but the appearance of the ligature is also wanting.

The Greeks and the Romans commonly wore their hair short: it was, however, combed with great care,[5] and sometimes perfumed; and this custom was prevalent even in the army.[6]

Baldness was accounted a deformity among the Romans;[7] and it is said, that Julius Cæsar wore a crown of laurel to conceal his want of hair.[8] It is, indeed, certain that, under the Emperors, such as were bald used a kind of peruke,[9] made

1 Veget. lib. I. cap. 20.

2 Κνημιδας χαλας, αργυρεοισιν επισθυριοις αραρυιας.
Ocreas pulchras argenteis fibulis aptatas. Iliad, lib. XI. ver. 17, 18, et alibi freq.

3 Εὐκνημιδες Αχαιοι. Iliad, lib. III. ver. 343. 370. et alibi freq.

4 The greaves were made of several kinds of metal. Homer mentions brass, copper, and tin. Among the Romans, they were frequently made of iron; and Hesiod says, those belonging to Hercules were made of a valuable kind of brass, ορειχαλκοιο. Scut. Her. ver. 122.

5 Senec. de Brev. Vit. cap. 12.

6 Suet. Cæs. cap. 67.

7 Ovid. Ars Amandi, lib. III. ver. 250. Tacit. Annal. lib. IV. cap. 57. Suet. Vit. Dom. cap. 18.

8 Sueton. in Vit. Jul. cap. 45.

9 Called *capillamentum*, or *galerus*, or *galericulum*. Sueton. Vit. Calig. & Othon. Juvenal, Sat. vi. ver. 120.

with false hairs fixed upon a skin.[1] This contrivance probably was not known in the time of Julius Cæsar, and, for that reason, he had recourse to the laurel crown.

The professors of philosophy let their hair and beards grow, to give themselves the air of gravity.[2] Slaves, for distinction's sake, wore long hair and beards; but, when any one of them was manumitted, he shaved his head and beard, and wore a woollen cap called *Pileus*.[3] Those escaped from shipwreck also shaved their heads;[4] and those who had been accused of a crime, but were acquitted, cut off their hair, shaved, and went to the Capitol to return thanks to Jupiter.[5]

The ancient Romans permitted their beards to grow, until Publius Ticinius Mænas brought barbers from Sicily, and first introduced the custom of shaving at Rome,[6] which prevailed till the time of Hadrian; and that Emperor, to cover certain excrescences on his chin, revived the fashion of wearing beards;[7] but, after his decease, it soon died away, and shaving was again resumed.

There was no set time for the young men of Rome to shave their beards: they sometimes did it when they assumed the toga virilis, or usually at the age of twenty-one; though Augustus, it seems, did not shave till he was twenty-five.[8] At the first performance of this operation, it was usual with the person shaved to hold a festival, and for his friends to send him presents.[9] They did not always shave the beard, but sometimes clipped it with scissors,[10] and sometimes they plucked it out with nippers, or small pincers.[11] They also made use of various arts to restrain the growth of the hair, and to clear it away where they thought it looked unhandsome; but all these practices were reckoned effeminate.[12] In great families, slaves were kept on purpose to dress the hair, and to shave; and these offices were

1 *Crines ficti*, vel *suppositi*. Mart. Ep. xiv. 50.
2 Horat. Sat. i. 3; Art. Poet. ver. 298; et alibi.
3 Juven. Sat. v. ver. 171; Plaut. Amphit. Act I. sc. 1.
4 Plaut. Rud. Act I. sc. 2.
5 Mart. Ep. ii. 74. Plin. Epist. vii.
6 About the year of the city 454. Plin. Nat. Hist. lib. VII. cap. 59.
7 Spart. Vit. Adrian. cap. 26.
8 Suet. Cal. cap. 10. Macrob. in Som. I. 6. Dio, lib. XLVIII. cap. 43.
9 Juven. Sat. iii. ver. 187. Mart. III. 6.
10 *Tondentes forfice*. Suet. Vit. Aug. cap. 79.
11 Called *volsella*. Suet. Jul. cap. 45, et alibi. Mart. VIII. 67.
12 Gell. lib. VII. cap. 12. Plin. Epist. 29.

sometimes performed by females.[1] For the use of poor people, there were barbers' shops,[2] which were much frequented, and where women also occasionally officiated.

The Greeks and the Romans generally went bare-headed; yet they were not destitute of a variety of head-coverings, which they wore on particular occasions: some of them appear to have been merely ceremonial; but others, again, were adopted, because they were useful. It is, unfortunately, true that we have little more than the names of most of them remaining; for which reason, very little can be said on this subject.

The Petasus[3] was a cap used by travellers, somewhat resembling the round hat of the present day; but, in its ancient state, the brims do not appear to have been so deep. Alexander the Great, we are told, used the petasus when he feasted; Caligula permitted the people of Rome to wear the petasus at the theatre, to shade their faces from the sun.[4]

The Romans had also another kind of cap, resembling a helmet, which they used when they travelled, called *Galerus.*[5]

Respecting the Casia and Crobilum, which were coverings for the head, we only know that the former was worn by the Lacedemonians, and the latter by the Athenians.[6]

The Infula, or *mitre*, was a white woollen *fascia*, or riband, or, as some say, a mixture of white and yellow, which was tied round the head, from one temple to the other, and fastened with a knot behind, so that the two ends of the bandage might hang down one on each side. This appears to have been a ceremonial ornament, and worn only by such as sacrificed.[7]

The Pileus,[8] or *woollen cap*, was used by the Greeks, and sometimes it was substituted for a lining to the helmet. This cap was worn by the Romans at the public games, and at festivals,[9] and by such as had been slaves, after they had obtained their freedom.[10] It was also used, for the sake of warmth, by the

1 *Tonsores*, Ovid, Met. XI. ver. 182; *tonstrices*, Cic. Tusc. ver. 20.

2 *Tonstrinæ*, Hor. Ep. i. Mart. Epigr. ii. 17.

3 Πετασος.

4 Dio, lib. LIX. c. 7.

5 Virg. Æn. vii. ver. 688.

6 See Montfaucon, as above.

7 See Montfaucon, as above.

8 Πῖλος.

9 Hor. Epist. i. ver. 13. Suet. Nero, c 57.

10 Thence called *pileati;* Liv. lib. XXIV. cap. 16. [Vide also, Persius, Sat. v. Ed.]

aged and infirm.[1] Homer gives to Laërtes, who is described in a rustic habit, a cap made with goats' skin, which he calls a helmet;[2] and probably it might have resembled one or other of the helmets of leather, which the reader will find mentioned below.

The Byrrhus was the name of a cap, or hood, used by the Romans in the time of the Lower Empire.[3]

The Romans often covered their heads with a portion of the toga, which they removed, as a token of respect, on meeting a person of superior rank;[4] the penula, the lacerna, and other garments, were also provided with hoods, which answered the purpose of hats, and might be drawn over the head, or thrown back upon the shoulders, at pleasure.

In time of war, the head-covering worn by the Greeks and by the Romans was the Helmet. Several kinds of helmets, according to Homer, were in use among the Greeks as early as the siege of Troy; but that which occurs most frequently is called by the Poet *Kynein*,[5] and corresponded with the *Galea* of the Romans. Upon the kynein, as well for the defence of the head as for ornament, there was a kind of cone, or, rather, elevated ridge, extending from the posterior part over the summit, and curving forward in the front. This protuberance, in the days of Homer, was decorated with horse-hair,[6] or some other substance made in imitation of it, which was called the *crest*. The crest belonging to the helmet made by Vulcan for Achilles, is called by Homer the *golden crest* and the *golden hair*;[7] and probably the Poet meant to express thin wires of gold resembling horse-hair. Plumes of feathers, in the after-ages, often supplied the place of hair; and this kind of crest seems to have been first introduced among the Grecians by Alexander the Great.[8] The helmets belonging to the chief commanders in the Grecian and Trojan armies, Homer tells us, were distinguished by their having three cones;[9]

1 Ovid. Ars Amandi. 2 Αιγειην κυνεην. Odyss. lib. XXIV. ver. 230. 3 [Vide p. lxxxvi. ante. Ed.]

4 Plutarch, in Vit. Pomp. Quæst. Rom. cap. 10. 5 Κυνεη

6 Ιππουρις, *setis-equinis-comans*, is an epithet continually applied to the helmet.

7 Χρυσεος λοφος, & εθειραι χρυσεαι.

8 Who, we are told, at the battle of the Granicus, was remarkable for a large plume of fine white feathers upon his helmet. Plutarch, in Vit. Alexandri.

9 Then called τρυφαλεια. The helmet of Achilles made by Vulcan, and that of Paris, are distinguished by this epithet; Iliad, lib. III. ver. 376; lib. XIX. ver. 382. 384.

and the helmet belonging to Agamemnon had four,[1] with a crest of horse-hair above them all.[2] The helmet of Meneläus is, in one instance, distinguished by the appellation of a *crown of brass*;[3] and probably it received this name from a wreath, or radiated ornament, placed upon it.

The helmets at this period were fastened beneath the chin with a strap or thong of leather, which, in some instances, was soft and thin, and decorated with embroidery: such a thong belonged to the helmet of Paris[4] at the time he fought with Meneläus; but this seems to have been a kind of foppery: the same, I presume, may be said of the crest appertaining to the helmet of Meges the Trojan, which, the Poet tells us, was "new tinged with Tyrian die."[5]

The ancient Grecian helmets were generally made of brass, though frequently ornamented with gold or silver: they had, however, others fabricated from less expensive materials; and two helmets of leather are particularized by Homer, exclusive of the pileus worn by Laertes mentioned above. The first of these belonged to Diomed: it was made of a bull's hide, and had neither a cone, nor a crest.[6] This kind of helmet, the Poet informs us, was called *kataityx*,[7] and generally used, as a safeguard for the head, by young men approaching to manhood.[8] I am happy to have it in my power to present to my readers the true form of this ancient helmet, taken from a curious bronze, the head being the full size of nature.[9]—When it is recollected, that Diomed was going as a spy to the Trojan camp, the prudence of the warrior will readily appear, in using such a head-piece, without any ornament to attract the sight. The Roman soldiers sometimes wore a cap, or helmet, of unwrought leather, which they called *cudo*;[10] this cap probably did not differ greatly from the kataityx.

The second helmet of leather mentioned by Homer was given by Meriones to

[1] Τετραφαλα. [2] Iliad, lib. XI. ver. 41, 42. [3] Στεφανη χαλκειη; ibid. lib. X. ver. 30, 31.

[4] Πολυκεστος ιμας : παλος, *acu-pictum ligamen tenerum*. Iliad, lib. III. ver. 371. [Mr. Strutt has, I think, transferred the epithet *soft* from the *chin* of the effeminate Paris to the thong of embroidered leather, the words being πολυκεστος ιμας απαλην ὑπο δειρην. Ed.]

[5] Νεον φοινικι φαεινος; recens, Puniceo colore fulgens. Iliad, lib. XV. ver. 538.

[6] Αφαλον και αλοφον; Il. X. ver. 258. [7] Καταιτυξ. Ibid.

[8] Ρυεται δε καρη θαλερων αϊζηων; Il. X. ver. 259.

[9] In the possession of Richard Paine Knight, Esq. who obligingly permitted me to copy it; which I did with great care: the reader will find it engraved, upon a reduced scale, at the bottom of the seventh Plate. [10] Sil. viii. 494. xvi. 59.

Ulysses: it is said to have been strengthened within with many thongs strongly interwoven, and without it was ornamented profusely with boar's teeth, white, and placed in curious order; in the middle, there was also inserted a *pileus*,[1] or *cap of wool*, to answer, I presume, the purpose of a lining. The Greeks frequently placed large ears erected and resembling those of fierce animals upon their helmets, to give them a more terrible aspect.

The form of several Grecian helmets may be seen upon the fifth, sixth, seventh, and eighth plates of the Introduction; and the most ancient is that which appears upon the dark rude figure at the top of the fifth plate; it is taken from a vase preserved in the British Museum; and, from the inscriptions upon it, which are in the Greek character, it is thought to be coeval with, if not anterior to, the Trojan war. The helmet upon the figure facing him, taken from another vase of great antiquity, seems to cover the whole of the face, excepting the eyes. Another helmet, something resembling this, but without either the cone or the crest, having a part in the front to defend the nose, is given at the top of the seventh plate; the original is brass; and, from its size, belonged to a man of large stature. There is something very singular in the helmet of the figure standing behind the man with the round shield upon the fifth plate: its form is not only exceedingly uncouth, but, one would think, it must have been very inconvenient to the wearer.

The warrior, who appears in two views at the bottom of the fifth plate, is taken from a very ancient bronze; beneath his helmet there is a kind of grating, or net-work, of metal, which covered the whole of his face, and seems well calculated to protect it from being injured by any weapon, excepting such a one as had a long and slender point.[2] Alexander the Great wore a helmet of iron, made by Theophilus, so excellently wrought and polished, that it was bright as silver; and to it was affixed a gorget of the same metal, set with precious stones.[3] The specimens of ancient helmets above-mentioned are sufficient, I trust, to prove that the nasal helmet of the Normans, and the helmets with face-guards which followed them, are by no means modern inventions, notwithstanding they may have received many considerable improvements in the latter times.

[1] Πιλος.

[2] Another bronze, with a helmet having a similar defence for the face, is in the possession of Richard Paine Knight, Esq. [These bronzes perfectly correspond with the representations of the Gladiators discovered at Pompeii, and I should consider these helmets to have been especially appropriated to the combatants in the Arena. Ed.]

[3] Plutarch in Vitâ Alexandri.

Before I quit this part of my subject, I wish to say a few words concerning the body-armour anciently used by the Greeks. The dark figure before-mentioned, upon the fifth plate, is undoubtedly of higher antiquity than those that accompany him; but, at the same time, the delineation is so rude, that one can hardly determine whether the figure be naked, or whether the white lines upon the breast and upon the thighs are intended as the indication of armour, and the other parts of the body covered with a garment fitted to the shape. The figure below, which is very ancient, is clothed with a short tunic, having no skirts on the sides below the girdle; it is remarkable, that the sleeve of the right arm is full of folds, and seems clearly not to belong to the tunic, while that of the left arm as evidently forms a part of it. The tunic, I presume, was made of leather, too thick and rigid to admit of sufficient liberty for the sword-arm; and, for that reason, the sleeve, probably, which belonged to the inner garment, was made of some more flexible material.[1]

Homer, speaking of the Greeks, frequently calls them the *brazen-tunic-wearers*,[2] and this species of tunic is rendered, in the Latin, *tunica loricata;* and, with equal propriety, in English, *tunic of mail:* it is, however, very extraordinary, that, where he speaks at large concerning the warlike habits of his heroes, he has not specified this tunic, nor given us the least hint respecting its form. In the long description of Agamemnon arming himself for the battle, at the beginning of the eleventh Book of the Iliad, we do not find it mentioned, unless the words by which this description is introduced may be thought applicable to it; "*He also clothed himself in splendid brass.*"[3] The passage will, however, admit of a much more general interpretation, and certainly, in my opinion, was so intended by the poet; for, immediately afterwards, he proceeds to particularize the several parts of that monarch's armour, and expressly says; "*first,*[4] about his legs he placed the handsome greaves, neatly joined

[1] The figure mentioned in the preceding note is clothed in the same kind of tunic, open at the side below the girdle, and the sleeve of the right arm apparently disjoined from the tunic: it is considerably smaller than this, and much neater respecting the workmanship. The protuberance on the top of the helmet is, literally, a cone elevated from the head, and without a crest; on either side arises a large ear like those represented upon the eighth plate, but rather higher in proportion to the middle; in the front, they bear the appearance of three cones; and probably this might be the form of the τρυφαλεια, or *three coned helmet,* so frequently mentioned by Homer. See page xcvi.

[2] Αχαιων χαλκοχιτωνων, *Achivorum æneis tunicis indutorum;* Iliad, lib. III. ver. 127. 131. et alibi frequentèr.

[3] Αργειους εν δ' αυτος εδυσατο νωροπα χαλκον. Iliad, lib. XI. ver. 16.

[4] Πρωτα. Iliad, lib. XI. ver. 17.

with clasps, or *fibulæ*, of silver;" and then passes on to the thorax, upon which he bestows no less than ten lines. There is no mention of the *tunic of brass*, in the request made by Thetis to Vulcan for a new suit of armour to equip her son; neither is it noticed in the description of the arms as they were made by that deity; nor in a subsequent passage, where Achilles is described putting them on. But let us suppose, that the thorax, and the *chalcochiton*, or brazen tunic, were only two denominations for the same armour, and we shall meet with no farther difficulty. If we look at the figure, holding a spear and a shield, upon the seventh plate belonging to the Introduction, we shall there see the ancient Grecian thorax. We find it large enough to cover, not only the breast, but all the front, at least, of the body, down to the navel: and probably it extended over the back in the same manner. The shoulder-parts are fastened in the front with thongs, or cords, to the bottom of the thorax, and might, I presume when those ligatures were unloosed, be thrown back at pleasure, so that the arms might easily be withdrawn, and the armour put off over the head of the wearer.[1] We also observe an appendage to the thorax, in imitation of the skirts of the tunic, made with broad straps, perhaps of leather, and plated with metal, reaching nearly to the bottom of the inner garment. Now, supposing the front of this thorax to be made of brass, which metal composed the greater part of the Grecian armour, we shall find no impropriety in the epithet the Poet so frequently bestows upon his countrymen. In fact, I conceive the thorax to have been a large breast-plate, affixed to a short and sleeveless tunic, made of leather, or some other appropriate material, to which the shoulder-guards were connected at the back.[2] Or, if it be thought that the thorax was fastened with straps and buckles, or with laces passing over the back, something resembling a woman's stays, I have no objection. We may, I think, with propriety, through the different aggrandisements of the thorax, trace the origin of the body-armour, which so completely enclosed the warriors of the later ages; but, even in that state, it was not unknown to the Greeks in ancient times, as the little bronze, twice represented upon the eighth plate, will sufficiently demonstrate.

The thorax of Agamemnon, according to Homer, was splendidly ornamented,

1 There are several passages in the Ancient Poets that justify this opinion in great measure.

2 These *shoulder-pieces* were also made of metal. Hesiod, describing the arms of Hercules, says, he placed upon his shoulders Αρης αλκτηρα σιδηρον, *the harm-repelling iron;* Scut. Hercul ver. 128.

having upon it ten rows of black *cyanus*,[1] twelve of gold, and twenty of tin, inclosed by three azure dragons[2] rising from either side to the summit of the pectoral, in the form of a rainbow. The thorax appertaining to Meneläus is said to have been double,[3] having, if I understand the Poet clearly, a zone, or girdle, plated with brass beneath it;[4] in like manner, also, we find that Agamemnon had a variegated belt,[5] strengthened with plates of silver, under his pectoral, which repelled the point of a weapon that had passed through the latter. The thorax was not always made of metal: the Egyptians used pectorals of linen curiously fabricated,[6] which, it is said, were not only lighter than those of metal, but better calculated to resist the point of the enemies' weapons. Alexander the Great, having obtained a pectoral of this kind from the spoils of the battle at Isis, wore it ever afterwards in preference to any other.[7]

Even the word *lorica*, or *mail*, may aptly enough be applied to the ancient thorax; for, if we examine the little figure, with the head thrown back, upon the eighth plate, we shall there find, upon the left side of the body, the indication of chain-mail; and the smoothness on the right side may, I think, be easily accounted for. This figure, in its original state, was evidently supported by another, whose left hand appears at the bottom of the thorax; and part of the right arm, broken off near the elbow, is seen on the opposite side; what is now wanting of this arm, when perfect, was brought forward; and, together with the hand, covered, I presume, that portion of the armour which is plain. In process of time, the thorax underwent variety of changes and enlargements, until it was formed into a complete body-armour; and in this state we see it exemplified by the figure represented in two points of view upon the same plate; where the back is equally as well defended from danger as the front.

The dark figure upon the fifth plate, which, as we observed before, is of very high antiquity, has no shield, but a piece of white drapery is cast over his left arm

1 Μελανος κυανοιο. Iliad, lib. XI. ver. 24.

2 Κυανεοι δρακοντες τρεις. Ibid. ver. 26.

3 Διπλοος θωρηξ. Iliad, lib. IV. ver. 133.

4 Ηδ' υπενερθεν ζωμα τε και μιτρη; Ibid. ver. 186, 187. Compare also lines 215 and 216.

5 Ζωνην θωρηκος ενερθε; Iliad, lib. XI. ver. 234; and, in the next line but one, it is called ζωστηρα παναιολος

6 Pages iv. and xvii. of this Introduction.

7 Plutarch, in Vitâ Alexandri.

to answer the purpose. The figure opposite to him, which is also very ancient, has a prodigious large round shield answering exactly to the *large shield*[1] which, Homer tells us, was used by the commanders at the Trojan war. The sevenfold shield of Ajax is almost proverbial. The shield of Agamemnon was surrounded with ten circles of brass inclosing twenty bosses of tin; and in the middle there was a bosse of black cyanus, having "the terrible aspect of the fierce-eyed Gorgon" upon it. The thong within the curve of the shield was of silver, and above it an azure dragon with three heads growing from one neck.[2] But the shield of Achilles was infinitely more superb, and abounded with sculptures, even to a great redundancy: the Poet seems to have been delighted with describing it; and has bestowed no less than one hundred and twenty lines of the eighteenth book of the Iliad to that purpose. In like manner, Hesiod thought the shield of Hercules a subject sufficient for a whole poem.

The Grecian shields varied not only in their form but in their size. We find one upon the fifth plate that is an *imperfect* sexagon; others we meet with that are nearly square, and rather larger in proportion; and others again are rectangular, and wider than they are high.

The sword-blades in general, according to Homer, were made of brass; but the hilts of the swords were embellished with studs of gold, or silver: and the scabbards were richly adorned with the same precious metals.[3] In one passage, however, the Poet speaks of young men who had swords of gold hanging from straps of silver.[4]

The sword-belt, or, more properly, *baldric;* for, it was worn over the right shoulder, and descended across the breast and back to the left hip, where it

[1] Σακος μεγα. [2] Iliad, lib. XI. ver. 33—40.

[3] The Poet says of Agamemnon:

Αμφι δ' αρ' ωμοισιν βαλετο ξιφος· εν δε οι ηλοι
Χρυσειοι παμφαινον· αταρ περι κουλεον ηεν,
Αργυρεον, χρυσεοισιν αορτηρεσσιν αρηρος. Iliad, lib. XI. verses 29, 30, 31.

Which passage may be rendered literally:

"*About his shoulders he hung his sword, in which were glittering studs of gold; and to the silver scabbard were fitted straps of gold.*" These straps, or *laminæ*, of gold were for the purpose of fixing the scabbard to the belt, or rather baldric, depending from the right shoulder. See the figure standing, plate VII.

[4] Μαχαιρας χρυσιας εξ αργυρεαων τελαμωνων. Iliad, lib. XVIII. verses 597, 598.

buckled; and was made fast to the scabbard of the sword, as the reader will find it represented by the figure holding a spear and a shield upon the seventh plate of the Introduction. This part of the military habiliment was variously decorated: Homer sometimes calls it "a variegated belt;"[1] and sometimes "a belt ornamented with curious workmanship;"[2] and sometimes "a splendid belt of Tyrian purple."[3] Plutarch tells us, that the sword-belt which Alexander the Great wore in all engagements was much richer in workmanship than any other part of his armour: it was made by old Helicon, and presented to him, as a mark of their respect, by the Rhodians.[4]

We learn from Herodotus, that the use of linen was very ancient in Greece: it was imported, he tells us, from Colchis and from Egypt.[5] The women, it appears, used garments of linen earlier than the men; and, at all times, in much greater quantities. Pliny, citing a passage from Varro, says, it had long been a custom in the family of the Serrani, for the women not to wear robes of linen;[6] which, being mentioned as a thing extraordinary, proves that linen garments were used by the Roman ladies in times remote. It is difficult, however, to determine at what time this article was first used as a shirt, or body-dress. A vestment of this kind, called *supparum*, was worn by the unmarried Roman damsels as early as the time of Plautus.[7]

The tunics of the women were larger than those of the men, and reached to the feet; excepting those worn by the Lacedemonian girls, which were not only very short, but divided at the sides so as to shew their thighs;[8] and this indecency was countenanced by the laws of Lycurgus. The Roman women had several kinds of tunics, which are mentioned by Plautus, but, unfortunately, without any description; so that little more concerning them than their names is now remaining.

The Regilla, according to Montfaucon, was a kind of white tunic, worn by virgins the day before their marriage.[9] The Impluviata and the Mendicula were tunics; but their colour, form, and texture, are totally unknown. The Ralla,

1 ζωστηρ παναιολος. Iliad, IV. ver. 186.

2 Ζωστηρ δαιδαλεος. Ibid. ver. 135.

3 Ζωστηρ φοινικι φαεινος. Iliad, lib. VII. ver. 305.

4 In Vitâ Alexandri.

5 In Euterpe, cap. 81.

6 Nat. Hist. lib. XIX. cap. 1.

7 Plaut. Rud. Act. I. sc. 2. Lucan. Phar lib. II. ver. 364.

8 Thence called φαινομηριδας.

9 Plin. Nat. Hist. lib. VIII. cap. 48.

which is thought to be the same as the Rara, and the Spissa, differed from each other; the first being of a thinner and looser texture than the latter. They had a tunic also, called Crocotula, the diminutive of *crocota;* which was an upper garment in use among the Grecian women, and received its name, Montfaucon says, either from *crocus, saffron colour;* or from *croce,*[1] the *woof* of any texture.[2]

The toga, in the infancy of the Roman empire, was worn by women as well as by men; in after times, the former assumed a different robe, called *stola,* which reached to the feet, having a broad fringe, or border, at the bottom.[3] Courtezans, and women condemned for adultery, were not permitted to wear the stola.[4]

The Roman women, married as well as unmarried, used girdles; and, besides them, they sometimes wore a broad swath, or bandage, round their breast, called *strophium;*[5] which seems to have answered the purpose of the bodice, or stays, and had a buckle, or bandage, upon the left shoulder.[6]

The Mitra, or *girdle,* of the Greeks, probably resembled the strophium of the Romans; the former was worn by the Grecian virgins. Hesiod applies an epithet to the Muses, signifying that they were *girt with golden mitres.*[7] Theocritus, in one of his pastorals, introduced a damsel complaining to a shepherd of his rudeness, saying he had loosed her *mitra,* or girdle; and he tells her, he means to dedicate the same to Venus.[8] The plated belt worn by Meneläus beneath the thorax was also called *mitra.*[9]

The Zone[10] was a part of dress of high antiquity: Homer describes the Goddess Juno binding round her waist a zone, elegantly formed, with an hundred foldings or fringes.[11] It probably differed from the *imas,* which she afterwards borrowed from Venus, and bound over the zone. The girdle that belonged to Venus was wrought, or embroidered, with the needle;[12] and the Poet tells us, "she loosed it from her breast." But I do not find any mention of clasps or buckles appertaining to either. From the common use of the zone, Hesiod calls his fair countrywomen *handsomely girded females.*[13]

1 Κροκη. 2 Lib. I. cap. 11 and 12.

3 This *limbus,* or fringe, was called *instita.* Hor. Sat. i.

4 Hence called *togatæ.* Ibid.; et Juv. Sat. ii. ver. 70. Mart. lib. I. Ep. xxxvi. ver. 8, 9.

5 Catull. LXIV. 65. 6 Called *spinther,* or *spinter.* Plaut. Men. Act III. Sc. 3.

7 Χρυσαμπυκες. Theog. ver. 916. 8 Idyll. xxvii. ver. 54. 9 See page ci.

10 Ζωνη. 11 Θυσανος; *fimbria;* fringes, welts, or borders. Iliad, XIV. ver. 181.

12 Κεστον ιμαντα, *acu pictum cingulum.* Ibid. ver. 214. 13 Ευζωνοια γυναικος. Scut. Hercul. ver 30.

The Peplus was a thin light mantle worn by the Grecian women above the tunic. This garment, according to Homer, was in great repute as early as the Trojan war; and was also worn by the ladies of Troy, who are called by the Poet *long-peplus-wearers*;[2] and speaking of the peplus of Minerva, when she loosened it, he tells us that it flowed upon the pavement.[3] Antinous presented to Penelope, a beautiful large and variegated peplus,[4] having twelve buckles of gold, with tongues neatly curved.[5] The magnificent peplus[6] of Juno was fastened with buckles of gold[7] upon her breast; but, generally speaking, I trust there was but one buckle used for this purpose; for Minerva, deriding the wound which Venus had received from Diomed, says to Jupiter: "She has been wantonly playing with one of the fair-peplus-wearing Grecian damsels, and has razed her soft hand against the golden fibula."[8]

If the Eanos of Juno be the same as the peplus, and such is the general opinion, it certainly was a garment totally distinct from the Kredemnon,[9] or *veil:* for Homer expressly tells us, that the Goddess had previously invested herself with the former, before she put on the latter. The peplus, however, was a very splendid part of the ladies' dress; and it is rarely mentioned by Homer without some epithet to distinguish it as such: he calls it the *variegated peplus*,[10] and the *painted peplus*,[11] alluding to the ornamental decorations, either interwoven or worked with the needle upon it, which consisted not only in diversity of colours, but of flowers, foliage, and other kinds of imagery; and sometimes he styles it the *soft purple peplus*,[12] which was then valuable on account of the excellence of the colour. From a passage in one of the Pastorals of Theocritus, it appears that the peplus was occasionally worn by the men, and fastened on the breast with a girdle.[13]

1 Πεπλος.

2 Τρωαδας ελκεσιπεπλους; or, perhaps, more literally, *drawing, or trailing peplus*, from its sweeping upon the ground. Iliad, VI.

3 Iliad, V. ver. 734.

4 Μεγαν περι καλλεα πεπλον ποικιλον. Odyss. lib. XVIII. v. 291.

5 Περοναι χρυσειαι κλησιν ευγναμπτοις. Ibid. v. 293.

6 Εανος αμβροσιος; Iliad, lib. XIV. ver. 178. The εανος is literally a *light thin vestment*, and is applied to the peplus.

7 Χρυσεησι ενετησι. Iliad, XIV ver. 180.

8 Ibid. lib. V. ver. 424.

9 Κρηδεμνῳ.

10 Πεπλος ποικιλος. Ibid. lib. V. ver. 735.

11 Πεπλοι παμποικιλοι, which literally signifies *a peplus all over variegated with painting*. Ibid. lib. VI. ver. 289.

12 Πορφυρεοις πεπλοισι μαλακοισιν. Ibid. lib. XXIV. ver. 796.

13 The Poet, speaking of Lycidas the Cydonian, a goat-herd, says, he had a white goat-skin upon his shoulders, and about his breast an old πεπλος, *peplus*, bound, ζωστηρι πλοκερῳ, with a *plaited, or interwoven, girdle*. Idyll. vii 171 218.

The Palla, or Amiculum, of the Romans, was the same kind of garment as the peplus, and with it the ladies sometimes covered their heads and their arms.

The Palliolum was a small cloak, or veil, worn by the women of easy virtue, when they walked in the streets of Rome, for concealment's sake.[1]

The *kredemnon,* which Juno put over her other vestments, was also used by the Phæacian virgins, who threw it aside when they amused themselves with playing at the ball.[2] This is usually considered as a thin light veil, worn over the head, and falling upon the shoulders. There was also a light kind of pallium used by the Grecian women, called *ampecone,*[3] and another *anabole*;[4] but we find nothing more concerning them than that they were upper garments.

The Chlamys, or Chlanidion, was also a species of mantle, and thought to have resembled the chlæna in its form, but it was lighter and softer in its texture. The chlamys was worn by both sexes.[5]

The Penula, which garment has already been described,[6] was worn by the women as well as by the men. The Emperor Alexander Severus forbad the matrons to use it in the city of Rome: they were allowed, however, to wear it at pleasure in the country.[7]

We learn from Theocritus, that the Theristrion[8] was a *veil,* or light summer cloak, worn by the women; and, from the thinness of the materials it was easily torn, especially in a crowd.[9] The same author informs us, that the Tompechanon[10] was a summer mantle, used by the females both before and after marriage, which does not appear to have covered the head, for they commonly wore the Tholian,[11] or hat, with this garment.

The Tarentine garment was used by the Greek women, and occasionally by the men; it is said by Lucian to have been white and comely, and so thin, that the form of the body and the limbs might be discovered through it.

The Roman ladies, in the latter times, had a fine robe, or mantle, which was called *cyclas* from the rotundity of its form.[12]

1 Hor lib. I. Sat. xi. Virg. Æn. XI. ver. 576. et alibi. 2 See page lxxxiii.
3 Odyssey, lib. VI. ver. 100, et infra. 4 Αμπεκονη, αναβολη. 5 Montfaucon, chap ii.
6 See page lxxxvi. 7 Montfaucon, chap. xii. 8 Θεριστριον. Idyll. xv. ver. 69.
9 Such an accident is described by the Poet; ibid. ver. 69.
10 Τωμπεχανον, ibid. ver. 39 & 71. 11 Θολιαν; ibid. Idyll. xv. ver. 39.
12 Juven. Sat. vi. ver. 259. Suet. Cal. cap. 52.

The Mavors, or Maforte, called also Ricinium, was a species of hood, or veil, used in time of mourning, which covered the head, and reached to the shoulders.[1]

The shoes of the ladies, and especially among the Romans, formed a very expensive part of their dress: in general, they were white;[2] but persons of opulence did not confine themselves to any colour; we find them black, scarlet, purple, yellow, and green; they were often not only richly adorned with fringes, and embroideries of gold, but set with pearls and precious stones of the most costly kind;[3] and these extravagances were not confined to persons of rank; they were imitated by those of lower stations, and became so prevalent, at the commencement of the third century, that even the luxurious emperor Heliogabalus thought it necessary to publish an edict, prohibiting the use of such expensive shoes, excepting to women of quality.[4]

The women wore the close shoe, or calceus, and the solea, and the crepida, as well in the city of Rome as in the country; but the form of their shoes does not appear to have differed materially from those of the men.

Gloves[5] seem to have been first invented to protect the hands of labouring people, when they were working among the bushes; and Homer has described Laërtes, the father of Ulysses, in his retirement, with gloves upon his hands;[6] but without giving us the least information respecting their form, their size, or the material with which they were composed; but most probably it was leather. Among the Romans gloves seem to have been more common than with the Greeks; and under the Emperors they were made with fingers,[7] though others were without them, and resembled the mittens of the present time.

From the representation which Homer has given of Juno attiring herself, we may form some faint idea of the fashionable dress among the ladies of quality in his time. He follows her to her toilet; and tells us, that she first combed her hair, and then with her fingers interwove, or braided, the shining locks.[8] This passage is paraphrased by Pope in the following manner; and though it will

[1] Cicero, Leg, lib. II. cap. 23. Serv. in Æn. I. ver. 268.

[2] Ovid. Ars Amandi, lib. II. ver. 271.

[3] Plin. Nat. Hist. lib. IX. cap. 35.

[4] Montfaucon, vol. III. part ii. cap. 5.

[5] Χειριδας, vel χειροθηκας; and in Latin *manicæ*.

[6] Odyss. lib. XXIV. ver. 229.

[7] Then called *digitalia*. Var. I. 55.

[8] Iliad, lib. XIV. ver. 176, 177.

not admit of a literal investigation, seems to convey the true meaning of the Poet:

> "Thus, while she breath'd of Heav'n, with decent pride,
> Her artful hands the radiant tresses tied;
> Part on her head in shining ringlets roll'd,
> Part o'er her shoulders wav'd, like melted gold."

The ornaments which were usually added we find in another part of the Iliad; where Andromache is represented, in excess of grief, tearing them from her head: unfortunately, however, little more than the bare names are recorded; they are four, exclusive of the kredemnon, or *veil;* the first is called the *desmata,*[1] distinguished by an adjective denoting splendour or elegance, and it is thought to have been an embroidered fillet, or ribbon; the second is named *ampyx,*[2] which is usually rendered a head-lace; the third is the *kecryphalon,*[3] generally taken for the caul of net-work which inclosed the hair; and the last is the *anadesme,*[4] which, from the epithet *intertwined,* or *woven,* applied to it by the Poet, may properly enough, in my opinion, be considered as a wreath or diadem.

Among the ancient Romans, the women's head-dress was exceedingly simple: they seldom went abroad; and, when they did, their heads were always covered with a veil; but, as riches and luxury increased, the lady's toilet was proportionally filled with ornaments for the person; so that it was called *The Woman's World.*[5]

They not only anointed the hair, and used rich perfumes,[6] but sometimes they painted it;[7] they also made it appear of a bright yellow colour, by the assistance of washes and compositions made for that purpose;[8] but they never used powder, which is a much later invention. They frizzled and curled the hair with hot irons,[9] and sometimes they raised it to a great height, by rows of curls one above the other, into the form of an helmet;[10] and such as had not sufficient

[1] *Δεσματα σιγαλοεντα*; Ibid. lib. XXII. ver. 468.
[2] *Αμπυξ*; in Latin *vitta;* ibid. ver. 469.
[3] *Κεκρυφαλον*; reticulum; ibid. ver. 469.
[4] *Πλεκτη αναδεσμη*; ibid.
[5] *Mundus muliebris;* Liv. lib. XXXIV. cap. 7.
[6] Ovid. Met. V. ver. 53
[7] Tibull. I. 9. 43; III. 4. 28.
[8] Val. Max. II. I. 5. Plin. Nat. Hist. lib. VII. 20. 33.
[9] *Calido ferro.* Virg. Æn. XII. ver. 100. Cic. Brut. 95.
[10] *In gradus formabant—in galeæ modum suggerebant.* Tertull. de Cult. Fœm 7.

hair of their own, used false hair to complete the lofty pile;[1] and these curls appear to have been fastened by hair-pins.[2] The Grecian virgins used to bind, or braid, their hair in a multiplicity of knots; but that custom, as well as painting the under part of the eye-lids with black paint, was discommended by an ancient Poet.[3] Persons of rank had slaves to perform for them the offices of the toilet:[4] they held the mirror in their hand themselves, to give directions; and Martial tells us, that, if the slaves unfortunately placed a hair-pin wrong, or omitted to twist the curls exactly as they were ordered, the mirror was thrown at the offender's head, or, according to Juvenal, the whip was applied with much severity.[5] It appears, indeed, that sometimes a number of women attended on these occasions, for no other purpose than to direct the operation.[6] The married women used a kind of bodkin,[7] which they managed very dexterously, to adjust and divide their hair into two portions; one turning to the right side, and the other to the left; and by this line of separation the married ladies were distinguished from those that were unmarried. The hair was adorned with ornaments of gold, with pearls, and with precious stones; and sometimes with garlands, or chaplets of flowers:[8] it was also bound with fillets and ribands of various colours, and of various kinds.[9] The ribands appropriated to the head-dresses of virgins differed from those of the married women.[10] And the ribands seem to have been a distinguishing mark of modesty; as, on the contrary, a broad fillet, or mitre, was of immodesty, being only worn by women of loose character,[11] excepting sometimes, indeed, by effeminate persons of the other sex.[12]—The net, or hair-caul, for the purpose of inclosing the hinder part of the hair, was in general usage with the Grecian and the Roman women. These ornaments were frequently enriched with embroidery; and sometimes made so thin, that Martial sarcastically called them *bladders*.[14]

[1] Hor. lib. I. Sat. viii. 48.

[2] *Crinales acus*, Propert. iii. 9. 53. Dio, lib. I. cap. 4.

[3] Frag. Naumachii, ver. 62; apud Poetas Minores Wintertoni.

[4] Hor. lib. I. Sat. ii. 98.

[5] Mart. Ep. ii. 66. Juvenal, Sat. vi. ver. 491.

[6] Juvenal, ubi supra

[7] *Acus discriminales.*

[8] Καλαι στεφαναι; Hom. Iliad, lib. XVIII. ver. 597. *Coronæ et serta;* Plaut. Ascn. Act IV. sc. i. ver. 58.

[9] *Crinales vittæ vel fasciæ.*

[10] Propert. IV. 12. Virg. Æn. II. ver. 168.

[11] Juvenal, Sat. iii. ver. 66. Serv. in Æn. IV. ver. 216.

[12] Cic. Rub. Post. 10.

[13] Called also *reticulum auratum;* that is, *a gilt caul*, or, rather, *ornamented with gold.* Juven. ii. ver. 96.

[14] *Vesica;* Mart. viii. 33.

Among the adornments of the head, I know of none that claim priority to the *ear-rings:* they have been fashionable, as Montfaucon justly observes, in all ages, and almost with all nations: we find them not only common to both sexes, but frequently worn by children also, and servants of the lowest class.[1] It is evident from Homer, that the Grecian women bored their ears for the admission of these ornaments. The Poet gives ear-rings to the Goddess Juno; and the words he uses on this occasion are literally these: "*In her well-perforated ears*[2] *she put the ear-rings of elaborate workmanship, having three eyes*" in each,[3] that is, three pendents, or jewels, either made in the form of eyes, or so called from their brightness. Just such a pair of ear-rings, for the Poet uses precisely the same words in both places, were presented to Penelope by Eurymachus, one of her suitors.[4] The extravagancy of the Grecian and Roman ladies in the purchase of these articles of adornment almost exceeds belief: Pliny says, "They seek for pearls at the bottom of the Red Sea, and search the bowels of the earth for emeralds to ornament their ears;"[5] and Seneca tells us, that "a single pair was worth the revenue of a large estate;" and that some women would wear at their ears "the price of two or three patrimonies;"[6] and this vanity was not confined to the fair sex; for, ear-rings of gold were worn by the young men of high rank.[7] In the Asiatic nations, it is well known, they are common to both sexes even in the present day. The fashion of the ear-rings, without doubt, was as variable as the materials they consisted of, which were silver, gold, pearls, emeralds, and every species of precious stones that could be procured. The ear-rings were not always worn for ornament only, but, out of superstition, as amulets, or charms.[8]

Another expensive ornament, among the ladies both of Greece and Rome, was the Monile,[9] or *necklace;* which was commonly made of gold, and set with gems. Homer mentions a necklace, curiously wrought with gold, intertwined with

1 Lib. II. cap. 3.

2 Ευτρητοισι λοβοισι; Iliad, lib. XIV. ver. 183.

3 Ερματα τριγληνα μοροεντα; ibid. verses 182, 183. *Inaures tribus-gemmarum-oculis insignes elaboratas;* Clarke.

4 Odyss. lib. XVIII. verses 296, 297.

5 Nat. Hist. XII. Præfat.

6 Senec. Vit. Beat. 17. "*Uxor tua locupletis domus auribus censum gerit.*" Vide Sueton. Vit. Jul. cap. 50; et Plin. ubi supra.

7 "*Auri tantum quantum puer mollitiæ insigne in auriculâ gestavit.*" Apuleius.

8 August. Civ. Dei.

9 Ορμον.

amber, which Eurymachus presented to Penelope.[1] The monile was also used by the men, but then it was usually twisted:[2] it was bestowed by the Romans upon the soldiers as a mark of honour and reward for their bravery. They had also chains composed of rings, which were worn about the neck by both of the sexes.[3] There was an ornament called *segmentum*, used by the matrons only, supposed by some authors to be a kind of necklace; but others take it for an embroidered riband, or fringe of purple, sewed upon their garments.[4]

The Bracelet for the arms was an article of adornment of high antiquity, and common both to the Greeks and to the Romans.[5] Bracelets were worn by the men, as well as the women, though not so frequently by the former; and those appertaining to the latter were probably richer, and adorned with precious stones.

The women sometimes wore ornaments round their legs called *periscelides;* but we know nothing respecting their form; perhaps they resembled the tinkling ornaments which were common enough in the Asiatic countries.[6]

Rings for the fingers are of great antiquity: it is thought, however, that the Romans derived the use of them from the Sabines.[7] At the time they were first introduced, none but Senators and Equites were permitted to wear them of gold; the privilege was afterwards extended to the Legionary Tribunes.[8] The plebeians wore rings of iron, excepting such a one as had been presented with a gold ring, for his valour in war, or for some other desert.[9] Under the Emperors, the liberty of wearing golden rings became more general; and was often granted for very frivolous reasons.[10] But Justinian gave permission to every citizen to use his pleasure respecting them;[11] and some were so finical as to have light rings for the summer, and heavier ones for the winter.[12] The ancient Romans rarely wore more

1 Ορμον χρυσεον ηλεκτροισιν ειρμενον; Odyss. lib. XVIII. ver. 294, 295.

2 *Torquis;* Virg. Æn. VII. ver. 351. Hence called *torques.*

3 Sueton. Galb. cap. 18.

4 Serv. in Æn. lib. I. ver. 658. Juven. Sat. vi. ver. 89. Ovid, Ars Amandi, lib. III. ver. 169.

5 Ψελλιον, χλιδων, et βραχιωνιστηρ; *armilla.*

6 See page xlvi.

7 Liv. I. cap. 2.

8 Ibid. lib. XXIII. cap. 12. Appian de Bell. Punic. cap. 63. Dio. XLVIII. cap. 45.

9 Cic. Ver. III. 80. Sueton. Jul. cap. 39. Macrob. Sat. ii. ver. 10.

10 Plin. Nat. Hist. lib. XXXIII. cap. 1. 4. Suet. Galb. cap. 14. Vitel. cap. 12. Tacit. Hist. lib. IV. cap. 3.

11 Novel. cap. 78.

12 Hence called *semestres.* Juven. Sat. i. ver. 28; et vii. ver. 89.

than one ring, and that upon the third finger of the left hand;[1] but afterwards the number was increased, and sometimes they had one or more upon each finger; but this was always considered as an effeminacy.[2] The rings were laid aside at night and when the wearer bathed; and, in the time of mourning, it was also indecorous for a person supplicating a favour to appear with a ring upon his finger.[3] The rings were not only of gold, but frequently set with precious stones of various kinds, and embellished with curious sculptures, such as the images or busts of the wearer's ancestors and friends, the portraitures of princes and famous men, the representation of great events, and a variety of other devices;[4] and they were of prodigious value. Nonius a Senator, it is said, was proscribed by Mark Antony for the sake of his ring, which was estimated at no less than twenty thousand sesterces.[5]

Rings were used for various purposes, and particularly for signets; they were also given as tokens, and in contracts and pledges, in any way.[6] It appears, that any free-woman might wear a ring of gold; and rings were worn by the females both before and after marriage.[7] A plain ring of iron without a gem, given to an unmarried woman, was a pledge of union; some say, the ring might be of gold.[8] A ring given by a person at the point of death was esteemed a particular mark of his affection.[9]

An iron ring was worn by a general at the time of his triumph.[10]

Face-painting does not appear to have been known among the Grecian ladies in Homer's time. In the dressing-room of Juno, as Eustathius justly observes, we meet with no washes for the face, no dyes for the hair, and none of the artificial embellishments since put in practice: the goddess had no mirror, and performed the duties of the toilet with her own hands.[11] A posterior Greek poet,

1 Hence called *digitus anularis*. Gel. X. 10. Macrob. Sat. vii. ver. 13.
2 Hor. Sat. lib. II. Sat. vii. v. 9. Mart. Ep. v. 62; et xi. 60.
3 Teren. Heaut. iv. 1. Liv. ix. cap. 7, et xliii cap. 16. Val. Max. viii. 1. Suet. Aug. cap. 101.
4 Cic. Cat. iii 5. Plin. Epist. X. Suet. Tib. 56. Cic. Sext. 61. Plin. Nat. Hist. VII. 26.
5 Ibid. lib. XXXVI. cap. 6.
6 Macrob. Sat. vii. Liv. Lib. XXVII. cap. 28. Justin. lib. II. cap. 12.
7 Plaut. cap. iii. sc. 5. Hor. Od. i. ver. 9. 23. Terentino Hecyra, IV. sc. 1.
8 Plin. Nat. Hist. lib. XXXI. cap. 1. Tertul. Apol. VI. Isidor. lib. XIX. cap. 32.
9 Justin. lib. XII. cap. 15. Val. Max. lib. VII. 88. et alibi.
10 Plin. Nat. Hist. lib. XXXIII. cap. 1.
11 Iliad, xiv. ver. 170, et seq.

directing his advice to a young virgin, counsels her against the waste of time in contemplating her form in the mirror, or in making many knots or braids with her hair; and, above all, to avoid the painting or blacking her eyes beneath the eye-lashes;[1] which was a fashion much practised in the Asiatic nations.[2]

The Roman women used variety of cosmetics, washes, and wash-balls, to improve the colour of their faces;[3] as well as different kinds of paints, some of which were composed of white lead, vermilion, and other pernicious ingredients, exceedingly dangerous to use.[4] They went so far as to cover the face with a thick kind of paste, which they wore at home.[5] Poppæa, the wife of Nero, invented an ointment to preserve beauty, made of asses' milk, and from her denominated *Poppæanum.*[6] The abominable fashion of face-painting was not confined to women: the men put the same in practice; and not only daubed their faces with paint,[7] but rubbed the skin with pumice-stones, to make it smooth.[8]

The women had plasters to eradicate the small hairs from the cheeks; and sometimes they pulled them out with an instrument of the tweeser kind;[9] their eyes and their eyebrows they darkened with a black powder;[10] and, to conceal any little deformity in the skin, they used patches in the form of a crescent;[11] but patches were often worn for mere ornaments.

In time of mourning, the Greeks cut their hair, and shaved their beards:[12] The Romans, on the contrary, when they mourned, allowed both to grow, and wore

[1] Frag. Naumachii, ver. 60, et infra. [2] See page xliv.

[3] Ovid, Met. Tacit. Ann. 51. Senec. Helv. 16.

[4] Plaut. Most. A. I. sc. 3. Ovid, Art. Am. l. iii. ver. 199. Hor. Epod. 10, 12. Martial, Ep. ii. 41, et alibi. [5] Juven. Sat. vi. ver. 462.

[6] Plin. Nat. Hist. XI. 41; et XXVIII. 12. [And Juvenal, as before. Ed.]

[7] Sueton. Otho, cap. 12. Cic. Pis. ii.

[8] Plin. Nat. Hist. lib. XXXVI. cap. 21.

[9] Called *volsellæ*, Mart. viii. 67.

[10] *Fuligine collinebant.* Tertul. de Cult. Fœm. V. Juvenal, Sat. ii. v. 93. Plin. Epist. vi.

[11] *Lunatam;* Mart. Ep. viii. 32, 33. Plin. ubi supra. [12] Seneca de Benef. V. 6.

the hair dishevelled, and sometimes covered it with dust and ashes;[1] and laid aside all their ornaments of gold and purple.[2] They also wore a black garment resembling the lacerna, called *pullata vestis.* It seems, however, that this vestment was not confined to the times of mourning, but was often used by the populace[3] on other occasions. The Ricinus, as we observed before, was a mourning garment worn by the women.

The slaves in Rome wore habits nearly resembling the poor people; their dress, which was always of a darkish colour, consisted of the exomis, or sleeveless tunic, or the lacerna, with a hood of coarse cloth; they wore the crepidæ for their shoes; and their hair and their beards were permitted to grow to a great length.[4]

The Roman boys being the sons of noblemen wore a hollow ball, or *bulla*, of gold, which hung from the neck upon the breast. Some think it was shaped like a heart; others that it was round, with a heart engraved upon it.[5] This device, according to Macrobius, was given to them, to put them in mind, as often as they looked upon it, that the heart was the seat of manhood. The bulla was made hollow for the reception of amulets against envy. Those belonging to the sons of freedmen and of poor citizens were made of leather.[6] Macrobius gives us the origin of this ornament, at least among the Romans; and, as the passage refers to another part of the young men's dress, I shall cite so much of it as will answer the present purpose. Tullus Hostilius, having conquered the Hetruscans, introduced at Rome, among other things, the *toga picta* and the *prætexta*, which were used by the Hetruscan magistrates; for, at that time, the pretexta was not given to the sons of noblemen, but was a habit of honour and distinction. Afterwards Tarquinius Priscus triumphed over the Sabines; and, in the oration which he made

1 Liv. i. 26, et vi. 16. Sueton. Jul. 67. Aug. 23. Calig. 24. Virg. Æn. xii. ver. 609. Catul. XLIV. 23.

2 Liv. lib. IX. cap. 7. Isidor. XIX. 31.

3 Montfaucon, vol. III. part i. chap. 7.

4 Gell. lib. VIII. 12. Hort. Sat. ii. 7. 54. Juven. Sat. iii. v. 170; et v. ver. 171, &c.

5 Cic. Verr. I. 58. Liv. lib. XXVI. cap. 36. Macrob. Sat. lib. I. cap. 6. [It was round. An original and beautiful bulla is in the exquisite collection of Samuel Rogers, Esq. Ed.]

6 *Bulla scortea*, vel *signum de paupere loro.* Juven. Sat. v. ver. 165. Plin. Nat. Hist. XXXIII. cap. i.

to the army, he bestowed much praise upon his son who, at fourteen years of age, had killed an enemy with his own hand. The eulogium being finished, he presented to the youth the pretexta and a bulla of gold, to shew, by those marks of honour, that his valour was superior to his years; the pretexta being an ensign of magistracy, and the bulla of triumph. Hence, adds he, the custom came of giving the pretexta and the bulla to the sons of noblemen;[1] or, as Pliny says, of giving a bulla of gold to the sons of those who had behaved valiantly in battle.[2]

The habits of the Priests we are by no means well acquainted with. The *Flamines*, it appears, received that appellation from a cap, or fillet, which they wore upon their heads.[3] They used the toga, and over that a purple læna, and sometimes a conical cap called *apex*.[4]

The Salii, or priests of Mars, on solemn occasions, danced through the city of Rome, clothed in an embroidered tunic, girt with a brazen belt; and over it they wore the toga pretexta, or the trabea; having on their heads a cap rising to a considerable height;[5] with a sword by the side; and holding in the right hand a spear, or a rod, and in the left one of the *sincilia*, or shields of Mars:[6] but, according to Lucan, this shield depended from the neck.[7]

The Luperci, or priests of Pan, at the Lupercal, ran up and down the city naked, having only a girdle of goats' skin about their waist, holding thongs of the same in their hands, with which they struck those they met, and especially the married women, to make them fruitful.

The Vestal Virgins wore a long white robe bordered with purple; their heads were decorated with fillets[8] and ribands;[9] at their initiation their hair was cut off, and buried; but it was permitted to grow again afterwards.[10]

The ancient Grecians, as well as the ancient Romans, used every method to encourage industry among the women. According to Homer, spinning and weaving constituted the chief employment of the ladies of the highest rank; and, indeed, the excelling in these qualities seems to have been one of the first recom-

[1] Macrob ubi supra.
[2] Plin. ubi supra.
[3] Varr. L. IV. c. 15.
[4] Lucan. lib. I. ver. 604. Virg. Æn. VIII. ver. 664.
[5] *Apex*, &c.; in Greek κυρβασια.
[6] Dionys. II. 70.
[7] Pharsal. lib. I. ver. 603.
[8] *Infulæ*, στεμματα. Dionys. II. 67; et VIII. 89.
[9] *Vittæ*. Ovid. Fast. III. 30.
[10] Plin. Nat. Hist. lib. XVI. cap. 44.

mendations a female could possess. But, in the more modern times, the women of quality of both nations became luxurious and indolent, and the management of the loom, with all its requisites, was committed to slaves. The goddess of Wisdom herself is described by the Poets as skilful in the production of fabrics of the finest texture, and also in decorating them with ornaments of various kinds, either interwoven by the mixture of different coloured threads, or embroidered with the needle; and this allegory was used, no doubt, as a stimulus for every woman to imitate so illustrious an example and become a good housewife.

Silk appears to have been unknown to the Romans during the existence of the Republic; it is afterwards mentioned; but the use of it was forbidden to the men.[1] Vespasian and his son Titus wore robes of silk at the time of their triumph;[2] but these, it is thought, were only embroidered, or embellished, with silk intermixed with other stuff; for, Heliogabalus is said to have been the first Emperor who wore a robe of pure silk.[3] It appears also, that the silk stuffs woven in India were esteemed at Rome too thick and close for use; and therefore they were unravelled, and wrought over again with linen or woollen,[4] and made so thin that the body might be seen through the garment.[5] In the time of the Emperor Aurelian, a vestment of pure silk was estimated at so high a price, that he refused to indulge his Empress on that account.[6] Silk-worms, it is said, were introduced at Constantinople as early as the reign of Justinian; but the Romans some-time after appear to be perfectly ignorant of the method of making silk.[7]

I shall conclude this chapter with the following description of a Grecian farmer's habit from Hesiod:[8]

> When gusty winter frowns upon the land,
> Such clothing use as I shall now command:
> Soft let the *chlena*[9] be; and to the ground
> The ample *tunic* shall descend around;

[1] Tacit. An. lib. II. cap. 33.

[2] See page vi. [Where the reference should be to Bel. Jud. lib. VII. cap. 5. sec. 4. Ed.]

[3] *Vestis holoserica:* Lamprid. in Vit. Heliogab. lib. XXVI. 29.

[4] Plin. Nat. Hist. lib. VI. cap. 22.

[5] *Ut translucerent.* These kind of garments were first made in the Island of Cos; hence *vestes Coe*, for their silken and transparent vestments; see page xxxvii.

[6] Vospisc. in Aurel. cap. 45.

[7] Procop. de Bell. Goth. lib. IV. cap. 17.

[8] Works and Days, Book II. ver. 153, et infra.

[9] Χλαινα.

In wearing these take largely of the fleece,
But sparingly of flax ; and work the piece
With care throughout, nor let the woolly part
Appear unseemly or devoid of art.
With *shoes*, well formed from an ox's hide,
The pile turn'd inwards, be your feet supply'd.
Have ready next, your shoulders to defend,
Should the rough storm or heavy rains descend,
A *cloak* of goats' skins, firstlings of the kind,
Sew'd with strong tendons,[2] and completely join'd.
Then for thine head a *pilon*[3] wrought with care,
Both ears inclosing cautiously prepare ;
For, piercing are the morning winds which blow
Chill from the North, and drive the falling snow.

[1] Πεδιλα βοος.

[2] Νευρῳ βοος ; literally, *the nerves of the ox.*

[3] Πιλος ; a cap, or hat.

A

COMPLETE VIEW

OF

THE DRESS AND HABITS

OF THE

PEOPLE OF ENGLAND,

FROM THE ESTABLISHMENT OF THE SAXONS IN BRITAIN
TO THE PRESENT TIME.

PART I.

THE CIVIL, MILITARY, AND ECCLESIASTICAL HABITS OF THE ANGLO-SAXONS, TO THE CONCLUSION OF THE EIGHTH[1] CENTURY.

CHAP. I.

THE STATE OF THE CLOTHING ARTS CONSIDERED.—HABITS OF THE MEN.—THE SHIRT.—THE TUNIC.—THE SURCOAT.—THE CLOAK, OR MANTLE.—THE HEAD-DRESS.—THE SHOES, STOCKINGS, &c.

Among the various arts, to which the necessities of mankind gave birth, none seems to have claimed more attention than those upon which the manufacturing of cloth depended; so that, if we had not the evidence of history in favour of our

[1] [The principal authorities upon which Mr. Strutt has relied for the Anglo-Saxon costume of the eighth century are the following illuminated MSS. in the British Museum, and the Bodleian Library at Oxford:—

1. The Book of Genesis, and other parts of the Mosaical History. Cotton Col. Claudius B. iv.
2. A Psalter in Latin according to the version of St. Jerome. Harleian Col. 603.
3. Book of Genesis, &c. Bodleian Lib. No. 5123. Junius xi.
4. A Calendar in the Saxon language. Cotton Col. Julius A. vi.

The four subjects on his first plate, inscribed "Saxon Rustics of the Eighth Century," are taken one

Saxon ancestors, we could hardly suppose them to have been altogether ignorant of the clothing arts, even at the time of their first arrival in Britain. They were, it is true, a rude, unlettered people; but it is equally certain, that they were by no means destitute of ingenuity; nor is it probable that, while they were making considerable advancement in other arts, they should totally neglect those, which were highly essential to their comfortable enjoyment of life. At the time of their establishment in England, we find that they were well acquainted with the manner of dressing and spinning of flax,[1] which they manufactured into cloth, and dyed of various colours according to their fancy; and, from the high price of wool enacted by the Saxon Legislature,[2] a strong presumptive proof may be drawn, that the making of woollen garments was also practised in this kingdom.

To what extent of delicacy they carried their manufactures cannot possibly be ascertained in the present day; but, that their skill in the art of weaving, so far back as the latter end of the seventh century, was by no means inconsiderable, we have the incontestable authority of an author of their own. Aldhelm, bishop of Sherbourne, writing in praise of virginity, uses the following lines by way of simile: "It is not the web of one uniform colour and texture, without any variety of figures, "that pleases the eye and appears beautiful, but one that is woven by shuttles filled "with threads of purple and various other colours, flying from side to side, and "forming a variety of figures and images in different compartments with admirable "art."[3] It appears, however, equally certain, that silks, and the finest linen, and

from each of these MSS. Now, No. 3 has been acknowledged to be as late as the close of the tenth, perhaps the commencement of the eleventh century. (Vide Archæologia, vol. 24, in which the illuminations are engraved, and the MS. described). No. 1 is considered to be not much its senior, and Nos. 2 and 4 Mr. Strutt himself has, in his reference at the end of the work, ascribed to the *tenth* century; and on his 23rd plate actually given two warriors from the former in their true chronological order. In my "History of British Costume," I have given my reasons for believing this Harleian MS. (603) to be of even a still later date, namely of the time of Harold II. It is necessary, therefore, that our readers should bear this notice in mind through the following chapters, as having placed this warning in front, I shall not encumber the text with continual corrections of the same error, more particularly as there does not appear to be any reason for supposing that much alteration took place in the dress of the Anglo-Saxons between the 6th and 11th centuries, for as early as the close of the 8th they were reproached with *putting on their garments in the manner of their pagan predecessors;* and the first serious innovation upon the ancient costume appears to have been that so bitterly lamented by William of Malmesbury, in the time of Edward the Confessor, when they began to ape the fashions of the Norman-French. Ed.]

1 Dr. Henry's History of Britain, Vol. II.

2 By some of the Anglo-Saxon laws it was valued at two-fifths of the price of the whole sheep. Dr. Henry, as above.

3 Aldhelm de Virginitate, MS. in the Library at Lambeth.

other cloths, made a considerable part of the imports from foreign countries, not only at this period, but even for some time after the Norman conquest: silk, we are assured, was used soon after the conversion of the Anglo Saxons to Christianity, to ornament the altars of their churches; and in a short space of time it became one of the luxuries of the wealthy in their dress; but there is no sufficient authority to support the supposition of its having been made in England during the Saxon Æra.[1]

When we look upon the delineations of the Saxons preserved in their manuscripts, (and there is no reason to believe that they are not the real transcripts of their own times), we see evidently, that not only the conveniences, but even the superfluities, of dress were adopted by them; and it appears that the decoration of the habit, with variety of redundant ornaments, was considered as an essential distinction of superior rank.

I shall close this short introduction with a few words upon the skill of the Anglo-Saxon ladies in the art of embroidering. The teaching of this art appears to have been one part of polite education among the fair sex, and their peformances therein were often of such importance as to excite the notice of the ancient historians; but we shall have occasion to speak on this subject more fully hereafter: in order to give some idea how far it was extended at this period, I shall only add here, that, in a charter which Wiglaf, king of Mercia, granted to the abbey of Croyland, cited by Ingulphus, mention is made of the king's golden veil, *embroidered with the History of the Destruction of Troy,* which he gave to the said abbey, to be hung up annually in the church upon his birthday.[2]

THE SHIRT.

THERE is sufficient authority to prove that the shirt was a garment in use among the Anglo-Saxons as early as the eighth century; but the difficulty, at present, is to distinguish it from the short tunic. The shirt was the clothing worn immediately next the skin, and rarely drawn by the artists of antiquity without some other covering; for which reason we cannot expect to see it in its perfect form. The sleeping figure, represented at the bottom of the second plate of this work, was drawn by the artist for a man in bed; the garment he wears greatly resembles the tunic

[1] Anglia Sacra, W. Malms. &c.

[2] Ingulphus, Hist. Croil. p. 487.

without its customary appendage, the girdle, saving only that it appears to sit closer to the body; and the folds of the sleeves, from the elbow to the wrist, are much smaller than they are generally depicted upon the tunic. From these circumstances, I have been led to conclude, that the garment here represented is the shirt of the Anglo-Saxons.[1] If this be not the fact, the appearance of a garment to sleep in is a good argument in favour of the decency of our ancestors in their uncultivated state, as the æra, we are now treating of, is usually called. We shall find, however, the shirt, as a night garment, was entirely rejected in the succeeding ages—ages, when one might have expected to have found mankind improved, and decency, at least, established upon a broader foundation.

From the colour of this garment, which in the original is white, I conceive it to have been designed to represent linen, of which material we may naturally conclude the shirt, at this time, was usually made, because the wearing of a woollen shirt was enjoined by the Canons as a very severe penance.[2]

I have observed, that the habit above-mentioned is white in the original, but the colour, when applied to dress, seems entirely to have depended on the caprice of the wearer; for other instances occur in which the garment of this kind is painted red and blue. We are not, however, to suppose that linen shirts, or even shirts at all, were in common use, especially at this period. The wearing of linen was certainly confined to the wealthy only, and seems to have been considered as a luxury of the times.

THE TUNIC.

This garment certainly is not of Saxon origin: we trace it in the monuments of highest antiquity; and, as far as we can judge of it, from the form and even from the name which it bore among our ancestors, it was derived from the Romans.[3] It was of two kinds; the short tunic, worn at times by all classes of people; and the long tunic, which appears to be the distinguishing mark of superiority of rank.

The short tunic, in its simplest state, bears no distant resemblance to the modern

[1] This figure is taken from a Saxon MS. in the British Museum, marked Claudius, B. iv.

[2] Johnson's Canons, A.D. 963. Can. 64.

[3] In the MS. from which the greater part of the specimens of the tunic are given upon the following plates, it is called ꞇunican. [It was also called Roc or Rooc.—Ed.]

shirt; it was apparently put upon the body over the head in the same manner, and the aperture at the top is sometimes drawn no larger than barely sufficient to admit the passing through of the head; but at other times we see it open upon the bosom, and adorned with a border, of which, perhaps, the frill of the present day may be considered as a remote imitation.

It was sometimes open from the hips downward on either side; and the wearer frequently appears to have no other garment to defend him from the inclemency of the weather: this form of the tunic might be adopted, because it gave full liberty to the limbs, and was of course more convenient when agility was required. Two specimens of the open tunic, selected from many which occur in the early Saxon manuscripts, are given upon the first plate of this work. The figure to the left represents a ploughman, and is the only instance, that I recollect, in which the tunic is depicted without a girdle round the loins.[1] The third figure upon the same plate is also a ploughman,[2] but I think of superior rank, and probably a free man; for the tunic open on the sides appears to have been, at this period at least, the distinguishing badge of slavery or servitude.

From the short tunic of the Saxons originated, I doubt not, the garment so commonly worn at this day by the rustics in all parts of England, and known by the name of round frocks, or carmen's frocks. The collars and wrist-bands of such frocks are very often curiously decorated with needle-work, and much in the same manner we shall see the Saxon tunic ornamented hereafter.

The short tunic rarely descended below the knee; and, being bound about the waist with a girdle, the loose flow of folds from the hips were by no means ungraceful: but frequent instances occur, especially where a person of superior quality is represented, in which this garment appears to be decorated with borders of various colours, embroidered, and sometimes set with precious stones; which, however they may have added to its finery, totally destroyed the elegance of its form. The third figure, on the second plate, exhibits an example of this kind, and several others may be found in the succeeding engravings.[3]

I have hinted before, that the short tunic was a garment worn by all classes of

[1] It is taken from a MS. in the Harleian Library, marked 603.

[2] This figure is taken from an ancient Saxon MS. in the Bodleian Library, at Oxford, marked Junius xi. and the figure in the middle of the plate is taken from the MS. mentioned in the last note but one, marked Claudius, B. iv.

[3] Three specimens of the short tunic, as worn without the mantle, are given on the second plate. The figure in the middle is from the MS. at Oxford, mentioned before, marked, Junius xi. The other two, and the figure sleeping at the bottom, are from Claudius, B. iv.

people, from the slave to the monarch; and, from the great frequency of its representation in the ancient delineations, it appears to have been more generally adopted by the nobility than the longer tunic, which was by no means so convenient for motion; and, indeed, it is rarely seen where the figures are represented walking, hunting, or in fact employed in any kind of exercise. I conceive it was only worn on state-days and other solemn occasions; and, whenever it is depicted, it appears to be the habit appropriated to people of the most exalted rank.

The sleeves of the longer tunic were sometimes loose, and open; at other times close to the arms; and most commonly to the wrist. This garment was bound about the waist with a girdle, and descended in loose graceful folds to the ancles. It is of various colours in the different delineations; but the more general colour appears to be white, which circumstance may lead us to conjecture that it was made of linen. The same observation, with respect to colour, will hold good concerning the shorter tunic, which is also very frequently painted white; however, we are well assured that the materials of that garment were varied according to the rank and wealth of the wearer. But, as the longer tunic was always confined to persons of superior stations, there can be little doubt that the materials of which it was composed were of the finest texture and most esteemed workmanship.

THE SURCOAT.[1]

The Surcoat was a garment worn over the tunic, and it was appropriated to persons of the highest distinction; from the nature of its construction it appears to have been an ornamental or state dress: like the tunic, it was put upon the body over the head, a sufficient aperture being left at the top for that purpose. The sleeves of the surcoat are usually depicted large and open, and do not descend beyond the elbow; some few instances must be excepted, in which they are made closer to the arm, and reach to the wrist: we see the surcoat perfectly represented in the third plate of this work, together with the longer tunic. To the dress of the monarch of this period is usually added the mantle, either as it is exhibited upon the fourth plate, or fastened with the fibula upon the right shoulder; frequent instances of which will be seen hereafter. I made choice of the present figure, because it shews the longer tunic and the surcoat distinctly, without any part of the

[1] [Properly, the super-tunic. Saxon, over-froc. Surcoat (sur-cote) was the Norman name for a similar garment.—Ed.]

latter being hid by the mantle. There is also a peculiarity with respect to the surcoat, as here represented, which occurs but once or twice more in any of the Saxon drawings that I have seen. It has the appearance of a double garment: that part of it which is most seen is blue, and the sleeves belonging to it are short and open: the under part of it which appears upon the knees, and descends in close sleeves covering those of the tunic, to the wrists, is yellow. The tunic reaches below the border of the surcoat to the ancles, and is painted red.

The surcoat is depicted of various colours; but, as it belonged to the nobility only, we may depend upon its having been made of the most costly materials, perhaps of silk, or finest linen; and we often find it ornamented with rich embroidery, and borders of gold.

The surcoat, as represented upon the third and fourth plates, reaches to the middle of the leg; but we find that a garment not so long, though perhaps of the same kind, was worn by persons of distinction over the shorter tunic. It descended below the waist, and appears to have been constantly ornamented at the bottom with a border of embroidery, as may be seen upon the seventh plate.

THE CLOAK, OR MANTLE.

There is no part of the ancient Saxon habit that appears to have varied so much in form and size as the Mantle. It is most usually depicted as a very partial covering, fastened with a fibula or buckle upon the right shoulder, whence it descended a little below the skirts of the shorter tunic, and, covering all the back, it was gathered into sloping folds over the left arm and part of the breast. This mode of wearing the mantle gave perfect liberty to the right arm, while the various actions of the left arm beneath it afforded a succession of forms, the lines of which were often very elegant. It is proper, however, to observe, that various instances occur, in which we find the order of wearing the mantle exactly reversed; the fibula being affixed to the left shoulder, and the right arm covered, while the left remains without any incumbrance. This might arise from the vanity of the wearer, to shew that he could use the left hand equally with his right, a skill which our ancestors certainly held in high estimation.[1]

The mantle, as above described, was generally worn with the shorter tunic; and

[1] To use the weapon with both hands is given as part of the character of a great hero in the ancient Chronicles of Norway. Pontoppidan's History of Norway, p. 248.

even personages of common rank are rarely depicted without it. I do not mean to say, that it was confined to persons of middling stations; it was also adopted by those of the highest distinction, and frequently worn with the longer tunic and surcoat, in which case it has the appearance of being longer than usual and more flowing.

The nobility, especially when habited in their state-dress, are often distinguished by a more ample cloak or mantle, which was usually fastened upon the breast with a fibula, and it covered both shoulders equally; sometimes it is delineated as descending nearly to the ancles in the manner represented in the fourth plate: at other times it appears to have been much curtailed, and extended but little below the verge of the shorter tunic, as may be seen upon the seventh plate. Both these mantles, from the manner in which they are fastened, must have been exceedingly inconvenient to the wearer in all cases where activity was required; whence we may reasonably conjecture that they were used as ceremonial or state-dresses only.

There was another kind of large cloak, or mantle, belonging to the Anglo-Saxons at this period; but, as it is rarely represented in their paintings, I am inclined to think it was by no means generally used. It was worn without any buckle, and appears evidently to have been made with an aperture nearly in the midst of it, for the head to pass through, over which it was put upon the shoulders; and, perhaps, (for I speak from conjecture only), it may be properly considered as a winter garment. The representation of it is given upon the fifth plate.

Youth of distinction are usually depicted with a small cloak resembling the herald's tabard. It was fastened with a fibula upon either shoulder, and, hanging down before, as probably it did behind in like manner, was open at the sides, and left both the arms at liberty;—this cloak did not reach below the girdle; the exact representation of it is given upon the fifth plate. Another drawing of a youth, apparently older than the former, is copied on the sixth plate. His cloak is fastened with a single fibula upon the right shoulder only, and it seems to have been no otherwise distinguished from the mantle worn by persons arrived at man's estate than by its size; for it is, as we may see upon examination, considerably smaller in proportion to his stature.

I do not apprehend that the Saxons always unbuckled their mantles when they took them from their shoulders, especially in case of any uncommon emergency.—From the manner in which they appear to have been buckled, there could have been no difficulty in putting them over the head, even in that state; this conjecture is strengthened by a drawing which I found in a Saxon manuscript of the tenth century, in which David is represented fighting with a lion; and, as his cloak would have been inconvenient to him during the combat, he is supposed to have taken it from his shoulders, and thrown it upon the ground, where it lies in the form faithfully represented at the bottom of the fifth plate.[1]

The mantle, worn by the figure with his arms extended in the middle compartment of the fifth plate, differs greatly from any of those already described. Part of it was bound about the waist, and reached below the knees; while the other part of it, passing over the left or right shoulder, covered the back, and descended to the middle of the leg. The same kind of mantle, but more perfectly represented, is exemplified upon the eighth plate.[2] This garment may probably be considered as part of the most superb habit of the monarch and grandees of this period; for, none but a superior personage is ever depicted with it; and it seems especially to have been appropriated to the representations of the Deity and other heavenly beings. If this observation should lead to the supposition that it was only a fancy-dress, it will be necessary to add, that the Anglo-Saxon artists do not, in any other instance, appear to have had the least distant idea of clothing their figures in dresses differing from those they were constantly accustomed to behold. But a stronger proof, that the garment under present consideration is not a dress of fancy, may be deduced from the resemblance it bears to that before-mentioned upon the fifth plate, which was executed by another artist of the same century, and because it also corresponds exactly with the same kind of mantle represented in many other Saxon manuscripts painted at different times, and probably in very distant parts of the country.

[1] The figure to the right upon the fifth plate, represented as running forward, is given to shew the manner in which the mantle sat upon the shoulders, when seen sideways. A back view of the same does not occur in any of the drawings of this period.

[2] I should not make any apology for giving this figure to the public, even if it was not so essential to the present work as I conceive it to be: extractedly, we may consider it as a curious specimen of the arts at the time in which it was painted; and, through the rudeness of the form, there is evidently to be traced an idea of grandeur and strength of imagination far superior to what might have been expected from a people so uncivilized as the Saxons are generally represented to be. Had the execution been equal to the conception, this figure would not have disgraced the pencil of a Raphael.

THE HEAD-DRESS.

The Saxon drawings of the eighth century contain no great variety of head-dresses, and the few we find delineated are very simple in their form. No regard seems to have been paid to beauty in their construction, nor much to common convenience; they scarcely covered the top of the head, and left the face exposed to the weather, and unshaded from the rays of the sun.

Personages of all ranks, the king only excepted, who (for distinction's sake) is always represented wearing his crown, are frequently depicted bare-headed; nor will it appear extraordinary, that the custom of going with the head uncovered should be prevalent among the Anglo-Saxons, when we recollect that long flowing hair was considered by them as an essential beauty, and the fondness to display the luxuriance of their locks might be the occasion of their paying so little regard to any extraneous ornament. This taste they derived from their ancestors; and so forcibly had fashion impressed it upon their minds, that they were not prevailed upon to curtail their hair for several centuries after their conversion to Christianity, notwithstanding it was a continual topic of declamation among the clergy, who reprobated the wearing of long hair as an unmanly and sinful custom.

The usual form of the hair, as we find it represented in the drawings of this remote æra, is not inelegant; it is parted upon the middle of the head, and flows on either side the face upon the shoulders; it appears to have been neatly combed, and is very rarely represented with curls, or braided; when it is so, it is evidently intended as a mark of the highest distinction, as may be seen on the eighth plate, where the figure is depicted with great exuberance of hair, far exceeding the usual quantity; it is also plaited or curled upon the crown and at the sides in a very curious and singular manner. The hair and beard of this extraordinary figure in the original drawing are blue, a circumstance not at all singular; repeated instances occur of the hair and beard being so coloured, not only in the book from which the present engraving is taken, but in a variety of other manuscripts some centuries posterior to it. This observation leads me to conjecture that the Anglo-Saxons either had some method of dying the hair blue, or filled it occasionally with powder of that colour. The custom of dying the hair of various colours is of much greater antiquity than the times I am now treating of, and it was especially prevalent in the eastern parts of the world.[1]

It has been said, that the Saxons always shaved their beards, leaving no part untouched by the razor but what grew upon the upper lip.[2] The authority of William of Malmsbury in particular on one hand, and the tapestry of Bayeaux on the other, is brought to prove this assertion ; which is certainly true, when applied to the time in which the celebrated tapestry was manufactured ;[3] but, in the more remote ages, and particularly in the eighth century, the very reverse prevailed among our ancestors. The greater part of the figures which accompany this chapter sufficiently demonstrate, that the upper lip and top of the chin were only shaved, and that the rest of the beard was permitted to grow to a considerable length ; it has the appearance of being very smooth and clean, and is continually represented as forked, or divided upon the chin, and terminating downwards in two points.

The cap, most commonly worn by the Saxons at this period, bears no distant resemblance to the ancient Phrygian bonnet. With the lower class of people, it has the appearance of roughness behind, and probably was composed of the skin of some animal dressed with the hair upon the hide, and the shaggy part turned outward. Such a cap is represented in the middle compartment of the first plate. When the man of quality wore this kind of covering, it was usually enriched with some species of ornament ; an instance of which is given upon the fifth plate.

Another cap, in the form of a perfect cone, was worn occasionally by the nobility ; but as this appears to have been a species of helmet, the description and representation of it will be given in the third chapter, where the military habits of this century are particularly considered.[4]

[1] Mohammed, the Arabian impostor, by the application of *Al Henna*, or Cyprus Indigo, and the herb *Al Catam*, gave a beautiful shining red colour to his hair and beard. His immediate successor, Abu Becr, followed his example, which is practised by the *Scenite Arabs* at this day. Modern Universal Hist. Vol. I. pages 252 and 379.

[2] Dr. Henry's History of Britain, Vol. II.

[3] That is, soon after the Norman conquest. We shall have occasion to speak more fully concerning this curious tapestry hereafter, when we come to the dress of the Normans.

[4] The crown and diadem, which are represented upon the third and eighth plates, will be fully described at the end of the Saxon Æra.

SHOES AND STOCKINGS.

The Saxons of the eighth century are seldom represented barefooted: shoes appear to have been very common, even among the lowest class of people. All the different forms of the shoes, retained in the drawings of this period, are given with the several figures which accompany the present chapter. They are usually painted black, and are sometimes fastened round the instep, without the appearance of any aperture farther than was barely necessary for the insertion of the foot. In general, they are divided in the middle; at other times they have evidently two divisions, one on each side; and the upper leather forms a flap, which covers the instep, and fastens upon it, where it is connected with the part attached to the soles. Some few instances occur, where sandals are represented, especially in a very ancient manuscript of the four Gospels;[1] but there is nothing particular in their form; and, from their being totally omitted in the more modern paintings of the Saxons, I conceive that the wearing of them was also quite abolished.

There is nothing more certain than that stockings were in use among the Anglo-Saxons as far back as the eighth century: but it will not be an easy task to discover the materials of which they were composed; nor to determine whether the ancient illuminators intended in general to represent the legs as bare, when neither marks nor folds are delineated upon them; for, there is rarely any distinction in such cases made by colour. One instance, however, I have procured in the boy upon the sixth plate; his legs, in the original painting, are blue, a circumstance which clearly proves them to have been covered, though there are no marks of the folding of the stockings. There are some faint indications of folds upon the legs of the rustic to the right, in the first plate, which, however, do not extend higher than the middle of the leg. The centre figure, upon the second plate, gives the most perfect representation of a covering for the legs; but, whether this was not a species of boot or buskin, in addition to the stockings, I cannot certainly discover.

Gloves seem to have been unknown at this period, though undoubted authority will be produced in the ensuing pages to prove that they were in use not long afterward; but even then as a luxury only, imported from the Continent, and confined to the highest class of people.

[1] This curious MS. is said to have been written at the instigation of St. Cuthbert, as early as the seventh century; figures, representing the four Evangelists, are rudely depicted and prefixed to the Gospels. They are faithfully copied in the third volume of Strutt's Ƿoꞃƀa Anᵹel-cynnan, or Manners and Customs of the English. [The figures were copied most probably from Greek paintings, and cannot be relied upon as authorities for Anglo-Saxon costume.—Ed.]

CHAP. II.

THE DRESS OF THE WOMEN OF THE EIGHTH CENTURY—THE UNDER-GARMENT—THE GOWN—THE MANTLE—THE COVERCHIEF, OR HEAD-DRESS—THE SHOES, STOCKINGS, &C.

THE great want of materials for furnishing a complete history of the Anglo-Saxons, and the confusion of circumstances arising from the various divisions of Britain under their government, has deterred many of our best writers from making deep researches into the abstracted remains of antiquity concerning them. The Saxon annals are hastily passed over; and we are led to conclude that they contained nothing worthy the serious attention of an accomplished historian.[1] The records of our ancestors, however, speak a contrary language; and even a partial examination of their drawings, though rude and imperfect in many instances, will demonstrate the strongest evidence of natural genius under some degree of cultivation, and convince us that more than the mere dawn of civilization had taken place among them.

The former chapter affords sufficient proof, that, as early as the eighth century, considerable advances had been made beyond the requisites of mere convenience, even to the appearance of luxury and magnificence in the garments of the men. We shall now pass on to the habits of the Anglo-Saxon ladies; and it gives me no small satisfaction to assure the female part of my readers, that they will find the strongest indications of modesty in the dress of their fair countrywomen, without the least tincture of barbarism, and without (let me not offend in speaking) that proneness to change of fashion which so forcibly characterises the later ages. Content with native simplicity, which is rarely inelegant, the Anglo-Saxon ladies adopted the fashions of their predecessors, and for several centuries posterior to the era I am now engaged in, the habits of the females appear to have undergone little alteration. The later Saxon manuscripts exhibit the same kind of garments, but progressively adorned with variety of ornaments of embroidery and needle-work. Ornaments of this kind depended entirely upon the skill of the ladies, and may more properly be considered as a display of their taste than a change of fashion; they also reflect great credit upon the fair artists, and testify by the gradual indications of improvement, that the elegant domestic employment of working with

[1] [Mr. Strutt made this observation before Mr. Sharon Turner had published his excellent "History of the Anglo-Saxons."—ED.]

the needle was holden by them in very high estimation. It has been already hinted in the preceding chapter, that the Anglo-Saxon ladies, so far back as the eighth century, excelled in the arts depending upon the needle: the history of their dress will therefore be, in some measure, a history of their ingenuity; and will, I trust, sufficiently demonstrate what has been asserted in their favour.

In the foregoing chapter it has been proved, that the shirt formed a part of the dress of the men; and surely we cannot hesitate a moment to conclude that the women were equally tenacious of decency in their habit, and of course were not destitute of body linen: the remains of antiquity, it is true, afford not sufficient authority to prove the fact; yet the presumptive argument, founded upon female delicacy, weighs so strongly in the scale, that, concluding it to be consonant with the truth, I shall proceed to the examination of those garments appropriated to the fair sex, for which I have indisputable evidence.

THE UNDER-GARMENT.

This part of the dress, for which I know not the ancient name, bears no distant resemblance to the longer tunic of the men.[1] It has sleeves exactly similar, which usually descend to the wrists, and are plaited in small folds to the elbow. Owing to its situation, it is never represented simply by itself; but, as far as one can judge of it from its general appearance, it was bound about the waist, and reached nearly to the ground, so as frequently to cover the greater part of the feet. It is depicted of various colours, but the most common colour is white; hence one may be led to conclude that it was made of linen, which opinion is farther strengthened by the smallness of the folds, and the frequent attempts to shew the appearance of the limbs beneath it. The under-garment, as it is partially represented in the drawings of this century, does not appear to have been ornamented even with the common decorations of needle-work, which are frequently found upon the other parts of the ladies' habits, excepting only in the single instance given upon the eleventh plate, where a female figure is represented sitting; the open sleeves compose a part of the under-garment, as the similarity of colour seems incontestably to

[1] [The tunic was worn by women as well as by men; but there was another garment, entitled the Kyrtle, which, in the will of Wynflæda, is mentioned amongst the "other linen web;" and in one place described as *white*. This would seem to have been an inner or under garment, as it was in the Anglo-Norman times, when "in kirtle alone" the ladies "served in hall." But in the Saxon word Syrca, transmuted into the lowland Scotch *sark*, we surely find evidence of that inner*most* garment so delicately alluded to by Mr. Strutt in the preceding paragraph.—Ed.]

prove; and an ornament of plaiting, formed by the needle in lines nearly circular, appears upon the shoulder; the corresponding part of the same garment is seen beneath the gown, but without the least indication of adornment.

The open sleeves are very rarely appropriated to this garment; they usually belong to the gown; but the close sleeves, with which it is most commonly delineated, are given in one instance upon the ninth plate; in two more upon the tenth plate; and most perfectly upon the twelfth plate, where the lady is represented in her full dress, and the four distinct parts of her habit are perfectly discriminated.

THE GOWN.

I HAVE often considered myself, when engaged in the abstracted researches of antiquity, in the situation of a traveller who has lost his way in a country totally unknown to him, and, finding no prospect of information, is reduced to the necessity of depending upon his own judgment with respect to the path he ought to pursue; and never did I feel the force of this similitude more than in the compilation of the present chapter. Uncertain how far the names I apply to the different parts of the dress, belonging to the females of this remote period, are consistent with reality, I am still necessitated, for brevity's sake, to adopt some names; and, should any of them eventually prove to be improper, I hope I may claim that indulgence which candour never denies, even to the errors arising from a minute investigation of subjects in themselves obscure and doubtful: I can safely assert, in my own defence, that I have exerted every endeavour to be as accurate as possible; and in all cases, where I am under the necessity of delivering my own sentiments, unsupported by authority, I submit them as such to the public, without presuming to impose upon my readers, or mislead them by any false hypothesis of my own. This apology I thought it my duty to make upon the present occasion, and beg it may be accepted in future; for I am confident that this is not the only part of the work in which the same difficulties will occur.

The part of the ladies dress, which I call the gown merely from the resemblance it bears to a garment so denominated in the present day,[2] is an exterior habit: it

[2] [Mr. Strutt, who has so modestly professed his ignorance of the proper name for this garment, has unconsciously hit upon the right appellation, our word *gown* being derived from the Saxon *gunna*, itself perhaps founded on the British *gwn*, latinized by Varro *gaunacum*. The gunna was of various lengths, as a Bishop of Winchester makes a present of "a short gunna, sewed in our manner." 16 Mag. Bib. page 82.—ED.]

seems to have varied little with respect to its general form, except in the sleeves, which are usually represented extending to the wrists; at other times they only reach to the elbows; and in one single instance seem to be totally wanting.[1] The gown is constantly bound about the waist with a girdle, and, when permitted to fall to its full length, descended to the ground; in which case it covered the under garment entirely: it is frequently adorned with ornaments of needle-work, which at this period were extremely simple, consisting only of variegated stripes or small sprigs, diverging from a centre, in imitation of foliage and flowers; specimens of which are given upon the bottom of the ninth plate.

The travelling habit of the ladies is represented upon the eleventh plate. The sleeves of the gown, if it be the gown, and not another garment over it used instead of the mantle as warmer and more convenient, are so long that they cover the hand, and reach some distance below the end of the fingers. I call this the travelling habit, because it is never represented but when the wearer is supposed to be performing a journey, and probably might be the winter dress of the time, as I think that of the lady seated, upon the same plate, was appropriated to the summer. She sits upon a bank beneath a tree in full foliage; and the gown she wears has no sleeves: the long loose sleeves which are there represented, as has been observed before, belong to the under garment; they were probably made of linen, and lighter than those which usually formed part of the gown. Upon the strength of this conjecture, I have ventured to give it the appellation of the *summer dress* at the bottom of the plate.

It is impossible, at this distance of time, to ascertain the materials which composed the gown. Judging, however, from the size of the folds, which are usually depicted much larger and thicker than those represented upon the under garment, we may fairly conclude that it was formed of some less pliant substance.[2]

There certainly was no particular colour appropriated to this part of the female dress. In the paintings of the Saxons, the colour of the gown was varied as far as the artists of the time possessed the power to diversify it. The girdle, which may properly be considered as an appendage to the gown, and invariably corresponds with it in colour, may easily be mistaken for part of it, though a small

[1] See the figure seated, upon the eleventh plate, where the long loose sleeves do not belong to the gown, but to the under garment.

[2] Silk, as we have seen in the introduction, was certainly worn as early as the eighth century, but we cannot suppose it to have been very general; perhaps the gown might, in some instances, be composed of woollen cloth of the finest manufacture. [A gown is mentioned made of otter's skin. Mag. Bib. p. 88.—Ed.]

degree of examination will be sufficient to trace it out in most of the female figures. It is, however, well ascertained by the figure, with her left arm elevated, upon the ninth plate, where one end of it is represented loose and flowing from the gown, and is the only instance in which I have seen it so depicted. A similar piece of drapery appears upon the middle figure of the same plate, which is evidently part of the coverchief, or hood, as the colour and situations sufficiently demonstrate.[1]

THE MANTLE.

It was observed in the foregoing chapter that no part of the habits appropriated to the men was subject to so much alteration as the mantle. The Anglo-Saxon ladies had also their mantle; and, indeed, it appears to have been a very essential part of their dress, for persons of distinction are rarely depicted without it; yet, with them, this garment was the least varied of any that pertained to their dress. The only material difference, during three or four centuries, colour excepted, which in most cases seems to have depended upon fancy, appears to have been in its size: there is none in the manner of wearing it, and very little, if any, in its general form.

The coverchief constantly hides the upper part of the mantle; for which reason it is impossible to discover how high it terminated upon the shoulders, or by what means it was fastened. I have never been able to trace out the least indication of fibula, broches, or bandages: judging from the usual appearance, I should suppose that its form was round, or rather, perhaps, oval; and that an aperture was made in it, at some distance from the middle, of sufficient size for the head to pass through when it was laid upon the shoulders; and, in proportion to the distance of the opening from the middle, the garment of course, when placed in its proper situation, would be longer on one part than the other, agreeable to the manner in which it is represented by the Saxon artists; for, in their drawings, we find it considerably longer and more ample behind, than at the sides and in the front. There are very few exceptions to be found against the universality of this fashion. Two instances, however, occur in the manuscript whence the larger part of the dresses, belonging to the eighth century, are taken, which merit particular attention, and for this reason I have engraved them both. The first may be found upon the ninth plate, in the figure, with both arms elevated, towards the left hand; and the second, where the lady is seated, upon the eleventh plate. In both these figures

[1] It is very common to see one end of the coverchief represented in the same loose situation; and it frequently gives a degree of elegance to the form of the figure.

the mantle appears in the front only, without the least indication of its passing over the shoulders, or hanging down on the back, according to the general custom. This might, it is true, have been a different garment, and used upon particular occasions; but I do not think myself justified to give it as such, and must therefore leave the reader entirely to his own judgment.

THE COVERCHIEF,[1] OR HEAD DRESS.

THE Coverchief, or, as it is often contractedly written, Kerchef, was an indispensable part of the dress appropriated to the Anglo-Saxon ladies. Its breadth was sufficient to reach from the top of the forehead to the shoulders, in such a manner as to cover the head completely, so that no part of the hair could be seen: it was then passed over both shoulders, and, when it was loose, hung down on each side as low as the knees. In this state it is represented upon the first figure, on the left hand, in the ninth plate. It was usually wrapped round the neck in such a manner as to cover the whole of the bosom: one end of it is sometimes left loose, and, from the manner in which it is drawn, flowing on one side or the other, manifests some conception of grace and elegance in the artist. An instance of this kind is given upon the middle figure, in the plate before referred to: but it is most generally represented with both ends concealed, as appears in several instances upon the figures which illustrate this chapter.[2]

The coverchief is generally distinguished from the mantle by a different colour; yet instances are not unfrequent in which the colours of both are the same; and upon a cursory view the two garments appear as one only: it is true, indeed, that the separation may be discriminated by attentive observation. An example of the apparent connexion of the coverchief and mantle is given, in the standing figure to the left, upon the tenth plate.

The coverchief, like most of the other parts of the Anglo-Saxon dress, is depicted of various colours; and probably was made of materials proportionable in richness to the rank of the wearer; but, that the materials differed in quality, the folds, which are sometimes small and abundant, and at other times few and large, sufficiently demonstrate.

[1] [*Couvre-chef* or *Cover-chief* is the Norman name of the female head-dress. The Saxons called it *Heafodes rœgel* (Head rail,) and the veil *wœfles*, from the verb *wœfan*, to cover.—ED.]

[2] See the seated figure, and the figure to the right, plate X. The standing figure, plate XI; and the lady in full dress, plate XII.

The cultivation of the hair, as we have already seen, was an important object among the men. The ladies are also said to have been great admirers of long hair ;[1] and though the head-dress, which they constantly wore in public, concealed the luxuriance of their locks, we have reason to believe that the management of them was not the least part of the female dress. In the manuscript, whence the larger part of the engravings already given are selected, a figure of Eve is depicted; and her hair, dishevelled as it is there represented, reaches to her hips without any bandage or apparent decorations. I do not mean to infer from this circumstance, that no ornaments were used in the adornment of the hair among the Saxon ladies of this period : the contrary may, I trust, be fairly concluded from the frequent mention made of half circles of gold[2] in the records of the succeeding centuries, and that without any indication of novelty. But, giving the artist the credit to suppose that he would not have deviated from the established rule of beauty, we shall readily grant that the great length and abundance of hair, given to this figure, is a presumptive proof, that in his day the growth and preservation of it was an object of attention among the ladies.

SHOES AND STOCKINGS.

It is impossible to ascertain the exact form of the shoes appropriated to the females of the eighth century : the only possible source of information is derived from the manuscript drawings of that period ; and in them the under garment is usually depicted of such length as to hide the greater part of the foot. In one or two instances, where the shoe is represented more perfectly than usual, it appears to have been fastened about the instep, immediately below the ancles, without any larger opening than was absolutely necessary for the insertion of the foot. In an ancient delineation, coeval with this æra,[3] there are several female figures introduced,

[1] Among the ancient Germans, long hair was considered as a very essential ornament to the person ; and no greater disgrace could be put upon a female than to shave her head : it was therefore the punishment usually inflicted for adultery.—Tacitus de morib. Germ.

[2] Or gilt at least : they are called in Saxon healꝼne bœnd ᵹẏldenne, and are supposed, with good reason, to be the hair-tiers of the women, as we shall see more fully hereafter.

[3] Prefixed to a MS. of Aldhelm's *Liber de Virginitate*, or poem in praise of Virginity, written in the eighth century. This MS. is preserved in the Lambeth Library.

whose shoes are very similar to slippers in use among the ladies of the present day.[1] One figure in the group, is represented with shoes differing from the rest; they appear to be fastened close to the ancles, and a dotted line is made upon the middle of the foot, from the instep to the end of the toes; but, whether it was intended simply as an ornament, or in imitation of lacing by which the upper leathers were drawn together, I cannot determine; the colour of these shoes is equally singular, being white. I met with only one instance in which the shoes of a female appeared to be open, like those appropriated to the men; this figure is given upon the tenth plate.

The colour of the shoes, with very few exceptions, is black; they are very plain in their form, and unadorned, in general, with ornaments of any kind.

The under garment of the women, as they are usually delineated by the Saxon artists, covered the greater part of the feet; we cannot, therefore, of course, expect to find any representation of stockings; neither is history more favourable with respect to information upon the subject; yet, I trust, it will be readily granted that the women would not appear with their legs uncovered, when a contrary example had been set them by the men, even supposing it was for the sake of decency only, and that the ideas of comfort and convenience were totally absented from the question.

[1] The form of these shoes or slippers so nearly corresponds with those of Aldhelm, whose portrait, extracted from the same drawing, is given upon the sixteenth plate of this work, that it was not thought necessary to repeat them.

CHAP. III.

THE MILITARY HABITS OF THE ANGLO-SAXONS OF THE EIGHTH CENTURY.—THE TUNIC.—THE MANTLE.—THE HELMET.—THE SHIELD.—THE SWORD AND THE SPEAR.—THE HORSE SOLDIER, THE FOOT SOLDIER, AND THE MILITARY OFFICER ATTENDANT UPON THE KING.

WHAT the real views of the Saxons might have been when they first came to the assistance of the Britons, cannot easily be ascertained: their friendship, however, was of very short date; and the scheme of forming a settlement in this island followed very soon after their arrival upon it; such an arduous undertaking could only have been executed by a people insensible of danger, whose courage and activity were superior to the severest difficulties. The offensive arms of the Saxons were not in the least superior to those of the Britons. They had no body-armour, an advantage the latter derived from the Romans; yet an handful of them soon secured a firm footing in this country; and in process of time, setting all opposition at defiance, they made themselves masters of the greater and most profitable part of it. The reason assigned for this extraordinary conquest by our best historians, and which appears to be founded upon fact, is the total neglect of military discipline among the Britons, who had been so long used to wear the yoke of foreign power, that the love of liberty, which stimulated the hearts of their forefathers to resist the Roman invaders, was extinguished in their breasts. An author of their own[1] has drawn their portraiture, at this period, with a sombre pencil it is true; for he describes them as a degenerate race of beings, sunk into such a shameful state of torpidity as to supplicate, even with tears, a continuance of their bondage rather than exert their own abilities to support themselves and oppose the progress of a domestic foe,[2] who were daily making inroads upon their territories. When the Romans refused to assist them, they had recourse to the Saxons, a fierce and active people, dependant upon their swords and inured to the practice of war. From this imprudent step, the origin of their total ruin may justly be derived.

The drawings of the eighth century represent the Anglo-Saxon soldier without any other defensive armour than the shield and the helmet; which latter seems in

[1] Gildas.

[2] The Picts, who ravaged all the northern provinces of Britain.

general to have been nothing more than leather.[1] His offensive arms are the sword and the spear. The bow was certainly known to the Saxons at this period, and they seem to have been very expert in the use of it;[2] but, as it does not appear to have been considered by them as a weapon of war, I shall defer the description of it to a future opportunity.

THE TUNIC.

There were few persons of distinction among the Anglo-Saxons of the eighth century, who did not bear arms.[3] The sword or the spear were the constant companions of that warlike people whenever they quitted their houses; and, if to these we add the shield and the helmet, we shall have the soldier completely equipped for the field.

The short tunic, as most convenient for action, was the constant military habit, and equally adopted by persons of every degree. They were made of linen, says an ancient Saxon author, and so well fitted to the wearer as to give every necessary freedom to his limbs in time of battle;[4] and this description corresponds exactly with the representations of the tunic preserved in the drawings of the time; the variety of colours given to this garment is no proof that it was not composed of linen; it is, however, very frequently painted white.

We must not conclude, that defensive armour for the body was totally unknown to the Saxons, because it was not adopted by them. We find the word *lorica* in the ancient Saxon authors; and this word is generally supposed to mean the coat, or, as it is sometimes called, the shirt of mail. A single instance, however, only occurs in the drawings of this period, where any martial garment is represented in the least analogous to the mail. It is evidently a royal habit; and, from its being the most ancient delineation of the kind, is highly deserving of particular attention. It is given upon the fourteenth plate of this work.

We shall have occasion hereafter to speak more fully concerning the body-

[1] It may be observed that the helmet, even in the representations of battles, is often omitted.

[2] In the MS. from which the greater part of the plates relating to the eighth century are taken, there is a figure of a young man shooting at a bird with a bow and arrow; he has several birds he is supposed to have killed hanging at his girdle. See Strutt's Chronicle, Vol. II. plate xv.

[3] To lay aside their arms, and walk abroad with a staff only, was enjoined in the ancient canons as a very severe penance. Canones dati sub. Edgaro.

[4] *Sicut solent habere milites tunicas lineas sic aptas membris ut expediti sint dirigendo jaculo, tanendo clypeam, librando gladium, &c.* Alcuinis, Lib. de Offic. Divin.

armour of the Anglo-Saxons, which makes it unnecessary to say any thing farther upon that subject in this place.

THE MANTLE.

I CONCEIVE the mantle to have been a distinguishing mark of military rank: the cavalry, which consisted of superior personages, are rarely depicted without it; and among the foot-soldiers it appears to have been appropriated to the officers only. But, in the representations of real action, it seems to have been laid aside by every rank of persons.

The military mantle was precisely similar to the mantle described in a former chapter,[1] which was fastened upon the right or left shoulder, and gave the sword-arm perfect liberty. The repetition, therefore, of what has been already mentioned is certainly unnecessary.

THE HELMET.

THE helmet, if it deserves the name, as it is commonly represented in the drawings of this æra, appears to have been nothing more than a cap of leather with the fur turned outwards: but personages of rank have a different covering for the head; its form is conical, and apparently it was made of metal, and gilt; for, the colour of it is most frequently yellow. Both these helmets may be seen upon the thirteenth plate of this work.

THE SHIELD.

THE form of the shield, at this period, is constantly oval: it is usually surrounded by a broad rim on the outside, and has a sharp boss protuberating from the middle; the chief material of which the shield consisted, I presume, was leather. One of the laws of Æthelstan prohibits the making of shields of sheep-skin, under the penalty of thirty shillings:[2] the rim and the boss were probably made of metal. The manner in which they were often ornamented appears in the several specimens that accompany this chapter.

1 See p. 7.

2 þe cƿæꝺon ꝥ nân ꞅcẏlꝺ ƿẏꞃhꞇa na lecᵹe nân ꞅceapeꞅ ꝼelle on ꞅcẏlꝺ. ⁊ ᵹıꝼ hıꞇ ꝺô ᵹẏlꝺe xxx. ꞅcill.—Leges Æthelstani apud Wilkins.

THE SWORD AND THE SPEAR.

The only offensive weapons, given to the Saxon soldiers of this æra, are the sword, and the lance or spear. The sword was so large and so long, that one would conceive it to have been a weapon ill calculated for close fighting. The chief dependance of the warrior rested, I trust, upon the vigour of his onset, or keeping his opponent at bay with the shield, while he struck at him with his sword. The blade of the sword was made of iron or steel; but the handle with the cross bar and knob at the end, was composed of some different kind of metal, as the colour indicates, which is often yellow: we may conclude that such of them as belonged to personages of the highest distinction were made of gold, or, at least, that they were gilt. The handles of the swords of state, as we shall see in the succeeding centuries, were certainly made of gold, and embellished with precious stones. The sheath, in which the sword was contained, and the girdle or belt, by which it was attached to the side, were also ornamented in the same splendid manner.

The lance or spear has nothing in its form to require a particular description, the representations of it, as given upon the thirteenth plate, will be perfectly sufficient. I shall only observe, that the head of the lance is sometimes barbed; and it will be needless to add any thing farther upon this subject for the present.[1]

THE HORSE SOLDIER, THE FOOT SOLDIER, AND THE MILITARY OFFICER ATTENDANT UPON THE KING.

The horse soldier appears, in the drawings of the eighth century, without either sword or shield. He is represented, completely armed, in the middle figure upon the thirteenth plate.

The foot soldier is exhibited, upon the same plate, in the action of striking with his spear. He has the sword and the shield added to his missive weapon.

The figure to the left, in the same plate, leaning upon his shield with his sword upon his shoulder, I take to be the principal officer of the king's guard. He is there represented, in the position he usually appeared, at the right hand of the throne, when the monarch held his court upon occasions of great solemnity.

[1] The several kinds of spear heads are given at the top of the thirteenth plate.

CHAP. IV.

THE ECCLESIASTICAL HABITS OF THE EIGHTH CENTURY.—A PARTICULAR DESCRIPTION OF THEM CANNOT BE GIVEN.—THREE FIGURES SUPPOSED TO BE ECCLESIASTICS; AND WHY.—A CURIOUS PORTRAIT OF ALDHELM, BISHOP OF SHERBORN, DESCRIBED.

THE ecclesiastical habits of this century can only be spoken of in a general way: the information, derived from the early Saxon historians, is insufficient to support a particular description of them; and the drawings of the time, such at least as have fallen under my examination, contain so few representations of ecclesiastical personages, and even those so undeterminate in general, that they afford little matter for discrimination.

Three figures are given upon the fifteenth plate of this work, selected from different manuscripts: the figure in the middle I take to be the most ancient; the artist intended it for a representation of David playing upon the harp; but the habit differs so widely from the secular dresses, abundant in the paintings of this period, that I am led to consider it as appropriated to the church, and a very early specimen of the kind;[1] but the particular parts of which it consisted I cannot pretend to explain.

The first figure to the left, upon the same plate, stands next in antiquity; it is extracted from a Saxon translation of the Pentateuch, and represents one of the priests that supported the Ark of the Covenant; for which reason I do not hesitate to give it a place among the ecclesiastical habits of this period.

The figure to the right is the most modern of the three; and the dress is much more determinate. He is represented presiding at the altar, and holds the sacramental wafer in his right hand, and the cup in his left. The surplice is ornamented with a cross;[2] and this is the most early instance, that I have met with, of its being so adorned in the drawings of the Saxon artists.

1 The near resemblance also, that it bears to the dresses of the four Evangelists, existent in a MS. coeval at least in date, may in some measure strengthen this opinion. It was a very common custom, with the ancient illuminators, to represent the portraitures of saints and pious personages in the ecclesiastical habits. This MS. has been already referred to (see the note to page 12); and is preserved in the Cottonian Library, the press-mark is Nero D. IV. The MS. containing the figure of king David, is in the same library; and the press-mark is Vespasianus A. I.

2 [In my opinion it is not a *surplice* but a *chasuble*, and the Y shaped ornamental border of the neck part is similar to that with which the vestment was occasionally furnished, resembling, more or less, the pallium of the Archbishop.—ED.]

THE PORTRAIT OF ALDHELM DESCRIBED.

THE most valuable delineation, however, that I have met with relative to this subject, and little inferior, in point of antiquity, to any of those above-mentioned, is the curious portrait of Aldhelm, bishop of Sherborn, given upon the sixteenth plate: the original is prefixed to his celebrated Poem in praise of Virginity. He is represented in his episcopal habit, with his right hand elevated, as bestowing his benediction, and his left rested upon a book, in which the poem is supposed to be contained. The alba, or white tunic, is enriched with an embroidered border; and the sleeves of his surcoat are adorned in the same manner, the greater part of which is covered with a mantle or surplice.[1]

Aldhelm was a near relation, if not a nephew, to Ina, king of the West Saxons. He received the early part of his education in the school of Macdulf, a learned Scot. He afterwards travelled, for his improvement, into France and Italy; and completed his studies, on his return to England, under Adrian, abbot of St. Augustine's monastery; and the learning he acquired rendered him famous not only in England, but also abroad.[2]

He founded the abbey of Malmsbury on the spot where he received his early education, and was himself the first abbot. Having resided thirty years at Malmsbury, he was made bishop of Sherborn, in Dorsetshire, where he died in the year of our Lord 709.

I shall not presume to detain the reader at present with any farther conjectural remarks; every part of the ecclesiastical habit occurs frequently enough in the drawings of the two succeeding centuries, and a fuller description of it will then be given.

[1] The original MS. whence this portrait is taken, was written early in the eighth century. It is preserved in the Lambeth Library, No. 200.

[2] Several ancient writers, of the first authority, have spoken highly in praise of the learning and piety of this prelate. Bede sums up his character in a few words: "*He was,*" (says that author) "*a man of universal erudition, his style was flowing and elegant, and he was wonderfully well acquainted with books both on philosophy and religious subjects.*" Hist. Eccles. Lib. v. Cap. 19.

THE END OF THE FIRST PART.

PART II.

THE CIVIL, MILITARY, AND ECCLESIASTICAL HABITS OF THE ANGLO-SAXONS, FROM THE COMMENCEMENT OF THE NINTH CENTURY TO THE ARRIVAL OF THE NORMANS.

CHAP. I.

THE HABITS OF THE MEN CONTINUED.—THE SEVERAL GRADATIONS OF RANK NOT POSSIBLE TO BE TRACED BY THE DRESS.—A PARTICULAR DESCRIPTION OF THE HABIT OF CHARLEMAGNE. —THE VARIATIONS IN THE SEVERAL PARTS OF DRESS DESCRIBED IN THE FORMER PART.— THE LEG-BANDAGES—THE SOCKS—THE BOOTS, OR BUSKINS—THE GLOVES, &c.

I HAVE already particularized, as far as lay in my power, the several parts of dress peculiar to the eighth century. I found it impossible, even from the minutest scrutiny of the Saxon delineations, to distinguish the various ranks of persons by their dresses with any tolerable degree of precision. The difference between the servant and his master in many instances may easily enough be discovered. The crown also continually determines the monarch; and the nobleman is known by his forming part of the king's court; but the difficulty lies in tracing the several gradations of rank from the free man to the sovereign. It appears to me, and I believe the various passages from history, which I shall have occasion soon to produce, will give some foundation for my opinion, that the chief, if not the only, distinction of quality at this period was made by the costliness of the materials which composed the dress, or the abundance of the ornaments with which it was enriched, rather than by its particular form or variety of parts.

The habits already described, with very few additions, and little variations in their general appearance, constituted the Saxon dress for the succeeding centuries. The chief alteration they underwent will be found to consist in such ornamental refinements of luxury as contributed abundantly more to show than to comfort or convenience.

The Saxon historians have been very remiss in describing the dresses of their own times: the only information we can derive from their writings is contained in a few casual observations which seem to have fallen inadvertently from their pens, and of course cannot be supposed to be very extensive. The silence, however, of our own authors is in some degree compensated by a French writer[1] of the ninth century, who has given us a complete description of the dress of Charlemagne; and, as the habits of the French and the Anglo-Saxons of that time were nearly, if not altogether, similar, it will throw much light upon the subject, and be extremely serviceable in the explanation of several parts of those drawings which will presently come under our consideration.

Charlemagne, as our author particularly observes, adhered strictly to the ancient manners of his own country, and treated all foreign innovations, that related to his dress, with the greatest contempt;[2] so that the description of his habit will convey to us the French dress of much higher antiquity; and we shall find that many of the parts of it agree well with the ancient Saxon habits, given in the former part of this work.

The dress that this great monarch wore in common consisted of the following parts, which I shall endeavour separately to explain.—The Shirt—The Drawers—The Tunic—The Stockings—The Leg-bandages—The Shoes—The Sword-belt, and the Sword. In the winter he added the Thorax, and the Venetian Cloak.

The Shirt is expressly said to have been made of linen.[3] Another ancient author speaks of shirts made of hair cloth.[4] We find in the canons of the Saxon church, that shirts of hair cloth and of woollen were enjoined by way of penance for crimes of considerable magnitude.

Shirt, or, as it was anciently written, *sherte*, is a word confessedly of Saxon origin; it answered to the Latin word *camisia*, and certainly was a part of dress worn next the skin.[5] Chaucer speaks of the shirt as a garment in which a new-born infant was first wrapped.[6] It makes part of the child-bed linen, and serves

1 Eginhart.

2 *Vestitu patrio, hoc est Francisco, utebatur;* and, a little after, *Peregrina verò indumenta, quamvis pulcherrima, respuebat.* Eginhartus de vitâ Caroli Magni à Schminckio Edit. cap. 23.

3 *Camisiam lineam.*

4 *Camisia cilicina.* Monach. S. Galli, Lib. 1. cap. 36.

5 See p. 8.

6 See Tyrwhitt's Glossary to Chaucer's Canterbury Tales, under the word *sherte*.

for the same purpose in the present day, and did so as far back as the eighth century at least.

The DRAWERS. This part of the monarch's dress is also said to have been of linen.[1] I have no proof from the ancient Saxon delineations, that drawers were in use in this country prior to the ninth century: about that time we meet with the first indications of them; for, the tunics of the soldiers are often represented so short, that much of their thighs are exposed to the sight: we find they usually terminated a little above the knee, where the bandage that fastened them at the bottom is frequently to be met with; and in some few instances below it.[2] We may, however, easily enough conceive that they formed a part of the Saxon habit at a still earlier period.

The TUNIC. Our author has not specified the materials that composed this part of the Royal dress; he informs us only, that it was ornamented with a border of silk;[3] but, as this monarch generally appeared in the military habit, it is highly probable that his tunic, according to the custom of the times, was made of linen. We are assured that it was the short tunic; for, the historian positively asserts that he wore the longer tunic but twice in his life.[4]

The STOCKINGS[5] are simply mentioned without any reference to the materials of which they were composed, or their length; they probably reached to the middle of the thigh, which we frequently find to be the case in the Anglo-Saxon delineations of this period. In another French author I find mention made of stockings and trowsers (if I rightly understand the word he there uses) of linen, which he tells us were of one colour, but ornamented with precious workmanship.[6]

[1] *Feminalibus lineis.* Eginhart. ut supra.

[2] See the middle figure, plate XVIII. of this work.

[3] *Tunicam, quæ limbo serico ambiebatur.* Eginhart. Des Carrieres, in his Epitome of the History of France, says his tunic was made of *woollen;* but upon what authority I know not.

[4] Having told us that Charles the Great despised all foreign dresses, he adds, *nec unquam eis indui patiebatur, excepto quod Romæ semel, Adriano pontifice petente, et, iterum Leone successore ejus supplicante,* longâ tunicâ *et chlamyde amictus, et calceis quoque, Romano more formatis, induebatur.* Eginhart. ut suprà.

[5] *Tibialia.*

[6] *Tibialia vel* coxalia *linea, quamvis ex eodam colore, tamen opere pretiosissimo variata.* Monach. S. Galli, Lib. I. cap. 36. [Probably the long or brech-hosan of the Saxons, so called in contradistinction to the short socca, as the conjunction *vel* seems to imply the uncertainty of the author under which term, stockings or troswers, to class them.—ED.]

The Leg-Bandages.[1] For a particular description of this part of the ancient French dress, which was also adopted by the Anglo-Saxons, we must refer again to the author quoted in the preceding article: he speaks of them as long fillets, variegated with checquer-work; and informs us that they were bound over the stockings cross-ways in such a manner as to keep them properly extended upon the legs.[2] A curious specimen of this kind of cross-gartering is given upon the seventeenth plate.

The Shoes are mentioned only in a general way. The author, above quoted, speaks of them as gilt outside,[3] and distinguished by long latchets; but their form is not even hinted. This defect is in some measure supplied by a more modern writer, who particularly describes the shoes of Bernard, king of Italy, the grandson of Charlemagne, as they were found upon opening his sepulchre: "The shoes," says he, "which covered his feet, are remaining to this day; the soles are of wood, and the upper parts of red leather, laced together with thongs: they were so closely fitted to the feet, that the order of the toes, terminating in a point at the great toe, might easily be discovered; so that the shoe belonging to the right foot could not be put upon the left, nor that of the left upon the right."[4]

The Sword-belt, and the Sword. Our author informs us that the monarch never appeared without these warlike accoutrements. Indeed he seems to have prided himself in their adornments, even at the times he neglected the other parts of his dress. The belt was composed of gold or of silver; and the hilt of the sword corresponded with the belt, except upon solemn court-days; he then wore a sword, the hilt of which was embellished with jewels.[5]

The Thorax was only used in the winter. It was made of otter's skin, and, according to our author, defended the breast and the shoulders from the

1 *Fasciolis crura.* Eginhart.

2 *Et super quæ,* i. e. Tibialia vel coxalia, *fasciolas, in crucis modum intrinsecùs et extrinsecùs ante et retrò longissimæ illæ corrigiæ tenebantur.* Monach. S. Galli, ut supra. The leg-bandages were made of linen and of woollen: for, an ancient author, quoted by Du Cange, informs us that the monks are commanded to wear linen bandages, and not woollen ones Du Cange, Gloss. in voce *Fasciola.*

3 *Calceamenta, forinsecùs aurata, corrigiis tricubitalibus insignita.* M. S. Galli, ut suprà.

4 Joan. Puricello in Mon. Basil. Ambrosianæ, p. 70.

5 *Et gladio semper accinctus, cujus capulus ac baltheus aut aureus aut argenteus erat; aliquoties et gemmato ense utebatur, &c.* Eginhartus, ut suprà.

cold.[1] The *thorax* is a garment of high antiquity. From Suetonius we learn that it formed part of the winter dress belonging to Augustus ;[2] but at that time it was made of wool. I must confess myself entirely at a loss respecting the form of the thorax. I find no resemblance of such a garment in the Saxon drawings.[3] Perhaps it was worn beneath the tunic; if so, the omission is easily accounted for.

The Venetian Mantle.[4] From what cause this garment derived its denomination cannot easily be determined. We may, however, fairly conclude that it was no innovation of dress among the French in the time of Charlemagne; sufficient already has been said to prove that he would not, by his own example at least, have been instrumental to the introduction of a foreign habit. We are indebted to our author for the name only of this garment; the description of it is derived from another writer, frequently referred to in the preceding pages: "It was," says he, "of a grey or blue colour, quadrangular in its form, and so doubled, that, when it was placed upon the shoulders, it hung down as low as the feet before and behind; but on the sides it scarcely reached to the knees;"[5] such was the dress in which this great man usually made his appearance. But upon

[1] *Et ex pellibus lutrinis thorace confecto humeros ac pectus hyeme muniebat.* Ibidem.

[2] *Hyeme quaternis cum pingui togâ tunicis, et subuculæ* thorace laneo, *et feminalibus et tibialibus muniebatur.* Sueton. in vitâ August.

[3] Unless the small cloak, which I considered (p. 8.) as a garment appropriated to youth of distinction, should be thought to bear any affinity to it. I can only add in its favour, that the wearers are often represented with both hands beneath it. The want of gloves might certainly have been so supplied; and the breast have been defended by it from the cold, but not the shoulders, as the author expressly declares they were. [Might it not have been a broad collar of fur, such as shortly afterwards was seen upon all royal mantles? In the work generally known as Titian's Book of Dress, Habiti Antichi e Moderne by Cæsare Vecellio, Venice, 1598, is an engraving of an ancient Doge from a fresco in the church of St. Mark, (built in 976), wearing a mantle different in shape to the later Ducal robe, but having on it "a collar of ermine like that," says the author, "which is worn by the Doges of our time." "*Un bavaro di pelle d'Armellini simile à quelli che usano i Dogi de nostri tempi.*" Taken in connection with the fact of Charlemagne's wearing a *Venetian* mantle it is at any rate an allowable conjecture.—Ed.]

[4] *Sago Veneto amictus.* Eginhartus. [May not the epithet *Venetian* be used here for *Lombard?* The dress of the Longobardi was precisely that of the Franks and Anglo-Saxons. Vide Paulus Diaconus. De Gestis Longobardorum.—Ed.]

[5] *Pallium, canum vel saphirinum, quadrangulum, duplex, sic formatum, ut, cum imponeretur humeris, ante et retrò pedes tangerit; de lateribus verò vix genua contegeret.* Monach. S. Galli, ut suprà. A garment, which I have called a winter garment, very similar to this, the reader will find described, page 8; and its representation upon the fifth plate.

solemn feast-days, and times in which the display of magnificence was required, his garments were extremely splendid. The tunic, he then wore, was interwoven with gold; his shoes were adorned with gems; his mantle was fastened with a fibula of gold; and a diadem of gold, ornamented with jewels, was placed upon his head: his sword and belt, and the hilt of his sword, as we have seen already, were also embellished in the same pompous manner.

In the description of the court dress of Louis le Debonnaire, the son of Charlemagne, who is said to have followed the example of his father, we find mention made of buskins of gold.[1] His sceptre is spoken of as a rod or staff of gold; and his mantle appears to have been woven with threads of gold.[2]

I have been the more particular in the description of the several parts of the dress of Charlemagne, because I conceive it gives us a just idea of the general habit of an Anglo-Saxon monarch of the same period, and that with little or no variation; for, excepting the *thorax* or *stomacher*,[3] there is no part of the dress of the French king that cannot easily be traced in the drawings of the Saxons.

The seventeenth plate contains the royal habit of the ninth century.[4] The tunic, as we there find it, is ornamented with an embroidered border; the stockings adorned with needle-work; and the leg-bandages, crossing each other upon them, agree exactly with the above description; the mantle also probably is similar to the state-mantle of Charlemagne, and, like that, it is fastened upon the shoulder with a fibula of gold: the sword and embroidered belt, with the shoes embellished with jewels, are all that appear to be wanting to complete the habit; the golden bracelets upon the wrists form indeed an ornamental part of the dress that the French monarch never adopted; at least we may judge so much from the silence of his historian.

1 *Ocreas aureas.* Theganus in vitâ ejus. cap. 19. I am well aware that the word *ocrea* signifies literally a greave, as well as a boot or buskin; but this part of the ancient Saxon habit, as it is represented in the drawings of the time, bears more resemblance in general to the boot or buskin than the greave.

2 *Baculum aureum, et chlamydem auro textam.* Thegan. ut suprà.

3 Perhaps this translation of the word *thorax* may be thought inadequate, because it is said to have covered his shoulders as well as his breast; and yet I know not any English word more proper to substitute in its place.

4 The Saxon MS. which contains this valuable delineation was written at the conclusion of the ninth, or very early in the tenth, century. It is preserved in the British Museum, and is marked Tiberius, C. VI.

I shall briefly mention the variations which took place in the several parts of the Anglo-Saxon habit already mentioned, during the ninth and tenth centuries, and then proceed to describe in a similar manner such other parts appertaining to it as have not been spoken of in the former part, and appear to be subsequent additions.

THE SHIRT.

To what has already been said concerning this garment[1] I shall now only add a few general observations. The *shirt* I have supposed to have been made of linen, because the wearing of woollen garments next the skin was enjoined as a severe penance ; but at the same time I meant it to be understood, that shirts of linen were confined to persons of superior rank, and they only could be affected by this injunction ; for, shirts of woollen, the want of which the tunic only often supplied, were worn by the common people, not by way of penance, but for comfort and conveniency ; and in the present day we have innumerable examples to prove, that use will soon reconcile the wearing of a flannel waistcoat next to the skin. The hair-cloth shirt, however, seems to have been considered as a very unpleasant garment by every rank of persons.[2]

[1] Page 3, and 28. The shirt is a garment of high antiquity, and it is called by several names in the ancient Latin authors, among which the most common are *Camisia, subucula,* and *interula*, the Saxon word Haam also signifies a shirt or body garment of linen, and appears to have been chiefly confined to the clergy. The ꞅẏꞃc or ꞅẏꞃic, and ꞅmoc, whence our modern word *smock* is evidently derived, seem rather to have been outer garments than such as were worn next the skin. [Why should it not have been applied to both, as it was in after times? The "Syrcas of Battle" mentioned in the song of Beowulf, for instance, are undoubtedly shirts of mail, but it does not follow that the word shirt was not used for an interior garment, also, as it has been for centuries. See note to page 14. – Ed.] The figure at the bottom of the second plate proves, that the SHIRT was a garment used for sleeping in. There are other night garments mentioned in the Saxon records, namely, the nihꞇeꞅ hꞃæᵹl or *night-rail,* and the liᵹ-ꞃæᵹel, or *night-gown.*

[2] In the Saxon version of Genesis, published by Junius, where Jacob, supposing his son Joseph to have been slain, is said to have *clothed himself with sackcloth,* it is translated ꞅcꞃiꝺꝺe hine miꝺ heꞃan, *he clothed himself with hair-cloth.*

THE DRAWERS AND TROWSERS.

THE *feminalia,* or DRAWERS, formed, as we have seen, an indispensable part of the royal habit in the ninth century ;[1] and it is equally certain, that they were no new invention at that time, nor confined to the nobility. Suetonius, an ancient Latin author, assures us, that the emperor Augustus wore *drawers* in the winter season ;[2] and the Saxon delineations of the ninth and tenth centuries give them to personages of inferior station.

They appear to have been made to fit the thigh with great precision, and were usually fastened some distance above the knee ; but several instances may be produced in which they descend below the knee, and then they bear no small resemblance to the breeches of the present day.[3]

The *coxalia,* or TROWSERS, were certainly a species of garment distinct from the *drawers,* and worn it seems in place of *drawers* and *stockings ;* for, in general, they appear to have been the two parts of dress comprised into one. The *coxalia,* from the name, must in some measure have been applicable to the hips ; and from the preceding description we find, that they covered the legs also, and were fastened upon them by the *leg-bandages.* A very perfect representation of the trowsers is given upon the eighteenth plate, where the figure to the right, intended for Job in his state of humiliation, is depicted without any other part of his habit.[4] The illuminator has, and I think with propriety, ornamented them with embroidered flowers ; the waistband is also adorned with work of a different colour, and they are edged with a border at the bottom corresponding with the waistband. The garment, as it is here given, one may reasonably conclude, was appropriated to persons of distinction only. Over the trowsers the *leg-bandages* were fastened from the feet, and reached to the middle of the leg, by which means they were secured at the bottom, and answered, as I have already observed,

[1] The word bꞃec, whence the brech of Chaucer, and *breeches,* in the modern language, derive their origin, occurs in the early Saxon writings, but whether it ought to be applied to the *drawers* or *trowsers* I will not take upon me to determine. [2] See the second note, page 31.

[3] As may be seen exemplified in the middle figure upon the eighteenth plate.

[4] [This figure is from the Royal MS. 6. c. vi. and assigned by Mr. Strutt himself to the *eleventh* century, and I should say it is of quite the latter part of it, and Anglo-*Norman.* ED.]

the double purpose of *drawers* and *stockings*, in the manner represented by the figure to the left hand on the same plate.[1]

In the description of Charlemagne's habit we find, that the drawers and trowsers are expressly said to have been made of linen, and probably were so in general when appropriated to the nobility and gentry; but that the same species of garment, consisting of coarser materials, was used by the inferior ranks of people, will, I trust, be readily admitted. The trowsers given to the figure of Job, above described, are blue, with a red waistband and borders; and the drawers of the middle figure are brown, which is no proof that they were not in both cases designed, by the illuminator, to represent linen; for linen at this period was frequently dyed of different colours.

THE TUNIC.

The form of the tunic, generally speaking, underwent little or no alteration during the whole of the Saxon æra. The short tunic continued in use among every class of people, and the longer tunic remained a mark of superiority of rank. We find them both occasionally varied with welts and borders of different colours,[2] and with embroideries also, and ornaments of needle-work, as the plates, appropriated to the ninth and tenth centuries, which accompany this work, will sufficiently demonstrate.

The wearing an upper and under tunic appears to have been common among the Anglo-Saxons, a custom they derived from high antiquity, and which, probably, never originated with them.[3] Agreeable to the manner of our ancestors, two coats, or two waistcoats, and very often both, form part of the present winter garments. The two tunics are very distinctly represented upon the figure towards the left hand in the eighteenth plate.[4]

[1] *Feminalia* is the Latin name which Eginhart gives to the drawers of Charlemagne, see the first note, page 29; and *coxalia* is the word here translated *trowsers*, which the reader will meet with in the last note of the same page.

[2] Reaꝼeꞅ-ꝼeneð, or fringed garments, are repeatedly spoken of; but I have never met with any thing like fringe in the Saxon drawings; perhaps the word ꝼneð, means only the welt or border.

[3] Augustus in the winter wore four tunics, according to Suetonius; see the second note, page 31.

[4] Roc or ꞃooc (whence *rocket*, a species of surplice, and the more modern word *frock*, are derived) was the Saxon name for the outer *tunic* or *surcoat*. [*Roc* or *froc* was, in my opinion, the *tunic*. The *surcoat* or *super-tunic* was the *over-froc*. See note 3, page 4, and the note to page 6.—Ed.]

The middle figure, upon the same plate, I have given as a singular instance of the appearance of buttons upon the front of the tunic. The manuscript it is taken from is certainly as ancient as the tenth century, and, probably, coeval with its commencement.[1] The figure is included in the ornamental part of an initial letter, and drawn with great precision.[2]

THE MANTLE.

The general form of the Saxon mantles has already been spoken of;[3] and the subsequent examples given upon the plates, appropriated to the ninth and tenth centuries, prove that little or no variation was made in them during that time. We trace in them, it is true, as well as in every other part of the Saxon habit, a luxuriancy of adornments with embroidery and borders of various colours, particularly of gold.

Early in the ninth century the French had adopted a short kind of variegated cloak or mantle, which is called by the writers of that period *saga Fresonica.* This garment was, however, highly reprobated by Charlemagne, who spoke of it in the following contemptuous manner; "Of what use are such trifling little cloaks? "when we are in bed they cannot cover us, when we are on horseback they are "insufficient to defend us from the wind and rain; and when we retire to ease "nature they will not secure our legs from the cold and frost;"[4] which rebuke, probably, soon put an end to the fashion of wearing such useless garments. The *sagum Gallicum*, or French mantle, on the other hand, was large and square, and said to have been often four times double.[5] But whether either of these garments were introduced into England by the Anglo-Saxons cannot easily be determined; perhaps the *bratt*, which is generally supposed to have been a short coarse mantle, was an humble imitation of the *saga Fresonica.*[6] The double mantle was certainly

1 This MS. is in the Royal library at the British Museum, and marked 6 B. VI.

2 This is the earliest specimen of the kind that I have seen. The tunic with buttons in the front will be seen frequently in the succeeding centuries. [I question this being more than a tunic with an embroidered or, at most, a studded band down the centre.—Ed.]

3 Page 7.

4 Monachus Sangallensis, lib. i. cap. 36.

5 See Du Cange in voce *Sagum.*

6 Urry, in his Glossary upon Chaucer, informs us that in Lincolnshire they give the name of *bratt* to a coarse kind of apron. A child's stomacher is called by the same name in Yorkshire to this day.

used by the Anglo-Saxons;[1] and I take it to be the same kind of garment as the reader will find described in the first chapter of this work,[2] which was put over the head upon the shoulders, and worn without any fibula or buckle; and this mantle seems to have been appropriated solely to the highest class of personages. It was not confined to the men; the women of quality frequently appear with it; but I do not recollect a single instance in which it is given to people of inferior rank.

The mantles at this period, those especially which belong to the females, were frequently lined with materials of different colours, if not of different quality, from the outer part; a remarkable instance of which may be seen in the lady represented upon the twentieth plate: the outer part of her mantle is rich crimson, the inner part or lining is deep blue.

THE HEAD-DRESS.

WE have already seen that long hair, and great abundance of it, was considered as a beautiful ornament of the person by our Saxon ancestors; and that the clergy, on the other hand, affecting self-denial, divested themselves of their locks, and preached vehemently against the cultivation of the hair.[3] It appears, however, that some of them were not insensible of the beauty of long hair, and wished to indulge their propensity to follow the fashion in some degree at least, which made the interdicting article necessary against concealing the tonsure by permitting the hair to grow, which is found in the Canons of the Saxon church.[4]

The hair appears to be shortened in the drawings of the ninth century, and in the beginning of the tenth to be generally curtailed. But when the Danes obtained an establishment in this country, they revived the customs of their ancestors, and long hair was again introduced, and the fashion of wearing it soon became very prevalent. It appears, that, towards the conclusion of the tenth century, the Danes were the greatest beaux of the time; they combed their locks at least once a day, and decorated them carefully, in order, say the ancient historians, to captivate the hearts of the Saxon ladies; and so strong was the attraction of those luxuriant beauties, that we find they frequently succeeded in their attempts.[5]

In the reign of Edward the Confessor, the hair was permitted to grow to a

[1] ꞇpẏꝼealꝺum menꞇıl.

[2] Page 8.

[3] See pages 10 and 21.

[4] Johnson's Canons, A. D. 960. c. 47.

[5] John Walingford, apud Gale.

very great length by almost every rank of persons, which induced Wulfstan, bishop of Worcester, to preach with great severity against such an effeminate fashion; and finding, perhaps, that his sermons had not the full effect that he wished them to have, an ancient author assures us, that, when any one bowed down before him to receive his blessing, he cut off a lock of his hair with a little sharp knife that he carried about him for that purpose, and enjoined him, by way of penance, to cut off the rest of his hair in the same manner, denouncing dreadful judgments against such as refused to comply with this requisition.[1]

Long hair, in the early ages, was a mark of high rank in France: by a certain law,[2] then existing, none but the nobility of the first class, and princes of the blood royal, were permitted to wear their hair at its full length: other personages were obliged to cut their hair round upon the middle of the forehead,[3] which made a manifest distinction. The beard also, at the same time, was held by the French in equal reverence: to touch the beard, was not only a mark of high respect, but stood in place of a solemn oath.[4]

The law for prohibiting the inferior rank of people from wearing of long hair does not seem to have ever taken place among the Anglo-Saxons; the frequent examples, which the reader may refer to in the plates which acompany this work, evidently prove the contrary. It will also be needless to enter into any farther description of the manner in which the hair and beard were worn by the Saxons during the ninth and tenth centuries; the same means of information will doubtless be found to be the most satisfactory.

We have already spoken of the cap, or rather, perhaps, *hat*, of the Saxons,[5] a word which occasionally occurs in their writings. The hat was, I doubt not, made of various materials; and by no means seems to be a part of dress universally adopted: from its general appearance, I have supposed it to have been made of skins, with the shaggy part turned downwards, and probably it often might be so: but they had also felt or woollen hats at this pĕriod, which their own records testify.[6]

1 Vita Wulfstani, Angliâ Sacrâ, vol. II.

2 Jus Capillitii.

3 *Ad frontem mediam circumtonsos.* Hence also the ancient kings of France are called by Claudian *crinigero flaventes vertice.* De laud. Stilici, lib. I, v. 203.

4 Aimoin, lib. I, cap. 4.

5 hæt.

6 Fellen hæt, a felt or woollen hat. See Lye's Anglo-Saxon Dictionary, under the word hæt.

THE STOCKINGS.

I HAVE already said that *stockings*,[1] certainly formed a part of the Anglo-Saxon habit as early as the eighth century: that they were of much higher antiquity is proved by an ancient Latin author.[2]

The stockings of the ninth century appear to have been of various kinds, and probably the materials, of which they consisted, were equally different. Stockings of linen, and linen-trowsers, which often supplied the place of stockings, are spoken of as worn at this period;[3] but, from the costliness of linen habiliments, we may easily conceive that they were confined to persons of wealth.

The Anglo-Saxons gave the same name of *hose* not only to what may properly be called the stockings, but also to the boots or buskins, and indeed to any part of dress applied to the legs. The word *skin-hose*,[4] however, seems to convey a perfect idea of stockings, and probably was the real name by which they were distinguished in the Saxon æra.

The stockings, appropriated to persons of quality, according to the drawings of the time, extended above the bottom of the short tunic, and were, I apprehend, made fast to the drawers upon the middle of the thigh. The inferior class of people appear to have worn shorter stockings, reaching only to the middle of the leg; and, from the largeness and unevenness of the folds, one may be led to conclude that they were composed of thick and coarse materials, perhaps worsted or yarn, and put upon the leg without any bandage or garter.

The stockings, worn by the nobility, always appear to set very close to the legs without any wrinkles or marks of folds above the leg-bandages: this circumstance distinguishes them from the *coxalia*, or trowsers, which did not fit the legs so exactly; and the marking of the folds are easily enough to be traced; a remarkable

[1] In the first chapter of this work the *shoes* and *stockings* are spoken of under one head; in the present chapter I have thought it best to divide them. The additional account of the *shoes* will be found under the article of BOOTS or BUSKINS.

[2] Suetonius; who tells us that stockings, *tibialia*, formed part of the dress of Augustus. See the second note, page 31, of this work.

[3] See the last note, page 29.

[4] Scınhoꞅe as it is written, in the Saxon charaters: the word banꞃıꝼꞇ seems rather to signify *buskins* than *stockings* and panhoꞅa Lye explains by the words *caligæ laciniosæ* which may be properly rendered greaves. Leaþeꞃ hoꞅa, or *leather hose*, is a name more generally applicable to *boots* or *splatterdashes* than to stockings, though I am well aware that *leathern stockings* are worn by the rustics in this country to this day. [Skin-hose means the same thing.—ED.]

instance of which is given in the figure to the left, upon the eighteenth plate, where the folds of the trowsers are very evident above the bandages of the leg.

The stockings are depicted of various colours in the drawings of the Saxons; but blue and red seem to be chiefly appropriated to the nobility.

THE LEG-BANDAGES.

THE garters, or more properly leg-bandages, of the Anglo-Saxons are called in their own writings by three different names;[1] which names, I doubt not, were given purposely to distinguish three different kinds of bandages then in use; and examples of all of them may, I think, be plainly pointed out from the figures which accompany this part of the work.

We have already spoken of the leg-bandages crossing each other, which formed part of the habit of Charlemagne,[2] and two representations of the manner in which these bandages were applied to the legs are given from Saxon drawings of the ninth century,[3] which are a sufficient proof that the fashion of cross-gartering prevailed at that time in England; and it appears to me to have then been confined to kings and princes, or the clergy of the highest order, and to have formed part of their state habit.—There was, I believe, only one bandage for each leg: the binding began at the toes, and was crossed backwards and forwards, being continued nearly to the knee; but how it was fastened there is not so clearly determined. The shoe of course hides all below the ancles: but in the portrait of Wulfstan, bishop of Worcester, who is represented in his study, and without his shoes, the cross gartering is very perfectly represented even upon the foot, and bound in the self-same manner.[4]

The next method of applying the bandages to the legs may be seen, very perfectly represented in the figure to the left, upon the eighteenth plate. This bandage, like the former, was made fast upon the foot, and then wrapped round it, every turn rising higher than the other, until it extended to the middle of the leg, or, in some instances, beyond it; the two ends were then crossed upon each other in the front, and turned down on either side below the calf, where they were severally

[1] Scanc-beaᵹaꞅ, Scanc-benꝺaꞅ, and Scanc-ᵹeᵹiꞃelan: they are called in Latin *fasciolæ crurum*.—See the first and second notes, page 30.

[2] Page 30.

[3] The one upon the seventeenth plate, and the other upon the nineteenth plate of this work.

[4] See the twenty-seventh plate of this work. [Where he is styled Archbishop of York, having held both Sees, A.D. 1002.—ED.]

fastened beneath the former windings of the bandages. This mode of gartering seems only to have been adopted by persons of superior rank.

The third and most common leg-bandages seems to have been a fillet or garter, simply fastened upon the stocking about the middle of the leg, and, perhaps, differed but little from the garter of the present day, saving only that there is not the appearance of more than one revolution, and sometimes it is made obliquely instead of being horizontal.[1] This kind of leg-bandage seems to have been worn occasionally by all classes of people, and particularly by the soldiers.[2]

We have already seen that the leg-bandages were made of woollen: they were also made of linen; because the ancient canons commanded the monks to wear linen bandages about their legs, and not woollen ones, to distinguish them from the laity; by which it should appear that woollen bandages were commonly adopted at that time.[3] In the Saxon Manuscripts the leg-bandages are depicted of various colours, and, in some instances, have the appearance of being adorned with spots or flowers of needle work.

THE SOCKS.

The *pedules*, or *socks*,[4] were a part of the ancient dress appropriated to the feet, as the name itself plainly indicates; and they are frequently mentioned by the writers of the ninth and tenth centuries. It has been thought that the *pedules* were probably that part of the stockings which received the feet, and not distinct from them;[5] and a quotation from an old author is given in Du Cange to support this opinion;[6] but, in proof of the contrary, variety of authorities might be produced; let one suffice: the *pedules* and the *stockings* are clearly mentioned as two distinct parts of the dress in the ancient Carthusian Statutes, quoted in the margin.[7]

[1] In many instances the stockings appear to reach something higher than the bandage, and are turned down over it. See the figure to the left, plate 23.

[2] See the middle figure, plate 19; and the figure to the right, plate 23.

[3] Du Cange, in voce *Fasciola.*

[4] The Saxon word ꞅlẏpe ꞅceo is said to mean a *sock* or *sandal;* but I do not see much analogy to either: the true word is ꞅoccaꞅ, whence the modern *sock* is evidently derived. [Certainly. The ꞅceo is a *shoe,* and the ꞅlẏpe ꞅceo (*slip-shoe,*) clearly a *slipper.*—Ed.]

[5] *Pedules;* pars caligarum quæ pedes capit.

[6] *Id etiam mandare curavit, ut de caligis* pedules *abscinderet, quatenùs præter pedes totus jaceret vestitus.* Du Cange, in voce *Pedules.*

[7] Among other parts of their habit the monks are ordered to have 2 *paria caligarum,* et 3 *paria pedulium.* Ibidem.

The socks, I apprehend, were generally worn with the trowsers, which, as we have seen before, did not cover the feet; and at times also with the stockings, especially by the clergy, who were obliged day and night to officiate in the churches.

In the Saxon delineations, those especially which belong to the tenth century, we find this part of the dress very frequently depicted. The sock usually rises a little above the ancle, and appears to be turned down towards the shoe, without being restrained by a garter or bandage, in the manner represented, upon the middle figure, in the eighteenth plate; and the socks are there drawn without the shoes; which is not often the case. A different kind of socks, ornamented with fringes or borders, are spoken of in the ancient records;[1] and a specimen of them, so adorned, is given upon the nineteenth plate. The reader is referred to the middle figure, where he will find the *stocking*, the *sock*, and the *shoe*, very distinctly shewn. The socks are said to have been made of woollen, and, generally speaking, they might be so; but, when they were adorned in the manner spoken of above, it is probable they might consist of some more precious materials.

THE BOOTS, OR BUSKINS.

THE buskins of Louis le Débonnaire, the son of Charlemagne, was certainly made of gold, or gilt at least.[2] In the drawings of the Saxon artists, this part of the leg-dress cannot easily be distinguished from the stockings, which frequently reach to the middle of the leg only. It is also remarkable, that, where the boots or buskins appear the most decidedly marked, they are never, that I recollect, depicted without the addition of shoes. The Anglo-Saxons gave the name of *hose* not only to the stockings and buskins, but also to the greaves or leg-armour; and the *hose* appear at all times to have been a part of dress distinct from the shoes, and bore a nearer affinity to the spatterdashes than to the boots of the moderns.

The *leather-hose* and the *pan-hose*,[3] names mentioned by the Saxon writers, I presume, are both of them leg-dresses of the buskin kind, the latter differing from the former by adornments only. The figure bearing a sword upon his shoulder, given upon the nineteenth plate, exhibits the most perfect example of the boots or

[1] *Pedules limbati.* [2] *Ocreas aureas.* See page 36, and the first note of that page.

[3] Pan-hoꞅa, which Lye renders *caligæ laciniosæ.*

buskins that has occurred in my researches ;[1] and probably they may have been intended to represent the *pan-hose*, or ornamented buskins.

The *leg-guards*,[2] which are also spoken of by the later Saxon authors, may be properly considered as the greaves or armour for the legs, and probably were made of metal, at least that part of them which came upon the front of the legs. We find no indication of any defensive armour of this kind in the Saxon drawings prior to the tenth century ; about which time some few instances occur. It is, however, very plainly marked upon the legs of the Danish chieftains, given upon the twenty-fourth plate ; the figures there represented are taken from a very curious Saxon reliquary, which, from the workmanship and other circumstantial proofs, is with good reason supported to have been fabricated about the close of the ninth century.[3]

High shoes, reaching nearly to the middle of the legs, and fastened by lacing in the front, and which may also properly enough be considered as a species of half-boots, were in use in this country as early as the tenth century ; and the only apparent difference between the high shoes of the ancients and the moderns seems to have been, that the former laced close down to the toes, and the latter to the instep only.[4]

I shall close this subject with some few additional observations concerning the *shoes* of the Saxons:[5] they appear in general to have been made of leather, and were usually fastened beneath the ancles with a thong which passed through a fold upon the

[1] [They appear to me on the contrary to be merely stockings with ornamented tops drawn over the longer hose, for they are worn with shoes, which surely would not be the case were they themselves boots or buskins. Indeed from the engraving one might deem the studded bands to be distinct ornaments. The boot or buskin of the Anglo-Saxons I take to be the high laced sort described by Mr. Strutt a few lines lower —Ed.]

[2] Scanc-beoꞃᵹ.

[3] This plate is more particularly spoken of in the third chapter of the present part of the work, where the military habit of the ninth and tenth centuries are fully described. [Not having seen the original it would be presumptuous to offer a decided opinion. I am under a strong impression, however, that the reliquary here mentioned is not of Anglo-Saxon workmanship, but a production of (at the earliest) the twelfth century, exhibiting the Anglo-Norman costume of that period in lieu of the Danish of the ninth century.—Ed.]

[4] An instance in which the high shoes are perfectly represented occurs in a MS. in the Harleian Library, marked 2908 ; but, as there was nothing farther remarkable annexed to the figure, I did not engrave it ; frequent specimens of the half-boots will necessarily occur hereafter.

[5] Leꞅcẏ, according to Lye, is a Saxon name for *shoes;* but from ꞅceo or ꞅcoh the modern word shoe evidently derives its origin.

upper part of the leather encompassing the heel, and was tied upon the instep. This method of securing the shoe upon the foot was certainly well contrived both for ease and convenience.

Wooden shoes[1] are mentioned in the records of this æra: but probably they derived that appellation from the soles only being made of wood, while the upper parts might consist of some more pliant materials; and shoes with wooden soles were worn by persons of the most exalted rank.[2]

The *calopedes*, spoken of by the ancient Latin authors, are thought to have been a species of wooden shoes; but perhaps bore a nearer affinity to *clogs* or *galloches*. The *sotulares*, or *subtalares*, appear evidently to have been a thick kind of shoes calculated chiefly for warmth, and were used by the clergy when they officiated in the churches in cold weather, or at night; and, as well as the *calopedes*, were, I conceive, large enough to receive the foot with the common shoe upon it.[3] Whatever the materials might be that composed the soles of the shoes at this period, it is certain that they were often rendered more durable by the assistance of nails: the nailing of shoes is a custom so prevalent among the rustics of the present day, that nothing farther need to be said by way of explanation.

THE GLOVES.

This article of dress certainly did not originate with our Saxon ancestors: the use of gloves was derived from the continent; and there is good reason to believe that gloves were unknown in England, prior to the close of the tenth century: that they were then confined to persons of the most exalted stations will, I trust, be readily granted, when we find, by the laws of Æthelred the Second,[4] for the regulating of commerce, that five pair of gloves made a considerable part of the duty paid to that prince by a society of German merchants for the protection of their trade.[5] There

[1] Tꞃıþen ꞅceo.

[2] See the description of the shoes of Bernard, king of Italy, the soles of which were of wood, p. 30 of this work.

[3] The *calopedes*, and the *subtalares*, of the Latin authors might probably answer to the ꞅlẏpe-ꞅceo and unheᵹe-ꞅceoꝼ, or short shoes, of the Saxons; both of which names will be proper enough, if we suppose them to resemble the women's clogs, easily slipped on, and shorter than the shoe by not rising above the heel.

[4] Æthelred the Second, surnamed the Unready, was crowned A. D. 979, and died A. D. 1016.

[5] Leges Æthelredi, apud Brompton.

is not the faintest indication of gloves in the various drawings of the Saxons that have fallen under my inspection ;[1] which I consider as a corroborating proof that they were not used, at least not in common, at the time those delineations were made, or they would not have been totally omitted.

There is no doubt, I believe, that gloves were occasionally worn by the Saxon clergy towards the close of the eleventh century, or perhaps rather earlier ; and they appear to have been made of linen : but I shall have occasion to speak more fully upon this subject in a subsequent part of this work.

[1] [There is an instance in the Harleian MS., 2908, which Mr. Strutt has overlooked when inspecting that volume. It is engraved in my History of British Costume, page 34, fig. b.—Ed.]

CHAP. II.

THE HABITS OF THE ANGLO-SAXON WOMEN CONTINUED.—THE SEVERAL PARTS OF THEIR DRESS NOT INCREASED IN NUMBER DURING THE SAXON ÆRA.—A RECAPITULATION OF THOSE PARTS OF THE FEMALE DRESS DESCRIBED IN A FORMER CHAPTER, AND THE ALTERATIONS THEY UNDERWENT FROM THE EIGHTH, TO THE CLOSE OF THE ELEVENTH, CENTURY.

It has already been premised that the Anglo-Saxon ladies were much less capricious, with respect to the fashion of their garments, than the men.[1] We have seen four distinct parts of dress appropriated to the females of the eighth century, exclusive of those belonging to the feet and legs; and the subsequent delineations, even to the close of the eleventh century, do not exhibit a single additional garment.[2] The little variation also, which those very parts of dress underwent during a period of nearly three centuries, is a manifest proof that our fair country-women were strongly attached to the manners and customs of their predecessors. It will therefore be sufficient, after what has been said upon this subject in a former part of the work, to recapitulate only the several parts of dress therein mentioned, and briefly point out the nature and extent of the variations I have found in them.

The Under Garment does not appear to have suffered the least change in its general form; the observations made upon this garment, from the drawings of the eighth century, may be equally applied to the remainder of the Saxon æra, excepting only that, towards the conclusion of the tenth, and in the eleventh centuries, we meet with some few instances wherein it is ornamented at the bottom with borders of different colours, which were probably worked with the needle. A specimen of this kind is given upon the twenty-first plate of this work: the reader is referred to the figure leaning upon her knee, and standing towards the right hand.

[1] See the second chapter of the first part of this work, p. 13.

[2] The halsado, a part of dress belonging to the neck, as the name, derived from hals the neck, denotes, and tæppet, an upper garment, are mentioned by the Saxon writers; but I am totally at a loss to apply the names to any of the parts of the ladies' habits, as they are represented in the drawings of the times; the *tippet* in particular is said, in some cases, to have been half rough or shaggy: in the Saxon language it is then called, healf hruh tæppet.

The Gown.[1] The drawings of the ninth century exhibit this part of the ladies' dress precisely the same as it appears in those of the century preceding. Towards the conclusion of the tenth century we find an alteration made in the gown, and especially in the sleeves, which are broader at the bottom, and in some instances resemble a fan when half opened. The sleeves of the lady's gown, given upon the twentieth plate, are of this kind; and something approaching to the same fashion are those of the lady towards the right hand upon the twenty-first plate. The ends of the sleeves, and the bottoms of the gowns, in both examples, are richly adorned with borders of different colours; the latter had also a collar of the same kind, and appears indeed to be entirely ornamented with sprigs and flowers of needle-work. The gowns of the tenth century were frequently lined with materials of different colours, if not of different texture, as may be seen in both the figures just referred to.[2]

The Mantles. There seem evidently to have been two sorts of mantles worn by the ladies of the ninth and tenth centuries: the first differed in no respect from the mantle described in a former chapter:[3] the second was bound about the waist, and thence was passed over the right or left shoulder, and flowed loosely at the side, as may be seen exemplified by the figure kneeling, upon the twenty-first plate.[4]

The figure to the left, upon the same plate, exhibits the former kind of mantle larger than I have seen it generally represented; it not only extends over the whole back, reaching to the ground, but is ample enough in the front to cover the arms and the hands also.

The Coverchief.[5] The variations of appearance, which occur in the drawings of this garment, seem evidently to have arisen from the mode in which it was fastened about the neck, rather than from any material difference in the form of the garment itself: sometimes it is gathered very close to the chin; sometimes it is more loose; and not unfrequently one end of it is left at liberty; but both of them very rarely are so. A singular instance of wearing the coverchief occurs upon the

[1] Perhaps the Saxon name for the gown was uꝼꞃee ꞅcꞃuꝺ, which properly signifies an upper garment. [It was *gunna*, vide page 15, note.]

[2] The gown of the lady, plate XX. is crimson; the lining deep blue. The gown and lining of the other lady, plate XXI are nearly similar.

[3] Chap. II. p. 17.

[4] The Saxon word Lach signifies also a *cloak* or *mantle*, and may be justly applied to this garment.

[5] The proper Saxon word for this part of the female dress was probably heaꝼoꝺeꞅ ꝩꞃiꝫelꞅ or hꞃæꝫel, which signifies *a covering for the head*, and is generally said to have been made of *linen*; the nihꞇeꞅ-hꞃæꝫl, or *night-rail*, was, I presume, the *night head-dress* of the ladies.

twenty-first plate; where it is represented as perfectly loose, and both the ends are passed over the shoulders so as to leave the collar of the gown and the front of the neck exposed to the sight.[1]

The manner in which the Anglo-Saxon ladies dressed their hair cannot by any means be ascertained from the drawings of the time. The coverchief, a part of dress that they are rarely drawn without, concealed it entirely. History is also deficient in point of information upon this subject; however, from the golden hair-tiers, and crisping needles,[2] to curl and platt the hair withal, which are mentioned in the writings of the Saxons, we may, as I have before observed,[3] fairly conclude that the ladies of this æra considered the adornment of their hair as an object of some consequence.

The Shoes. On this subject I can add but little to what has been said already.[4] During the ninth and tenth centuries, they appear to have varied more in colour than in the century preceding: we meet with them red, brown, light orange, and blue; but the more general colour continued to be black,

Clogs[5] are mentioned in the Saxon writers as worn by the women; but I have not met with the representation of them in any of the drawings of this period.

[1] The þæꝼelꞅ, or þeꝼelꞅ, from þæꝼan to *cover*, signifies a *veil*, and is mentioned in the Saxon writings; but I have not met with any part of the head-dress distinguishable from the *cover-chief*, that seems to bear any analogy to it.

[2] hæꞃ-neꝺl. [3] Page 19. [4] Pages 19, and 20.

[5] Wiꝼeꞅ ꞅceoꝼ, clogs or shoes with wooden soles, which Lye explains by the word *baxeæ*.

CHAP. III.

THE MILITARY HABITS OF THE ANGLO-SAXONS FROM THE COMMENCEMENT OF THE NINTH CENTURY TO THE ARRIVAL OF THE NORMANS.—THE COAT OF MAIL.—THE BREAST-PLATE.—THE GREAVES.—THE HELMETS.—THE SHIELDS.—THE SWORDS; AND THE SPEARS.—THE MILITARY HABITS OF THE DANES DESCRIBED FROM A CURIOUS SAXON RELIQUARY.

THE civil and military habits of the Saxons differed little from each other prior to the introduction of body-armour; for, as every man of rank, the clergy excepted, considered himself a soldier, the bearing of arms was esteemed by him as an indispensable privilege, and therefore he was rarely found at any great distance from home without such accoutrements as became his character. Body-armour, though spoken of by the early writers, was not, so far as we can judge from their own delineations, brought into general use among the Anglo-Saxons before the conclusion of the tenth, or rather the commencement of the eleventh, century.

The TUNICS of the Saxon soldiers are said to have been made of linen;[1] and in some instances, in the drawings especially of the tenth and eleventh centuries, they are depicted partly open at the sides, and so short as scarcely to reach to the middle of the thigh. This habit, I presume, was appropriated to the light infantry of the time; for, the same observation does by no means hold good respecting the horse-soldier.

The MANTLE, when it was used, does not appear to have undergone the least alteration during the whole of the Saxon æra.

THE COAT OF MAIL.

THE word *lorica* frequently occurs in the writings of the most ancient Saxon authors; and, when it is applied to the defensive armour of the body, appears to be perfectly synonymous with the military habit, called in English the *coat* or *shirt* of *mail*.[2] The *lorica* consisted of plates or wires of iron, brass, or some other introduced among the Saxons; and, from the frequency of its appearance in the

[1] See page 22.

[2] The Saxon word býꞃn or býꞃna; the ꝺehꞃýnꝺeꝺ-býꞃn, or *mail, with rings*, seems to be that species of it that was formed of wires intersecting each other. [And why not of rings as the word itself distinctly asserts? ED.]

metal, interwoven with each other, as we may learn from a curious ænigma, written towards the conclusion of the eleventh century by Aldhelm, bishop of Sherborn; it may be translated thus: "I was produced in the cold bowels of the dewy earth, "and not made from the rough fleeces of wool; no woofs drew me, nor *at my birth* "did the tremulous threads resound; the yellow down of silk worms formed me not; "I passed not through the shuttle, neither was I stricken with the wool-comb; "yet, strange to say! in common discourse I am called a *garment;* and I fear not "the darts that are taken from the long quivers."[1]

It is highly probable that the coat of mail, at the time of its first introduction into this country, was a very cumbrous habit, which might prevent its being hastily brought into use among our Saxon ancestors, who seem to have placed their chief dependence in battle upon their own agility and personal courage: for this reason they were usually clad in garments of the lightest kind, contrived in such a manner as least to impede the exercise of their arms.[2]

A very ancient and a very singular representation of body-armour is given upon the fourteenth plate of this work. It is of the eighth century, and the first specimen I have met with of the kind, and, as far as one can judge from its appearance in the delineation, consisted of small rings of wire interwoven with each other, or quilted upon a tunic or jerkin of leather in such a manner as to be rendered pliable.[3] I speak, however, with great diffidence upon this subject, because I have no historical authority to support my opinion.

Towards the conclusion of the ninth, or about the commencement of the tenth, century, a body-armour, differing from the coat of mail already described, was introduced amongst the Saxons, and from the frequency of its appearance in the

[1] The original runs thus:

De Lorica.

Roscida me genuit gelido de viscere tellus;
Non sum setigero lanarum vellere facta;
Licia nulla trahunt, nec garrula fila resultant;
Nec croceâ seres texunt lanugine vermes;
Nec radiis carpor, duro nec pectine pulsor;
Et tamen, en! *vestis* vulgi sermone vocabor;
Spicula non vereor longis exempta pharetris.

B. Aldhelmi Ænigmatum, published at Mentz, A. D. 1561: and in a MS. in the Royal library, marked 15. A. XVI.

[2] See page 22.

[3] In either case, this species of the *lorica,* or *mail,* may properly be applied to the ȝehꞃýnȝeꝺ-býꞃn, or *armour with rings,* mentioned by the Saxon authors. [Certainly; as I have noticed at the foot of the preceding page: but the figure here mentioned is from a MS. of the close of the *tenth* or beginning of the *eleventh* century, and not of the *eighth.* Vide note 1, page 1.—Ed.]

drawings of that period, we may fairly conclude that it was more generally adopted. I have selected two specimens which vary in some degree from each other: they are given upon the twenty-third plate. And whether this armour was composed of thin plates of metal, fastened upon the interior garment or tunic, which appears below in such a manner as to move upon each other, or whether it was entirely detached from the tunic, cannot easily be ascertained; but, whatever the materials were of which it was composed, certain it is that they were by no means confined to colour. This part of the military habit is sometimes blue, as it appears upon the figure to the right; and sometimes of two separate colours at once, as upon the figure bearing the standard, where the upper part of it, which encompasses the body and descends to the hips, is a deep reddish brown; the lower part, which forms three rows like the scales of a fish and covers the thighs, is of an orange colour, and corresponds with the tunic; in other instances it is painted red, and sometimes green. This variety of colour, however, does not amount to a proof that the habit itself was not formed of metal plates.[1] The Saxon artists were certainly very skilful in colouring of metals, and inlayed them with much ingenuity; and if, at the same time, we recollect how highly our ancestors held their military accoutrements of every kind in estimation, it will not in the least excite our astonishment that they should pride themselves in the beauty of their adornment.

Upon the twenty-second plate is exhibited an armour of the same kind, but probably much more ancient; the original statue, finely carved in alabaster, was found in Monmouthshire, near a place called *Porth Sini Kran.* From the description given of it when it was perfect, we find that the figure "held in his right hand "a short sword, and in his left a pair of scales: in the right scale appeared a maiden's "head and breast, and in the left (which was outweighed by the former) a globe."[2] It was afterwards broken, and presented, in the mutilated state in which it appears

[1] [I consider these illuminations to represent the leathern armour called *corium* and *corietum*, of which description was that recommended by Harold (according to Ingulf, p. 68.) to be worn instead of the heavy tunic of iron rings by his troops when pursuing the Welch into their fastnesses. Similar armour appears in the Bayeux tapestry, on the figures of Guy Count of Ponthieu and Odo Bishop of Bayeux, and specimens are to be found as late as the thirteenth century. See plate LXV. of this work.—Ed.]

[2] This account is copied from bishop Gibson's additions to Camden's Britannia, in which is given a very imperfect representation of the figure itself. The learned prelate seemed inclined to think the statue was intended for a female, and perhaps the goddess *Astræa;* but Mr. Gough, with infinitely more probability, conceives it to have been part of a tomb, and the figure of *St. Michael* weighing a human soul against the world. [This statue is now acknowledged to be of a much later date, and to represent St. Michael, either in scale armour or covered with feathers as he was frequently depicted.—Ed.]

at present, to the Ashmolean Museum, at Oxford, where it remains to this day.[1] The mail was certainly gilt when the statue was in perfection; for, evident marks of the gilding are still visible in the interstices of the armour.

THE BREAST-PLATE.

If the *thorax*, mentioned as a part of the habit of Charlemagne, had not been expressly spoken of as a winter garment only, and said to have covered his shoulders as well as his breast, I should readily have concluded it to have been a species of body-armour, and analogous to what is called, in the modern language, the *breast-plate.*[2] I have met with several words that appear to be perfectly applicable to this kind of armour; and they very frequently occur in the Saxon records.[3] If the application be granted, it will amount to a proof that the breast-plate was known to our ancestors: but how far it was generally adopted by them cannot so easily be determined; it certainly does not appear in their drawings; from which circumstance I am led to conclude that it was not in common use at the time those drawings were made, because, on the other hand, the breast-plate occurs continually in the military paintings, subsequent to the Norman Conquest, when we know that it formed almost an indispensable part of the soldier's habit.

The Saxon authors are by no means explicit with respect to the form of the *breast-guards*, mentioned in their writings, nor concerning the materials of which they were composed; they are spoken of in a cursory manner, and the only qualities applied to them, that I recollect, are that they were *rigid*, and *rough* or *shaggy*,[4]

[1] The plate which accompanies this work was engraved from a drawing accurately made from the original figure.

[2] See page 35.

[3] halſ-beaꞃh, halſ-beoꞃᵹ, or *neck guard.* Bꞃeoſꞇ-beꝺen *defence for the breast,* and Bꞃeoſꞇ-ꞃocc, which seems to be perfectly the *breast-plate.* [In the Bayeux tapestry, both Normans and Saxons are seen armed in the tunic of rings with a cowl or hood to it drawn over the head. This I take to be the Saxon *halsberg* or neck guard, as it effectually protects that part of the wearer. (From whence the Norman *halbers* and *haubert* or hauberk, latinized alberium or halbercum.) Besides which, many of these halsbergs are furnished with a square pectoral either quilted or covered with rings and surrounded by apparently a metal border, and which may very properly be entitled to the name of *breast beden* or breast-defence. The epithets *rough* or *shaggy* apply only to the *breast-roc,* which as its name suggests, must have been some sort of tunic. The Danish *roc* was a rough or hairy garment worn at sea in bad weather. The prototype of the modern P-jacket or North-Easter.—Ed.]

[4] Sꞇiðe ⁊ ꞃuᵹe Bꞃeoſꞇ ꞃoccaſ.

which indicates their formation from wool or hair, but totally precludes the idea of their having been made of metal.

THE GREAVES.

THE *greaves*, or *leg-guards*, are decidedly mentioned by the early Saxon writers;[1] but, as I observed in a former chapter, there is not the least indication of such kind of armour in the drawings prior to the tenth century.[2] The twenty-fourth plate, on which the representation of Oscytil the Dane and two of his companions is given, contains the first specimen of the leg-guards that I have met with; they form a partial covering only to defend the front of the leg; and, as far as one can judge from their appearance, they were made of thin plates of metal fitted to the skin and attached to the stockings, though the manner in which they were fastened is not shewn: we see, however, that they reached from the instep to the bottom of the knee, where the foldings of the hose are evidently to be traced. These figures are taken from a curious reliquary, of which they form part only of the front; the whole subject represents the murder of Theodore, abbot of Croyland, and the attendant monks by the Danes.[3] The reliquary itself was formerly preserved in the abbey of Croyland, and there is, I trust, no doubt of its having been the work of a Saxon artist;[4] it bears every mark of authenticity, and probably was fabricated not long posterior to the event it commemorates.[5] If we suppose the sculptor in giving the leg-guards to the Danes intended them as marks of distinction, it will not be unreasonable to conclude that they were first introduced by that people, or, at least,

1 The word hoſe is sometimes thought to mean the *greaves;* but the Scanc-beoɲᵹ may properly be rendered *leg-guard;* and of course it is synonimous to the *greave.* 2 Page 43.

3 The abbot is represented officiating at the high altar; and the figure with the sword, intended, as it is supposed, for king Oscytil, is in the act of striking off his head. The workmanship is admirable; the figures are chased in gold upon a blue ground; the heads are of silver, and protuberate in high relief. This event took place A. D. 890.

4 [As I before mentioned (page 43, note 3,) I entertain the greatest doubt of this reliquary being of Anglo-Saxon workmanship. The lines supposed by Mr. Strutt to indicate greaves upon the legs of the figures in question, would, I suspect, on examining the original turn out to be only the artist's attempt to describe the swell of the calf of the leg. Such being more or less visible in nearly all the illuminations or enamels of the 12th century, and in this instance exaggerated in the engraving. There is no instance of anything like a greave in any Anglo-Saxon, Anglo-Norman, or Danish figure I ever saw, and I conceive the Saxon Scanc-beorg, leg-guard, to be another term for the leathern bandage before noticed.—ED.]

5 Probably under the direction of abbot Goodric, the successor of Theodore.

more commonly adopted by them than by his own countrymen; and this may in some measure account for the omission of the *greaves* in the Saxon paintings, where the figures are constantly drawn conformably to the common customs of the country.

THE HELMET.

THE ancient Saxon artists made no distinction between the *royal helmet*[1] and the *crown:* the monarch is depicted by them in his court, and in the field of battle, with the same kind of head covering, even when every other part of his dress is marked with decisive variation: the paintings indeed of the subsequent centuries exhibit the royal helmet with some indications of improvement; and, upon the twenty-eighth plate, it is given in its most perfect state; the figure there represented is the portrait of Edward the Confessor, taken from an original impression of his great seal: we may observe an ornament upon his helmet, analogous to the crown or diadem of that time. The crown, considered simply as a civil ornament, and detached from the helmet, was worn by the Saxon monarchs long before the reign of the Confessor; but the royal helmet is never, that I remember, delineated without the appearance of the crown.

The helmet, appropriated to the nobility of the eighth century, is usually depicted in the form of a cone; and it was probably made of brass or some other kind of metal.[2] The same species of helmet appears in the drawings of the two succeeding centuries, but we find it gradually improved, if ornaments of gold or gilding, and embellishments of precious stones, may be deemed improvements.

I do not believe that the helmet was universally adopted by the military at any period of the Saxon æra; for the soldiers of every class, the king alone excepted, are frequently represented bare-headed; especially in those drawings that bear the greatest marks of antiquity. The head-covering, which occurs most generally in the Saxon drawings, bears more resemblance to a *cap* or *hat* of leather or woollen than to a helmet; and I am induced to think that occasionally it answered the purposes both of the hat and of the helmet. The *hat*[3] is mentioned in the records of the ninth and tenth centuries as a covering for the head, and sometimes spoken of as being ornamented with a crest.[4]

[1] Cẏne-ƿealm, or ƿelm.

[2] The Leþeꞃ-ƿelme, or *helmet* of *leather*, is mentioned by the Saxon writers, but perhaps the term is more applicable to the *hat* mentioned in the next note, which was sometimes made of leather, and sometimes of woollen.

[3] hæꞇ and Fellen-hæꞇ, that is a *felt* or *woollen hat*.

[4] Camb on hæꞇꞇe, and Camb on helme, the word camb signifies a *comb* or *crest*.

THE SHIELDS.

In the first part of this work I observed, that the general form of the Saxon shields was oval:[1] the same form prevailed, with few exceptions, until the Norman Conquest, when a new system of tactics was introduced, which required of course a changement in the military habiliments. The uniformity of appearance respecting the form of the shields cannot be applied to their size; for, the size is continually varied, not only in the drawings of different centuries, or different manuscripts of the same century, but even in the different delineations which occur in one and the same manuscript; especially in those manuscripts that belong to the tenth and eleventh centuries, where the shield, in some few instances, is represented full as tall as the bearer, and of sufficient latitude to cover him entirely from the sight of his enemy. The size most commonly represented is such as would cover the head and body completely; some are much smaller, and some so diminutive as not to exceed the length of the lower arm. The variation of the size is also supported by historical authority. We find mention made of *little shields*,[2] and *smaller shields*.[3] In the will of prince Æthelstan, the son of the second Æthelred,[4] the *shoulder-shield*[5] is included among the legacies, and it is distinguished from the *target*.[6] It was, I apprehend, a shield of the larger sort, and might receive its appellation from being usually slung upon the shoulder.

With respect to the materials which composed the Saxon shields, the silence of history prevents my enlargement. We have already seen that leather was certainly used by the shield makers,[7] and it might compose the body of the shields in general; but the rims and bosses were certainly made of metal, which, as far as one can judge from the colour, was often gilt or plated with gold. Some few instances indeed occur in which the whole shield appears to have been covered with gold or metal gilt.

The ornamental adornments of the Saxon shields, in addition to the bosses and rims or borders of gold and silver, appear to have been very few, and those very simple; and, as they are given upon the several military figures which accompany this work, they do not require any farther disquisition.[8]

1 Page 23. 2 Lýtel ꞅcýlꝺ. 3 Ꝺa læꞅꞅan ꞅcýlꝺaꞅ.
4 The original, dated 1015, is in the possession of Thomas Astle, Esq.
5 Mıneꞅ boh ꞅcýlꝺeꞅ. 6 Mıneꞅ ꝺaꞃᵹan. 7 Page 23.
8 See plates XIII. XIV. and XXIII.

THE SWORDS; AND THE SPEARS.

THE form of the Saxon sword was not subject to much variation, as the reader may easily see by referring to the several military figures which are given in this work.[1] There are, however, several sorts of swords specified in the Saxon records; such as the *shining sword*;[2] the *sharp-pointed sword*;[3] the *dull*, or perhaps rather, *pointless sword*;[4] the *two-edged sword*;[5] the *broad sword*;[6] and the *small sword*, or *dagger*.[7]

When I described the habit of Charlemagne, I observed that, at the time he neglected every other part of his dress, he prided himself in the beauty and adornments of his military accoutrements. His sword, which was his constant companion, and the belt, from which it was suspended, were enriched with gold or silver; and, upon particular occasions, ornamented with jewels.[8] The same kind of pride was prevalent among the Anglo-Saxons; and their arms are frequently distinguished by epithets, alluding to their beauty or their goodness: nor is it indeed the smallest matter of wonder, that a warlike people should consider their weapons as the most essential part of their habit.

Every man of rank possessed a number of swords suited to different occasions. Upwards of a dozen, the property of prince Æthelstan, are bequeathed in his will; and the sword-cutler appears to have been an artist held in high estimation. In the ancient records, his name is frequently added to the arms he fabricated, as a mark of their superior excellence.[9]

The sword itself, I presume, was anciently made of brass; but, in the more modern times, of iron or steel; and, in some instances, it was polished:[10] but the

1 See plates XIII. XIV. XIX. and XXVIII.

2 Fagum-sweordum.

3 Swurdes-ord.

4 Sweordum aswefde.

5 Sworde twý ecgedes.

6 Brad-swýrd.

7 hæp-seax, or hýpe-seax, literally *hip-seax*. [The word *seax* has been the subject of much dispute. It has been described as a curved sword carried by the ancient Saxons, and that the name of the nation was derived from it. Mr. Sharon Turner has exploded the latter hypothesis. With regard to the former, I have elsewhere remarked that no instance of a curved sword occurs either in Anglo-Saxon drawings, or sepulchral remains. Æder-seax signifies a lancet, literally, Vein-seax. Sword is itself Saxon. Seax would seem to imply a knife or dagger.—ED.]

8 See page 30.

9 Thus, in the will of prince Æthelstan, spoken of in the former page, one of the legacies is *a silver-hilted sword which Wolfricke made*.

10 It was then called the *shining sword*. See note 2, above.

hilts, which admitted of more adornments, were composed of great variety of materials. Silver-hilted swords are particularly specified in the will of prince Æthelstan, mentioned above; and swords with hollow hilts,[1] or rather hilts ornamented with fret-work: hilts of gold are also spoken of by the writers of this æra. A sword, with its hilt, and the belt belonging to it, embellished with jewels, taken from a Saxon manuscript of the tenth century, is given upon the twenty-ninth plate of this work.

The manner in which the sword was girded upon the side is exemplified by the figure, with the spear and shield, upon the thirteenth plate. Some few instances indeed occur in the Saxon drawings, in which it is suspended from the shoulder; but this does not appear by any means to have been a prevalent fashion.

The sword-belts are frequently spoken of by the Saxon authors, as adorned with gold, silver, and jewels; yet, singular as it may appear, they are rarely so represented in the manuscript drawings of the time, or distinguished at all from the common girdle with which the tunic was usually bound about the waist. An ornamented belt, intended to represent, I presume, the studding of jewels, and the only one I have met with so perfect, is given upon the twenty-ninth plate: the sheath of the sword, when it is represented, is generally black; for, variety of instances occur, in which the sword appears to have been worn without any sheath at all. Its ornaments, generally speaking, are few and simple, consisting of a few lines only at the top, with a cross between them. We must, however, except the sword-sheath of the Danish chieftain upon the twenty-fourth plate, which seems to be more superbly adorned.

The Spears have been spoken of in a former chapter;[2] and the various forms of the spear-heads, as they appear in the manuscript drawings of the Saxons, are given upon the thirteenth plate. The spear was by no means confined to persons of superior rank; but seems to have been borne by every person who was able to purchase it. As a weapon of war, it is frequently given to the foot-soldiers; and the cavalry are very rarely depicted without it.

There are three sorts of spears mentioned by the Saxon writers, namely, the war-spear, the boar-spear, and the hunting-spear: but in what particulars they differed from each other cannot easily be determined.[3]

[1] ⁊ þær ſpurder mid ðam pẏttedan hiltan.

[2] Page 24.

[3] Wig-ſpere—bar-ſpere and hunting ſpere.

THE MILITARY HABITS OF THE DANES.

There is not a sufficiency of authentic materials remaining at present to afford a particular illustration of the Danish habit; but, as all the Northern nations were subject to the same manners and customs, there can be little reason to suppose that the Danes and the Saxons should have differed essentially in their modes of dress.—The early writers, who have spoken largely concerning the transactions of the Danes from their first invasions of England to their establishment in the island, are silent upon this head; and their silence may be considered as a corroborating proof that the habits of the Danes were at that time similar to those of the Saxons; at least, so much so as not to require a separate description.[1] We learn however from history, that the Danes paid great attention to the cultivation of their hair and the adornment of their persons; in short, they seem to have been considered as the complete beaux of the tenth century. The three Danish chiefs, given upon the twenty-fourth plate of this work, are richly habited.[2] Their tunics are embellished with embroidered collars and borders; and their hair is combed and platted in a very particular form. The figure striking with the sword is the portraiture of Oscytil, who bears the title of king in the Saxon records; his tunic is open before, and discovers the under-tunic. The folds of the *femoralia*, or drawers, are also very distinctly marked. The ornaments upon his breast, I am apt to believe, are intended to represent the *thorax*, or breast-plate; and probably it was constructed of linen, folded many times, and quilted together; for such was the manner in which the *thorax* was anciently made.

The *greaves*, which are very plainly marked upon all the three chieftains, have already been spoken of;[3] and, excepting them, and the opening of the tunic of Oscytil in the front, there is no difference between the habits of these figures and the habits of the Saxon nobility of the same æra.

The Danish *swords* were made in the same manner with those of the Saxons; but the scabbard, whence the middle figure upon the twenty-fourth plate is drawing his sword, is more richly ornamented than any I have met with of equal antiquity.

The *battle-axe* has been generally attributed to the Danes, and considered by

[1] [Nearly all the information that can be gleaned upon the subject of Danish, or Norse, military costume will be found in the 24th Vol. of the Archæologia, in Sir Fred. Madden's erudite and interesting paper on the chess-men found in the Isle of Lewis in 1831.—Ed.]

[2] See note 4, page 53.

[3] Page 53. [See note as before.—Ed.]

modern writers as a certain mark, by which the representations of that people may be distinguished from those of the Saxons; this opinion cannot however, I conceive, be supported by good authority. In the Saxon drawings, it is no uncommon thing to see the battle-axe given to the military figures, and in cases where the artists certainly intended to delineate their own manners and habits, without the least reference to those of the Danes; however, if it should be said that the Danes more generally used the axe as a weapon of war than the Saxons did, I will by no means dispute the point;[1] for, indeed, I do not recollect an instance in which the Danes are represented in a military capacity without one or two of the soldiers having a battle-axe.

The *axe*, and the *double-axe*, or *bipennis*, are both of them frequently mentioned by the Saxon writers:[2] the form of the first may be seen on the twenty-fourth plate, and that of the latter upon the twenty-ninth plate of this work.

[1] [There can be little doubt of the axe having been the characteristic weapon of the Danes and Northmen. The Welsh bard Gruffyd ap Merredydd speaks of

"——— the men of Lochlyn (Denmark)
With their keen-edged axes."

And Giraldus says the Irish had "broad axes excellently well steeled, the use of which they borrowed from the Norwegians and Ostmen." We learn also from the same writer that the Danish shields were usually painted *red*, for he tells us the Irish carried "red shields in *imitation* of the Danes."—ED.]

[2] The *axe* is called in Saxon bıll; and the *double axe* ꞇpı-bıll, or ꞇpẏ-bıll.

CHAP. IV.

THE ECCLESIASTICAL HABITS OF THE NINTH AND TENTH CENTURIES.—THE ARCHBISHOP, BISHOP, ABBOT, MONKS, AND INFERIOR CLERGY.

THE eighth century afforded very few materials towards the illustration of the ecclesiastical habits.—From a manuscript of the tenth I have taken the figure of an archbishop, engraved upon the twenty-sixth plate: he is depicted in the full dress, the mitre excepted; the place of which is supplied by a *nimbus*, or circle of glory. The several parts of the habit are very distinctly marked, and divested of that load of ornamental enrichments which appear upon the garments of superior clergy in the succeeding centuries.[1]

The portrait of Wulfstan, the second archbishop of York of that name, given upon the twenty-seventh plate, is extracted from a manuscript of the eleventh century; and the striking difference which appears in the habits of the two Metropolitans does not, I apprehend, arise from any material change having been made in the ecclesiastical vestment during the elapsment of half a century; but rather from the one being drawn in his official habit, and the other in the dress he was accustomed to wear in his retirement from the duties of the church: agreeable to this idea, we find archbishop Wulfstan depicted as seated in his study, and writing in a book which is open before him. The portrait is prefixed to a code of synodial decrees for the reformation of the church, which were probably drawn up by him, and afterwards confirmed by Æthelred the Second.[2]

1 The MS. in which the original drawing is preserved, belonged formerly to the monastery of St. Augustine at Canterbury; and was probably presented to the cathedral church by abbot Elfnoth, when it was dedicated anew, and the name of St. Augustine added to that of St. Peter, to whom for several centuries it had been solely appropriated. The portrait of the abbot appears in the frontispiece, presenting the book itself to his new-adopted patron, who is depicted in his *pontificalia*, seated in his chair of state, and attended by the assistant clergy, and receiving it from him. The nimbus, or circle of glory, about his head, denotes his having been honoured with the title of *Saint*. Augustine was the first archbishop of Canterbury, and the founder of this monastery, which received its name from him. Abbot Elfnoth died A. D. 980.

2 Wulfstan, or Wulstan, was the twenty-second archbishop of York; he came to that see A. D.

The habit of the Anglo-Saxon monks is exemplified by two figures, given upon the twenty-fifth plate: the border of the cowl, the bottom of the sleeves, and the lower verge of the outer tunic belonging to one of them, are ornamented in a peculiar manner; but, whether such ornaments were merely optional, or were a mark of superiority of the rank or order of the wearer, I cannot pretend to determine: the garments of both these figures are white, and the outer tunic is lined with red. It is necessary, however, to observe, that the outer garments, appropriated to the Saxon monks of this æra, though uniform in their general appearance, were not confined to the colours just mentioned: in other manuscripts of the same period they are frequently painted black, and in some instances dark brown and grey; but the inner tunic, so far as one can judge of it from the small portion of the sleeves usually seen below the outer garment, was white: we must indeed except the attendant clergyman, bearing the crosier of abbot Elfthnoth, on the twenty-sixth plate; his tunic is light blue, and the outer garment, or *surplice*, is white.

I do not apprehend that the external habits of the inferior ecclesiastics were limited to precise form or colour; we find them differing materially in both, and even in the same painting, where more than one are depicted: thus in the twenty-sixth plate there are two attendants represented behind the archbishop; the garment of the one is blue, and that of the other is green.

The *calopedes*, and the *subtalares*, were species of coverings for the feet: they seem both of them to have been chiefly calculated for warmth;[1] and they were much used by the clergy in the performance of their nocturnal duties, and in the winter; so were also the *socks* in addition to the *stockings*, or rather *trowsers*,[2] which covered not only the legs, but the thighs also, and were well adapted to answer the end proposed by the interdiction confirmed in the council of Chalcuith, which runs in the following manner: "Let no minister of the altar presume to approach it to celebrate mass with naked legs, lest his filthiness should appear, and God be offended."[3]

In the canons, instituted under the patronage of king Edgar, the priests are commanded "to wear, at the celebration of mass, a garment called the *corporale*,[4] in addition to the *subumlem*,[5] under the *alba*;"[6] and it is farther insisted upon, "that all these garments shall be kept clean and in good order. Another clause

1002, and died May 28, A. D. 1023. The MS. from which this portrait is extracted was probably written, and the drawing made, during the life-time of the prelate.

1 See page 48.

2 See pages 38, and 46.

3 This council was held A.D. 785. Wilkins, vol. I. p. 147.

4 The same, I presume, as the *camisia* or *shirt*. See page 37.

5 Or inner tunic.

6 ALBA, *vestis seu tunicæ species, à candore sic nuncupata.* Du Cange in voce *Alba*.

expressly commands "that no priest shall come into the church or chancel without his *surplice*."[1]

The ancient ecclesiastical laws required the inferior ministers to shave their beards to distinguish them from the laity; but this restriction does not appear by any means to have extended to the superior clergy; for, they are more frequently depicted by the Saxon artists with beards than without them; perhaps the wearing the beard was a privilege confined to the higher order of ecclesiastics. I am also inclined to think that the mandate, contained in the forty-seventh canon, published during the reign of Edgar, forbidding such persons as entered into holy orders to permit their hair to grow, was confined to those who had, at the same time, received the tonsure; for, in the drawings of that period, the ecclesiastics are generally represented with their hair sufficiently long to cover the whole head, and fall upon the shoulders.

The garments appropriated to the church, were chiefly made of linen; particularly the *surplice*, the *alba* or *tunic*, and the *shirt*. Woollen shirts, it is true, are spoken of by the Saxon writers; but it is equally true that the wearing of them, whenever it was enjoined, was considered as a very severe penance. It is, however, very probable that the external garments of the dignified clergy were made of silk; such especially as we find ornamented with borders and fringes of gold, and adorned with needle work. These garments, we are assured, were sometimes edged, if not lined, with furs and sables; but, as this subject will be more fully treated upon in a subsequent chapter, it is unnecessary to dwell any longer upon it in the present instance.[2]

1 Oꝼeꞃ-ꞅlipe in the Saxon; See Lambard de Leg. Saxon.

2 [The fact is that we are at present greatly in the dark respecting early ecclesiastical costume. It is a subject replete with interest, and I am happy to find that a most intelligent antiquary has for some time past been directing his attention to it, and will shortly favour us with the result of his enquiries.—Ed.]

CHAP. V.

THE MOURNING HABITS OF THE ANGLO-SAXONS NOT KNOWN.—HOW THE BODIES OF THE DEAD WERE APPARELLED.—THE MANNER IN WHICH CHARLEMAGNE WAS BURIED.—THE APPEARANCE OF THE BODIES OF EDWARD THE CONFESSOR, OF DUNSTAN ARCHBISHOP OF CANTERBURY, AND OF WITHBURGA, SISTER TO ETHELDRIDA ABBESS OF ELY, UPON OPENING OF THEIR TOMBS.

I HAVE already mentioned the difficulties which occur in the attempt to investigate the various ranks of people among the Anglo-Saxons from their habits:[1] that distinctions of this kind did exist, we can hardly doubt; but the want of sufficient materials, from which they might be exemplified, stands as an insuperable bar to obstruct the researches of the curious. The article of dress forms only an accidental part, as it were, of the Saxon history; and the names of such portions of it as do occur were considered by the authors as well known to their readers; and of course a minute description of them was thought unnecessary. The general form of the Saxon garments is not sufficiently varied, in the drawings of the time, to throw much light upon the subject; and particular colours, such as purple and scarlet, which anciently were determinate badges of distinction, do not appear to have retained their prerogative among our ancestors; for, they are indiscriminately worn by every rank and class of people. One would naturally suppose, that the mourning dresses would have been decidedly different from the common habits of the time, and on this supposition expected to have found that difference marked in the manuscript drawings. This, however, is by no means the case: the representations of burials and of the previous ceremonies thereupon dependant are frequently enough to be met with; but, from the minutest examination of the attendant figures, I cannot trace the least material alteration made in the habits of either sex upon this occasion: *widows' garments*[2] and nuptial garments,[3] are mentioned, it is true, in the Saxon records; but by what particular marks they were distinguished from the usual dress cannot be discovered.

The funeral customs of the Anglo-Saxons, so far as they relate to the treatment

[1] Pages 27, and 28. [2] ƿẏdepan-ꞃeaꝼ. [3] ᵹẏꝼtlic-ꞃeaꝼ

and habit of deceased persons, are in various instances described by their writers, and frequently represented in the drawings contained in their manuscripts; I shall not therefore be at any loss to investigate this subject, as fully at least as the nature of the present work requires.

The corpse, being washed with pure water, was covered with the *camisia*, or *shirt*: it was then clothed with such garments as the rank of the person required, and finally enveloped in a sheet or wrapper of linen cloth:[1] the face, however, was usually left uncovered by the wrapper till the time of burial, in order, I presume, that the friends and relations of the deceased might be gratified with a sight of the corpse previously to its being desposited in the tomb. A dead body in its funeral habit may be seen at the bottom of the twenty-ninth plate of this work; and again, entirely covered in the manner it was buried, at the top of the same plate. Before the face of the deceased was enveloped with the wrapper, it was covered with a *sudarium*, or napkin; and this seems to have been the constant practice.[2]

The ablution and clothing of the corpse were performed with every due regard to decency. In a manuscript of the eighth century[3] we meet with several representations of this ceremony: it appears to have been performed by two persons whose sex, I apprehend, accorded with that of the deceased. They are drawn as kneeling, one at the head, and the other at the feet of the dead body; and over them was placed a large sheet to conceal them from the attendants, and prevent any interruption during the performance of the ceremony: this sheet in some instances was supported by the attendants, but still in such a manner as to exclude the body from their sight: it is to be observed, that the wrapper or winding-sheet, is frequently painted white; but in several instances blue, red, and pink.

The corpse represented on the twenty-ninth plate seems to be habited in the shirt only; but it was a common custom with our Saxon ancestors to clothe the bodies of the deceased in those habits of dignity and splendour to which they

1 The Saxon word is ſcẏꞇan, which signifies a sheet; it may, therefore, with the strictest propriety, be called in English the *winding-sheet*.

2 The *sudarium* is constantly mentioned by the Saxon writers, when they minutely describe the funeral habit of the time. An ancient historian informs us, that, upon the opening of the tomb of Acca, bishop of Hagulstad, who died A.D. 741, besides the bones of the prelate, were found the *casula*, or *surplice*, the *tunic* and *sudarium*, with which the corpse had been habited previous to its interment. Hist. Simon Dunelm. sub anno 741. The proper Saxon word for the *sudarium* was ſpaꞇ-claꝺ; but in Alfred's translation of Bede's Eccles. Hist. Onꝺpleꞇon is used to express the words *vultus indumento*. Lib. 4. c. 30.

3 Claudius, B. IV. [*Tenth Century*. Ed.]

had been entitled in their life-time: and this practice was not confined to personages of exalted rank; it extended also to those of inferior degree, as well of the clergy as of the laity: kings were buried in their royal robes; knights in their military garments; bishops in their pontifical vestments; priests in their sacerdotal habits; and monks in the dress peculiar to the order to which they belonged.

The manner in which the obsequies of Charlemagne were performed is recorded by a cotemporary author.[1] We have no description of the kind so perfect among the Saxon writers; and, as the forms of sepulture adopted by the French at that period corresponded exactly with those of the Saxons, I shall translate the passage as a curious relique of antiquity; and trust, that it will throw much light upon the funeral ceremonies of this country. His body was washed with great solemnity, and carefully prepared for the burial.[2] It was then clothed with a garment of hair-cloth next the skin; which ceremony it is said ought always to be secretly performed.[3] He was afterwards habited in the imperial vestments; and his face was covered with a *sudarium* or *napkin*, over which a diadem was placed upon his head; and in the diadem was enclosed a portion of the wood which composed the holy cross.[4] His sword enriched with gold was girt about him; and in this dress he was seated upon a gilt throne.[5] His shoulders were reclined on the back of the throne; and his head was supported in an erect position by a golden chain fastened to the diadem.[6] In his hands he held the holy gospels embellished with gold, which rested upon his knees; he was then placed, together with the throne on which he was seated, within the cavity of the sepulchre.[7] The gilt travelling pouch,[8] which he used to wear when he went to Rome, was laid by him; and the sceptre of gold, with the golden shield which Pope Leo had consecrated, was suspended before him.[9] These ceremonies being performed, the sepulchre was filled with aromatic drugs of various kinds, together with considerable quantities of gold; it was then closed and sealed.[10]

[1] Monachus Egolimensis, page 282.
[2] More solenni lotum et curatum.
[3] Cilicium ad carnem ejus positum est, quod secretò semper induebatur, &c.
[4] Et in diademate lignum sanctæ crucis positum est.
[5] Sede aureâ;—it is afterwards called *cathedra*.
[6] Reclinatis humeris in cathedrâ, et capite honestè erecto ligato aureâ catenâ.
[7] In curvaturâ sepulchri.
[8] Pera peregrinalis.
[9] Sceptrum aureum et scutum aureum quod Leo papa consecraverat ante eum posita sunt dependentia.
[10] Et repleverunt sepulchrum ejus aromatibus, pigmentis, et balsamo, et musco, et thesauris multis in auro.—Et clausum et sigillatum est sepulchrum ejus.—Monach. Egolimensis, p. 283.

Linen of the finest quality[1] was prepared for the obsequies of Edward the Confessor; and his best mantle[2] was appropriated to the envelopement of his body. When his tomb was opened about six and thirty years after his interment, the mantle which covered the corpse was found entire; and, being removed, his body appeared clothed in the regal vestments, with the ornaments belonging to it, together with the *sudarium* which covered his face and head, in a perfect state. The old mantle was taken away as a precious relique, and the body, with all its other ornaments, was re-wrapped in a mantle of silk.[3] And, in the year 1688, several pieces of gold-coloured and flowered silk were drawn out of the tomb, which probably were part of the envelopement just mentioned.[4]

The body of Dunstan, archbishop of Canterbury, after his decease was completely apparelled in his pontifical habit; the mitre, and other insignia belonging to his office, such as the ring and bracelets, are mentioned among the adornments; and the sandals, which were put upon his feet, are particularised for their beauty and elegance. In this array the body was finally inclosed in a fair linen cloth, and so committed to the tomb.[5]

The body of Withburga, sister to queen Etheldrida, abbess of Ely, when examined by the order of abbot Richard, several centuries after her sepulture, was found with a cushion of silk beneath her head; and the veil, together with all the vestments in which she had been interred, were perfectly whole and as good as new.[6]

[1] Preciosis lintheis.—Ailredus abbas Rievallis de vitâ et miraculis Edw. Confess.

[2] Optimis palliis corpus involvitur.—Ibid. [3] Vestimento holoserico.—Ibid.

[4] See the Introduction to Mr. Gough's Sepulchral Monuments, vol. 1. p. 48.; and his account of Edward the Confessor's tomb, &c. in the body of the work, p. 1.

[5] An ancient author, who was present at the opening of Dunstan's tomb long after his interment, informs us, that they found the body of the saint—"more summi pontificis, infulatum, annulatum, palliatum, spindulatum, sandaliis venustissimè adornatum."—Eadmeri Epistola de corpore Dunstani, Anglia Sacra, vol. II.

[6] Pulvillo serico ad caput apposito, velo et totis vestibus integrâ novitate renitentibus, &c.—Malmesb. de gest. Pont Angl. l. 4. p. 167.

CHAP. VI.

A GENERAL REVIEW OF THE MATERIALS WHICH COMPOSED THE SAXON HABITS.—THE ART OF WEAVING.—THE ART OF EMBROIDERY.—THE ANGLO-SAXON LADIES FAMOUS FOR THEIR SKILL IN THIS ART.—THE SUBJECTS EXECUTED BY THEM.—THE USES TO WHICH EMBROIDERED GARMENTS WERE APPROPRIATED.—THE TANNER'S ART.—THE DYER'S ART.

LINEN certainly formed a very large part of the Anglo-Saxon habits: it was an article indiscriminately worn by every class of people whose circumstances allowed them to purchase it; and it was particularly appropriated to such garments as were worn next the skin. The use of linen is of high antiquity among the Saxons; for, a writer of their own, who flourished during the eighth century, informs us that the military tunic in his time consisted of linen.[1] Another ancient writer, describing the manners of the Longobards, says their vestments were loose and flowing; that they consisted chiefly of linen like those of the Anglo-Saxons, and were ornamented with broad borders woven, or embroidered with various colours.[2]

The garments of the women, such I mean as were of superior rank, consisted chiefly of linen; and many of the vestments belonging to the clergy were certainly composed of the same material. Linen was also in common use among the religious devotees: it is noted by Bede as a rare instance of humility and self-denial in Etheldrida, abbess of Ely, that she never would wear linen garments, but contented herself with such as were made of wool.[3]

It is impossible, from the drawings of the Anglo-Saxons, to ascertain how large a portion of their garments consisted of linen: the colour will by no means determine the matter; for, we are well assured, that many of their woollen vestments were white, and their linen habits were frequently dyed of various colours. The shirt and other interior garments were certainly made of linen, because the wearing of woollen vestments next the skin was enjoined as a penance.[4]

[1] Alcuini lib. de offic. div. See page 22, note 4.

[2] "Ornato institis latioribus, vario colore contextis."—Paul Diaconus de gestis Longobardi, lib. iv. cap. 23.

[3] Bede, Eccles. Hist. lib. iv. cap. 19.

[4] See pages 4, and 33.

WOOLLEN CLOTH occasionally composed the external garments of all ranks of persons; and was, I trust, in much more general use than any other production of the loom; there is good reason therefore to believe, that the manufactory of woollen cloth was carried to very high perfection by the Saxon artists. I am indeed inclined to think, that the fineness of the materials, and the costliness of the workmanship, rather than any particular colour or form of the garments, made the chief distinction of rank among the Anglo-Saxons.[1]

SILK, as we have observed before, was in use among the Anglo-Saxons soon after their establishment in Britain; but so expensive an article, we may reasonably suppose, must have been confined to the highest rank of people. Coronation vestments and mantles, the external garments of the dignified clergy, and the robes of the queens and princesses were often made of this valuable material; it was also used for the adornment of the altars, and other religious purposes.[2]

HAIR CLOTH was certainly manufactured by the Anglo-Saxons: it seems to have been chiefly in use among the clergy; it formed part of their bed, and was even worn next the skin by way of severe penance. The hair-cloth shirt composed part of the funeral habit of Charlemagne,[3] and might probably be often used upon such occasions in this country.

The art of weaving was not confined simply to the working of cloth of one colour; it was well understood in all its branches: we have already seen, that, so far back as the eighth century, variety of colours forming different figures were produced from the loom.[4] In an ancient Saxon translation, or rather paraphrase, of the Pentateuch,[5] the garment which Israel made for his son Joseph, called in our modern version *a coat of many colours*,[6] is rendered *a tunic* adorned *with rings*;[7] and, agreeable to this idea, the illuminator, in the representation of Joseph, has given him a short blue tunic, covered with dark rings encircled in white narrow borders; and such a dress was probably worn by the Anglo-Saxon young men of distinction; it has every appearance in the drawings of having been the product of the loom without any extraneous aid.

How far the art of variegating the colours and ornamenting of cloth without the assistance of the needle extended cannot be ascertained.[8] It is certain,

1 See page 28.

2 Anglia Sacra.

3 See page 65.

4 See page 2.

5 Cotton MS. Claudius, B. IV.

6 Genesis, chap. xxxvi. ver. 3.

7 hrinȝ ꝼaȝe tunecan.

8 The words *intexo, intertexo, contexo*, and even *texo*, frequently used by the ancient authors, will admit of a more extensive construction than that of weaving only, and may signify not only the manu-

however, that garments ornamented with needle work were held in the highest estimation by the Anglo-Saxons; and it is equally certain, that the Saxon ladies excelled in the performance of these elegant manufactures. I have already slightly spoken upon this interesting subject;[1] and I presume that the following enlargement will not be thought improper in the present instance:

The Anglo-Saxon ladies of the first quality employed much of their time in carding of wool, spinning, and working with the needle; and some of them also encountered the labours of the loom: these exercises do not appear to have been so general among the Continental ladies, as in England; however they were occasionally practised abroad; and Eginhart assures us, that the daughters of Charlemagne were no strangers to the use of the distaff.[2] The four princesses, daughters of Edward the elder, and sisters to Æthelstan, are highly celebrated for their skill in spinning, weaving, and embroidering;[3] and Edgitha the wife of Edward the Confessor was perfectly mistress of the needle.[4]

The eulogiums bestowed upon our fair countrywomen on this account are not confined to our own authors: we may add the additional testimony of several foreign writers. I shall, however, content myself with the selection of two passages, which will, I trust, be thought sufficient to prove how highly the Saxon embroideries were esteemed upon the Continent. "The French and Normans," says an ancient author, "admired the beautiful dresses of the English nobility; for," adds he, "the English women excel all others in needle-work, and in embroidering with gold."[5] Another writer tells us, that "the Anglo-Saxon ladies were so famous for their skill in the art of embroidery, that the most elegant productions of the needle were called by way of eminence *The English Work*."[6]

The operations of the needle were not confined to the mere variegation of

facturing of brocades, but the adornments of the needle also. In this light I consider the following passages: "Unum regium pallium auro textam."—Carta regis Æthelstani. "Unum vestimentum de serico aureis aquilis intextum."—Ingulphus, Hist. Croyland. And particularly the standard of Harold the Second; in which, says Malmesbury, was the figure of a man fighting, "auro et lapidibus arte sumptuosâ contextam."—De Gestis Regum Angliæ, lib. II. *Acupictus*, or wrought with the needle, is a term sometimes used; and properly expresses the work of *embroidery*: in Saxon it is called ȝolð-ꞅioꝼða; that is, *sewed* or *embroidered with gold*.

1 See pages 3, and 13.

2 "Filias verò lanificio assuescere."—Eginhart, Vita Caroli Magni, cap. 19.

3 Malmesb. de Gestis Rerum Angliæ, lib. II. p. 26.

4 Ibid. lib. II.

5 Gesta Gulielmi Ducis apud Duchen. p. 211.

6 "Anglicum opus."—Guil. Pictavens. p. 211.

colours; they extended to the representations of flowers, foliages, buildings, birds, beasts, and men; and sometimes even to historical subjects,[1] which were embroidered upon cloth with threads of gold and silver intermixed with silk, cotton, and worsted, of such colours as the nature of the design required. The outlines of the subject to be worked were first drawn upon the cloth; but this part of the operation was not always performed by the ladies, whose office it was to fill up those outlines with the needle. The celebrated Dunstan, when a young man, was considered as an artist of some degree of eminence for drawings of this kind, and assisted a lady in designing the embellishments which she embroidered with threads of gold upon a sacerdotal vestment.[2] It is highly probable (though I speak indeed from conjecture only), that there were Saxon artists who made this branch of the art of embroidery their profession, and not only drew the outlines upon the cloth, but furnished the fair workwomen with designs, by way of patterns, shaded and painted in their proper colours.

The costly manufactures of the needle were chiefly appropriated to the regal and ecclesiastical vestments. The mantles used by the Anglo-Saxon monarchs at their coronations and upon other great solemnities were frequently embellished with superb embroideries. The golden veil of Wiglaf king of Mercia, on which was represented the destruction of Troy, has already been spoken of.[3] The vestment which Cnut the Dane presented to the abbey of Croyland was made of silk, embroidered with eagles of gold;[4] the coronation-mantle of Harold Harefoot the son of Cnut, which he gave to the same abbey, was also made of silk, and embroidered with flowers of gold;[5] and the garments of Edward the Confessor, which he wore upon occasions of great solemnity, were sumptuously embroidered with gold by the hands of gentle Edgitha his queen.[6]

Religious zeal produced many splendid works of this kind, which were dedicated to the service of the church. The altars enriched with embroideries, and the sacerdotal habits of the clergy beautified with needle-work, bore testimony at once to the piety and skill of our fair countrywomen. Queens, princesses, and other ladies of high rank, employed their time to this benevolent purpose; and memorandums of their donations are frequently enough to be met with in the ancient records of the church.[7]

[1] The Destruction of Troy was embroidered upon the veil of Wiglaf king of Mercia. See page 3.

[2] Osburnus de Vitâ Dunstani, Anglia Sacra, vol. II. p. 95. [3] See page 3.

[4] "Unum plenum vestimentum de serico aureis aquilis intextum." — Ingulphus, Hist. Ab. Croyland. [5] Ibid. [6] Guil. Malmesb. de Gest. Reg. lib. II. cap. XIII. p. 51.

[7] Annales Eccles. Winton in Angliâ Sacrâ, p. 290.

The tanner's art must certainly have been well understood by the Anglo-Saxons; for, *leather* not only formed part of their habits, but was used for a variety of other purposes; and connected with it was probably the art of dressing the skins of animals with the hair upon them. The garments of the nobility and dignified clergy, (such of them especially as were appropriated to the winter), were often fringed and even lined with furs of various kinds: those of sables, of beavers, and foxes were the most esteemed;[1] the inferior sorts were made from the skins of cats and of lambs; but we shall have occasion to speak more fully upon this subject hereafter.

From what has been said in the foregoing pages, it is evident that the art of dying cloth of various colours must have been carried to a considerable degree of perfection at this period. A modern author informs us, that a scarlet dye, extracted from a small insect of the kermes or cochineal kind, was discovered about the commencement of the eleventh century, and found its way into England soon afterwards;[2] but, if the manuscript paintings of the Saxons be faithful respecting the colours of their garments, a scarlet dye of much higher antiquity was known and used in this country. Scarlets and reds of various kinds, purple, green, yellow, pink, brown, and several other colours, are exhibited upon the habits of the figures that appear even in the earliest manuscripts.[3]

[1] "Sabelinas, vel castorinas, vel vulpinas, &c."—Anglia Sacra, tom, II. p. 259.

[2] Dr. Henry's History of Britain, vol. II. book ii. chap. 5.

[3] The words ꞇƿe-bleo, ꞇƿi-bleo, or ꞇƿeo-bliᵹ, which signify twice or double-dyed, occur in the Saxon MSS.

CHAP. VII.

THE ORNAMENTAL PARTS OF DRESS CONSIDERED.—BODY-PAINTING.—COLOURING OF THE HAIR. —CROWNS AND DIADEMS. —HEAD-TIRES.—EAR-RINGS.—GIRDLES.—POUCHES.—BRACELETS.— RINGS.—BUCKLES AND SPURS.

EXCLUSIVE of the embellishments immediately connected with the garments of our Saxon ancestors, we meet with a variety of ornaments which may properly be considered as parts of their dress, and ought of course to be particularly described; but, before I enter upon this part of the work, I beg leave to offer the following short observations to my Readers, which I hope will not be considered as improper or unnecessary, because it must be granted, that the subjects from which they are taken owed their very existence to the prevalent admiration of personal adornments.

Body-painting and puncturating of the skin with ornaments of various kinds were both of them practised by the Britons. The origin of these barbarous customs cannot be traced with any degree of certainty, nor the period of their introduction into this island determined; but we have undoubted authority in favour of their high antiquity.[1] Among the various usages that the Saxons derived from the Britons, these fashionable adornments of the body may certainly be included. Soon after the conversion of the Saxons to Christianity, the practice of painting the body fell under the ecclesiastical censure; and it was prohibited by a law enacted as early as the year 785.[2] This interdiction, however, did not produce a total abolition of skin-painting, as we may learn from Malmesbury, an historian of good authority; who, enumerating the prevalent vices among the English at the time of the Norman Conquest, ranks in the dark catalogue that of marking their skins with puncturated paintings by way of ornament.[3] In the subsequent centuries, the puncturating of the skin and body-painting seem to

[1] Cæs. bell. Gall. cap. 10. Pliny, Nat. Hist. lib. XXII. cap. 1. Herodian, lib. III. cap. 46.

[2] Wilkins's Concilia, tom. I.

[3] "Picturatis stigmatibus cutem insigniti." Will. Malmesb. de Gest. Reg. Anglorum. Lib. III. p. 57.

have been entirely abolished, except those vestiges of the latter that we find to this day retained by the ladies ; such, I mean, as paint their faces, and make use of various arts to give the skin a more delicate appearance than is natural to it.

It has been previously observed, that, in the manuscript paintings of the Saxons, the figures frequently appear with blue hair ;[1] in some instances, which indeed are not so common, the hair is represented of a bright red colour ; and, in others, it is of a green and orange hue. I have no doubt existing in my own mind, that arts of some kind were practised, at this period, to colour the hair ; but, whether it was done by tinging or dying it with liquids prepared for that purpose according to the ancient Eastern custom, or by powders of different hues cast into it agreeable to the modern practice, I shall not presume to determine. All that has been said upon the subject relates entirely to the men ; for, the hair of the Saxon ladies was so effectually concealed by the coverchief, or veil, that we have not a fair opportunity of forming our judgment concerning them. It is probable, however, that the same kind of arts were adopted by them, and for the same purpose ; for, the only female figure that I recollect, represented with her hair dishevelled, is Eve, in the Saxon manuscript of the Pentateuch so often referred to ; and her hair is painted blue.[2]

Crowns and Diadems. These ornaments are frequently enough to be met with in the manuscript paintings of the Saxons ; and, from the close of the seventh century, we may be able to ascertain their form with some degree of accuracy ; but we have no source of information previous to that period, except we refer to the coins of the Saxon monarchs, the workmanship of which is so exceedingly rude, and the lines in many instances so undetermined, that it is hardly possible to distinguish the ornament of the head from the hair itself. Ethelbert, the fifth king of Kent, is thought to have been the first Saxon prince that coined money.[3] His profile, executed in a very unskilful manner, appears upon his coins. In these one may trace the faint resemblance of a *fillet*, or *tiara*,[4] upon his head, fastened on the hinder part, where the two ends of it are plainly to be discovered. Something like a garland or crown of laurels decorates the head of Cuthred, king of Kent, upon his coins ; but a diadem, embellished with jewels, is seen upon the coins of Offa the Great. A radiated diadem, or crown, which was fastened at the back part of the head by a fillet or ribband, appears upon the head of Egbert the Great ; and on the coins of

[1] Page 10. [2] This figure is more fully described, p. 19.

[3] He reigned from A. D. 568, to A. D. 616. [4] The Saxon word ꞇýꞃ signifies a *tiara*.

Ludican, the eighteenth king of Mercia, a diadem of the same kind without the ribband, but adorned with jewels. The first representation of what may properly be called a crown I met with upon a coin of Ædred, the son of Edward the elder ;[1] it is a circle of gold surmounted with three small globes, without any indication of farther embellishment.[2] That the crown, however, was a regal ornament among the Saxons for two centuries at least prior to the time of Ædred, the ancient manuscript drawings bear sufficient testimony; as the reader may see by referring to the third plate of this work. The crown appears with some small variation, and embellished with jewels, in the ninth century, as may be seen upon the seventeenth plate ; and two specimens more of its form are given upon the twenty-ninth plate; which are all the material variations I have met with in the Saxon drawings. The Diadem, or *circle of gold*,[3] was worn occasionally by the Saxon monarchs after the introduction of the crown ; an example of which is given upon the eighth plate : it was worn also by princes and noblemen of very high rank, and that even in the presence of the king. In an old Saxon poem, written in celebration of the victory obtained by Æthelstan and his brother Edmund over Anlaf the Dane, and Constantine king of Scotland, at Brunanburh, Edmund is said to have worn a *long tiara*,[4] which, I presume, was meant to express the diadem, or golden circle ; besides the diadem given upon the eighth plate, the reader will find two more upon the twenty-ninth plate, one of which appears to be studded with jewels.

The Head-tire. We are altogether at a loss respecting this ornamental part of the ladies' head-dress, because it never appears in the drawings of the Saxons, being at all times completely hid by the coverchief, or veil ; but head-tires, or half circles of gold, were certainly used by the fair sex at a very early period of the Saxon æra, because mention is frequently made of such ornaments in the ancient wills and charters.[5] We may, however, I doubt not, very justly conclude that the head-tires, which occur in the ancient Norman drawings, were ornaments of the same kind : they appear to have been only half circles rising up in the front, and were probably fastened on the hinder part of the head with a fillet or ribband. The most ancient specimen of the half circle of gold, that I have met with, is given upon the thirty-

1 He reigned from A. D. 946, to A. D. 955. These observations are made from a very perfect coin of this monarch in the possession of Mr. Thane.

2 Cẏne-bænd, the *king's diadem*, seems to be the proper Saxon word for the crown.

3 heaꝼoꝺ-beᵹh *head-bracelet*, and ᵹeheaꝼoꝺ-ꞃinᵹe *head-ring*, are the Saxon names for the diadem.

4 Lanᵹne-ꞇẏꞃ.

5 This ornament is called in Saxon healꝼne bænꝺ ᵹẏlꝺenne. See p. 19.

eighth plate: the reader is referred to the middle figure holding a child in her arms.[1]

Fillets or *hair-bandages*,[2] *hair-needles* or *bodkins*,[3] and a *diadem* or circle of gold for the top of the head,[4] are all enumerated among the ornaments belonging to the Saxon ladies.

EAR-RINGS.[5] The names only of these ornaments occur in the Saxon records; but, as they are spoken of without the least indication of novelty, we may conclude that they formed part of the ancient head-dress. The ear-rings, like the head-tires, are always so completely concealed by the coverchief, that the form of them cannot by any means be ascertained.

The GIRDLE, or BELT, formed an indispensable part of the Saxon habit; and it was equally common to both sexes: it was bound about the waist; and frequently with the men answered a double purpose, that of confining the tunic, and of supporting the sword. In other instances, however, the sword was supported on the left side by a second belt, which passed over the right shoulder, and crossed the body both before and behind.

The girdles which belonged to the ladies of high rank were usually enriched with embroideries, and set with precious stones; nor were those belonging to the kings and noblemen less costly. The girdle of Charlemagne was composed of gold or of silver;[6] others are spoken of as studded with gold;[7] and others again as adorned with jewels.[8] The sword, with the embroidered or studded girdle, is represented at the bottom of the twenty-ninth plate.

POUCHES. There is not the least appearance of pockets belonging to the garments of the Saxons; though certainly some contrivance of the pouch or purse kind must have been in use among them; for, it is hardly possible to conceive that they could have dispensed with them entirely; accordingly, we find mention in the

[1] The MS. from which this figure is extracted, was written at the conclusion of the eleventh, or early in the beginning of the twelfth, century. It is preserved in the Cotton Library at the British Museum, and marked Caligula, A. xiv. [I take this figure to be Anglo-*Norman*.—ED.]

[2] *Redimicula vittæ*. Aurelii Prudentii Psycomachia, in MS.

[3] hæꞃ-næꝺl *crinalis acus*, in MS.

[4] *Verticis aurum*, in MS.

[5] Eꞃ-ꞃınᵹ, or eꞃıunᵹ.

[6] See p. 30.

[7] *Baltheus bullifer*, or *studded belt*, is mentioned by Aldhelm, Lib. de Virginitate; which book was written at the conclusion of the seventh century.

[8] When Ælfred knighted his grandson Æthelstan, he girded a girdle ornamented with jewels upon his loins, with a Saxon sword in a sheath of gold—*gemmato baltheo, ense Saxonico cum vaginâ aureâ.* Will. Malmesb. de gest. Reg. Ang. Lib. 2. Cap. VI.

old authors of leather bags or purses, and purses for money.[1] They were probably worn under the garments, for I never found anything in the least analogous to them in the Saxon drawings. In the description of the burial of Charlemagne, the gilt travelling pouch, which he used to bear when he went to Rome, is particularly mentioned; but the size or form of it is not ascertained.[2]

Bracelets. These ornamental parts of the Saxon habit were of two kinds, the bracelets for the arms, and the bracelets for the neck:[3] the first were common to both sexes; but the latter were appropriated chiefly, if not entirely, to the service of the ladies. In the early part of the Saxon æra, the wearing of bracelets appears to have been confined to persons of distinction; and, when made of gold, were considered as proper presents for the sovereign or his consort; and accordingly at times bequeathed to them in the wills of the wealthy. They were also frequently bestowed as badges of high honour upon the civil and military officers of the state by kings and princes of the blood royal; for which reason they are called, in the poems of that age, the "*bracelet-givers.*"[4] In the succeeding centuries, the fashion of wearing bracelets became more extensive; and it was afterwards adopted by the inferior classes of the people.

The clergy inveighed against the useless luxury of these adornments; and William of Malmesbury, speaking of the vices generally prevalent among the English at the time of the Conquest, adds to the number that of "loading of their arms with bracelets of gold."[5]

The bracelets of both sorts were probably made of a variety of materials, according to the fancy or wealth of the wearer; but those that are particularised by the Saxon authors are said to have been made of gold; and were, at times, so heavy as to become exceedingly cumbersome. An arm-bracelet, mentioned in the testament of a Saxon nobleman,[6] weighed one hundred and eighty mancuses of gold, or about twenty ounces Troy-weight; another, bequeathed to the queen, thirty mancuses of gold, or about three ounces and a half; and a neck-bracelet forty

[1] Leþeꞃ coꝺꝺaꞅ a *leathern purse*, Sceaꞇ-coꝺ a *money purse*. [2] See page 65.

[3] The Saxon words beaᵹ, beah, beh and bıᵹ signify a *bracelet;* and, when they stand by themselves, a *bracelet for the arm:* if the word ꞅpeoꞃ, or ꞅpuꞃ, which is the *neck*, be added, the signification of course is a *neck-bracelet*. healꞅ mæᵹeð is another name for the *neck-bracelet*. The Latin names chiefly used are *armilla, monile,* and *torques.*

[4] Æþelꞅꞇan cẏnınᵹ eoꞃla ꝺꞃıhꞇen beoꞃna beah ᵹẏꝼa, *Æthelstan the King, Lord of Earls, the child of the bracelet-giver*. Chron. Sax. sub an. 938.

[5] *Armillis aureis brachia onerati.* Guil. Malmesb. de gest. Reg. Angl. lib. III. page 57.

[6] Testamentum Byrhtrici et Ælfswythæ uxoris ejus. Hickesii. Dissert. p. 51; and the appendix to Lye's Saxon and Latin Lexicon.

mancuses of gold, or nearly five ounces. The bracelets of gold upon the arms of the soldiers, belonging to a magnificent galley which was presented by earl Godwin to Hardicnut, weighed eight ounces each.[1]

RINGS for the fingers were in common use among the Anglo-Saxons at a very early period.[2] In their form they differed but little from those of the present day. The *signet*, or seal-ring, as it occurs in a manuscript of the tenth century, is given upon the twenty-ninth plate.[3] Rings are rarely represented in the Saxon drawings, so that we cannot determine clearly upon which of the fingers they were worn, or whether upon more than one finger at once: we are equally at a loss to know if these ornaments were confined to one hand, or indiscriminately worn upon both: the *gold-finger*,[4] or ring-finger, is spoken of by the Saxon authors. In a manuscript of the tenth century[5] a drawing occurs, in which the servant of Judah is represented as bringing to him the staff, the bracelet, and the ring, which he had left as pledges with Tamar his daughter-in-law; the servant wears the bracelet upon his right arm, and the ring upon the third finger of the left hand, which, it is highly probable, was its proper situation.[6] Rings were common to both sexes, and, I trust, by no means confined to the nobility; they were also made of various metals, and frequently adorned with engravings and chasings agreeable to the taste of the times.

SPURS. It is not possible to ascertain the time that spurs were first introduced among our Saxon ancestors: they appear in the earliest drawings of their Horsemen; and were, I doubt, not of much higher antiquity than any of their manuscripts now existing.

Certain it is, that the rowel at the end of the spur was totally unknown to them, excepting which the general form of the Saxon spur differed but little from the spur in present use; and it was fastened upon the foot by a leathern thong[7] much in the same manner: instead of the rowel, the hinder part of the spurs were lengthened to a sharp point,[8] in the manner they are represented upon the feet of the middle figure in the thirteenth plate; and this form is not materially varied in any of the Saxon drawings.

1 Malmesb. lib. II. c. 12; and Simon Dunelmensis, de gest. Reg. Aug. sub an. 1040.

2 hpinc, hpinʒ, and hpincʒ, are the proper Saxon names for the *ring*.

3 See fig. 15. 4 ʒolð-ꝼýnʒeꝛ. 5 Claudius, B. IV. British Museum.

6 The whole of this drawing is copied upon plate XV. of the hoꝛða Anʒel-cýnnan, or Manners and Customs of the English, vol. I.

7 Called in the Saxon ꞅpuꝛ-leðeꝛa.

8 And this point was called in Saxon the ꞅpuꝛ-ꞅpeꝛe, or *spur-spear*.

Spurs, answering to the above description, have been found in different parts of England: such as have fallen under my examination were made either of iron or of brass; though it is probable they might occasionally have been constructed of more precious metals. The spurs, however, of Bernard king of Italy, grandson to Charlemagne, are expressly said to have been made of brass.[1]

[1] Joan. Puricello in Mon. Basil. Ambrosianæ, p. 70.

CHAP. VIII.

GENERAL OBSERVATIONS.—THE VARIOUS MANNERS IN WHICH THE ANGLO-SAXON MONARCH IS DEPICTED.—THE APPEARANCE OF THE ANGLO-SAXONS WHEN ABROAD, AND IN THEIR RURAL EXERCISES.—THE MANNER IN WHICH THEIR BATTLES ARE REPRESENTED.—THEIR STANDARDS.—THEIR APPEARANCE ON HORSEBACK.—THE MANNER IN WHICH THE LADIES RODE ON HORSEBACK.—GENERAL APPEARANCE OF THE LADIES.—DOMESTIC AND STATE HABITS.

WHEN the king is represented in his robes of state, and seated upon his throne, he generally holds a sceptre in his left hand. When he has no sceptre, the place of it is usually supplied by a sword; but in some few instances he is drawn without either the sceptre or the sword; and on the other hand, when he is represented in a judicial character, he has both of them, the sceptre in the left hand, and the sword in the right. When the sword is not held by the king himself, we constantly find it borne by an officer of the court upon his shoulder; and the officer stands at the king's left hand.

The sceptre, in the early manuscripts, has the appearance of a long staff surmounted with a round knob, as in the third plate of this work; or a sort of ornament resembling a fleur de lis: in other instances it is shorter: see the seventeenth plate. In a manuscript of the tenth century, where Pharaoh is represented receiving Jacob in a friendly manner, his sceptre is surmounted with a dove.[1]

The martial habit of the monarch has been already described; but, when he is supposed to be abroad, and not depicted in armour, he is constantly represented in the short mantle and tunic; and, saving the crown upon his head, which is always given him for distinction-sake, his habit differs no way from the military habits of the officers specified in a former chapter.

The men, when they are represented walking or engaged in any rural exercises, constantly appear in the short tunic; to this in general is added the smaller kind of mantle which left one arm at perfect liberty. They are, at times, depicted without the mantle, especially when they are supposed to be in the field of battle; they are often represented, within their houses, and at the king's court, with hats or bonnets on; and as often abroad without any covering for their heads. The

[1] Cotton Claudius, B. IV. See the hoꞃꝺa Anᵹel-cẏnnan, vol. I.

sword, or the spear, they seldom left behind them when they went abroad; they are frequently seen with both; and in warlike excursions the shield is also to be added.

Religious subjects in general engaged the pencils of the Anglo-Saxon artists. The representations of battles of course were seldom attempted: the few that do occur are rudely enough depicted; and the soldiers on both sides are exhibited in perfect confusion, fighting hand to hand, as if every man was individually engaged for himself, without the least consideration of his being under the conduct of a leader.

The Saxon standards were small, and their form in general was nearly square;[1] they seem to have been made of some inflexible material, which was fastened at the top of the pole in such a manner as to turn with the wind. It is remarkable that the standard is not to be found in the most ancient Saxon manuscripts, though there is good reason to think that the use of it was of high antiquity. John Brompton speaks of the Saxon standards as painted, or perhaps, rather embroidered, with gold;[2] and the same author expressly tells us, that the standard of Cuthred, king of the West Saxons, was a golden dragon.[3] The standard of Harold the Second had upon it the representation of a man fighting, sumptuously interwoven with gold and precious stones.[4]

The Anglo-Saxon horsemen are almost constantly depicted with the short tunic, and the small mantle which covered one shoulder only; they usually have a spear, and sometimes a shield; but rarely a sword. The form of the bridle, and the trappings of the horses, differed little from those of the present day, the saddle excepted, which was hollow in the middle where the man sat, and elevated before and behind. The Saxons constantly rode with stirrups depending by straps of leather from the saddle, in every respect resembling those in common use at this time.

It has been asserted that the English women, prior to the fourteenth century, rode on horseback astride like the men. This is an error, however, which appears to have originated among the modern historians; for, the testimony of antiquity abundantly proves the contrary. The Saxon and the Norman women, whenever

[1] I remember only one or two instances where the Saxon standard is depicted otherwise; which may be seen in the first volume of the hoɲꝺa Anᵹel-cẏnnan, or, Manners and Customs of the English.

[2] "*Vexillis auro resplendentibus depictas.*" Chron. J. Brompton, part III.

[3] *Draconem aureum.* Ibid.

[4] *Vexillum—in quod erat hominis pugnantis figura auro et lapidibus ante sumptuosá contexta.* W. Malmesb. de gest. Reg. Angl. lib. II.

they are represented on horseback, are seated sideways upon the horse, agreeable to the present custom.

Both at home and abroad the women are frequently depicted without the mantle, but never without the coverchief, or veil, which, in some instances, is loose, and then the wearer appears to be walking; the sleeves of the tunic, which the ladies wore when they were travelling from place to place, were long enough to cover the hands entirely, and supplied the want of gloves; which part of dress does not appear to have been adopted by the women of this country for several centuries, posterior to the æra we are now treating of.

To the list of ornaments belonging to the dress of the Anglo-Saxon ladies, given in the foregoing chapter, may with great propriety be added the article of *beads*. They do not appear, it is true, in the Saxon manuscript paintings; but there is every reason to suppose that they constituted part of the paraphernalia of females of ancient times, because they are frequently found in the places of their interment,[1] and were probably worn by them about the neck according to the modern practice.

Superior personages of both sexes, when represented in their own dwellings, and especially when they are seated, are usually depicted in their full dresses: the servants and common attendants are drawn without mantles; and the male servants constantly with the short tunic, frequently bare-footed, and rarely with any covering for the head.

We now close the description of the Saxon dresses, which we have traced through nearly four centuries; and I doubt not but the reader will, upon the perusal of the foregoing pages, be convinced that the assertion which is made at the head of the work, concerning the skill of the Anglo-Saxons in the clothing arts, is fully justified by the authorities produced in their favour. I have dwelt the longer upon this important subject, because so little notice has been taken of the Saxons by our best authors: on the contrary, they have passed over the history of this extraordinary people with unjustifiable haste, as if there was nothing remaining of their manners and customs worthy the perusal of a modern reader, the contrary of which is manifestly the case. Their habits, as we have seen, were more simple and less varied than those of the succeeding æras; and the alterations which were made in their dress, under the government of the Normans, justly forms a new epocha in the history of Great Britain.

[1] See the Nænia Britannica, by the Rev. J. Douglas.

END OF THE ANGLO-SAXON ÆRA.

PART III.

THE CIVIL, MILITARY, AND ECCLESIASTICAL, HABITS OF THE ANGLO-NORMANS, FROM THE ACCESSION OF WILLIAM THE FIRST TO THE THRONE OF ENGLAND, TO THE CONCLUSION OF THE TWELFTH CENTURY.

CHAP. I.

THE MANNERS AND DRESSES OF THE SAXONS CHANGED BY THE NORMANS.—A BRIEF REVIEW OF THE CLOTHING MATERIALS.—THE PROGRESS OF THE CLOTHING ARTS.—LAWS RELATIVE TO THE MANUFACTURING OF CLOTH, &c.

THE total subversion of the Saxon government, which followed soon after the establishment of the Normans in England, would not in all probability have been so easily effected, had it not been facilitated by the innovations previously introduced by Edward, surnamed the Confessor. During the long residence of that prince in Normandy, he imbibed a strong partiality for the dress and manners of the Normans; and upon his accession to the throne of England he continued to adhere to them: his example was followed by the nobility; and, as the fashions of the great are usually adopted by those of inferior degree, the people may be said to have been in some measure Normanized, if I may be allowed the expression, before the Conquest. William the Norman, however, and his successors, taking the advantage of those innovations which the love of novelty had voluntarily produced, by the cruel exertion of tyrannical policy, abolished the ancient customs of the country, and completed the introduction of their own; so that under the government of the Normans not only the dress and manners, but the laws, and even the language of our Saxon ancestors, were entirely changed.

It does not appear that any new materials for clothing were introduced by the Normans at the time of their first establishment in Britain. The fact, I trust, is they had none that were unknown to the Saxons; and, generally speaking, the best existing were the produce of this island. Linen formed the body-garments both of the Saxons and of the Normans; and woollen cloth the external parts of their habits. The hair of animals was certainly manufactured into cloth in this country previous to the Conquest; and, in some instances, worn by way of severe penance as a garment.

We have already seen that furs of various kinds were known to the Saxons: it must, however, be acknowledged that they were brought into more general use by the Normans.

The shoes, and other parts of the Saxon dress, were occasionally made of leather; but how far it constituted the body-garment of that people cannot easily be ascertained. Tunics and mantles of leather were worn by the Norman rustics, as appears by the manuscripts of the twelfth century: the skins of which they were composed were dressed with the hair upon them, and the shaggy part turned outward. Shepherds are often depicted with garments of this kind. The leathern mantle appears also to have formed part of the habit of the early Pilgrims.[1]

Silk was much more generally used in England after the Conquest, than it had been previous to that event. It was purchased by the Norman prelates, not only for their own garments, but for the adornment of their churches;[2] neither was it confined to the church and the clergy; but it was worn also by kings, queens, princes, and other personages of high rank, especially upon solemn occasions.[3] There is not, however, the least reason to suppose, that silk was manufactured in England at this period: it was probably imported from Spain, Sicily, Majorca, and other countries.

It has been sufficiently proved in the former part of this work, that the clothing arts were carried to no small degree of perfection by the Anglo-Saxons:— it will also appear by the following pages, that these arts were not by any means impaired, but rather improved, by the Norman Conquest; and this circumstance was chiefly owing, I presume, to the great number of weavers who came over from Flanders in the army of the Conqueror, and settled in this kingdom; for, even at that remote period, the Flemings were so famous for their skill in the manufacturing wool, that one of our ancient authors says, "the art of weaving seemed to be a peculiar gift bestowed upon them by nature."[4] After their settlement in England,

[1] See plate XLIX.

[2] Anglia Sacra, vol II. p. 416. and 421; W. Malmesb.—Hist. Cænobii Burg. a Jos. Sparke. edit. p. 100, &c.

[3] Maddox, Hist. Excheq.

[4] Gervas. Chron. page 1349.

where they found the most excellent materials for their manufactures, they pursued their original occupations with great advantage to themselves and to the kingdom. The body of clothiers who came over with the Conqueror, were increased by several considerable emigrations from Flanders into this country; particularly in the reigns of Henry the First, and of Stephen.[1]

For the farther improvement of the clothing arts, the weavers in all the principal towns in England were formed into gilds, or corporations; they had also several extensive privileges granted to them, for which they paid certain sums of money into the Exchequer. In the fifth year of the reign of Stephen, the weavers of Oxford paid a mark of gold for their gild; in the twelfth year of the same reign, those of Winchester fined two *chaseures*, or hounds, for the same purpose; and, in the fifteenth, those of London sixteen pounds. In the twelfth year of Henry the Second, the weavers of Winchester paid one mark of gold as a gresome, and two marks, as their annual rate; for the rights of gild and the privilege of choosing their own aldermen. In the same year, the Fullers of the same city, who had formed another corporation, paid six pounds for their gild.[2]

In the reign of Richard the First, it was enacted that all woollen cloths should every where be made of the same breadth, namely, two ells within the lists, and of the same goodness in the middle as at the sides; and that no merchant should stretch before his shop or booth,[3] a red or black cloth, or any other thing by which the sight of the buyers might be deceived in the choice of good commodities: it was also enacted, that the ell measure should be of the same length throughout the kingdom, and that it should be made of iron: by the same law the merchants were forbidden to vend cloth of any other colour than black in any part of the kingdom, excepting in cities and capital burghs; and that in all cities and burghs four or six men, according to the size of the place, should be appointed to enforce the observations of these regulations by seizing the persons and goods of all that should transgress.[4]

These laws were strictly adhered to till the reign of John, when the merchants and manufacturers purchased licences to make their cloth as broad or as narrow as they pleased; and this indulgence was productive of great sums, which were paid into the Exchequer.[5]

The ancient historians of this country say nothing respecting the art of bleach-

[1] J. Brompton, Chron. page 1003. Gervas. ut suprà.

[2] Maddox, History of the Exchequer, chap. XIII. sec. 3. p. 323.

[3] *Seldæ suæ.* Mat. Paris.

[4] Hovenden. Annal. p. 440, col. 2. Matthew Paris has it, *corpus illius capiatur, et in carcerem detrudatur, &c.* Hist. Angl. p. 191.

[5] Hovedon, p. 467, col. 2.

ing of linen cloth: their silence upon this head cannot, I presume, be construed into a positive proof that this art was unknown to the Saxons and the Normans, especially when we recollect, that fine white linen is frequently mentioned by them. With respect to the fuller's art, we have ample proof that it was very extensive in the time of the Normans, as far back as the twelfth year of Henry the Second: the fullers of the city of Winchester, as we have seen above, formed themselves into a corporation, and paid a large sum of money for their gild.

The dyer's art was carried to a great degree of perfection in the Saxon æra, if the testimony of their manuscript-paintings are to be credited; and history itself will abundantly support this opinion respecting the succeeding centuries.

The tanner's, the furrier's, the goldsmith's, and the jeweller's arts, so far as they relate to dress, will appear to have been practised with great success by the Normans; and, so far as one can judge from record, with no less honour than profit.

CHAP. II.

THE HABITS OF THE MEN GENERALLY CONSIDERED.—THE INTERIOR PARTS OF THEIR DRESS NOT CHANGED.—THE TUNICS; THE SUPER-TUNIC;—THE GOWN.—THE MANTLE.—THE COVERINGS FOR THE HEAD, AND HEAD-DRESS.—THE GLOVES.—THE STOCKINGS.—THE BOOTS.—THE SHOES.—THE GIRDLES.—THE APRONS, &C. OF THE ANGLO-NORMANS.

THE Normans and the Flemings, who accompanied the Conqueror into England, and those who followed him in great numbers after his establishment upon the throne, are said by our early historians to have been remarkable for the beauty and elegance of their persons, and not less so, for their ostentation and love of finery. Personal decorations, we are assured, formed an essential part of their study; and new fashions of course were continually introduced by them.[1] How far the people of England at large departed from the simplicity of their ancestors during the government of the elder William cannot be perfectly ascertained: we may easily enough conceive that the Norman habits were adopted by the greater part of the nobility, and especially by those who attended upon his person, or frequented his court.

The reign of his son and successor William Rufus is stigmatised by the writers of that period for many shameful abuses and ridiculous innovations, which were then made in the dresses of the people. The *mania* was caught from the court, where Rufus himself first set the example, and it extended rapidly through the whole kingdom; the clergy, as well as the laity, were infected with the malignant influence; and their fondness for novelty, not to say absurdity, is equally reprobated by the Monkish writers;[2] but nothing seems to have attracted their censure so generally as the sharp pointed shoes then introduced, and the preposterous length to which the men permitted their hair to grow—so that, says Malmesbury, "they resembled women rather than men." He adds farther, that "they also adopted a mincing gait and loose dresses, and seemed to pride themselves in the effeminacy of their appearance."[3]

[1] Malmesb. lib. V. p. 98. Hen. Hunt. p. 222. [2] Malmesb. lib. IV. p, 72.

[3] Tunc fluxus crinium, tunc luxus vestium, tunc mollitia corporis certare cum fæminis, gressum frangere, gestu soluto, &c.—Malmesb. de gest. Reg. Anglorum, lib IV. cap. I. page 69; and, in another part, criniti nostri, obliti quid nati sunt, in mulieribus sexûs habitum capillorum longitudine seipsos transformant. Hist. Novel. page 66.

These enormous vices (for as such they are considered by the ancient writers) were so generally adopted by the churchmen and the laity, and so powerfully supported by the court, that all the endeavours of the more serious part of the clergy to suppress them in the life-time of Rufus were exerted in vain. They met, however, with a temporary restraint during the reign of Henry the First, who, after the death of Rufus, ascended the throne of England. This judicious monarch discountenanced the ridiculous modes of dress which were prevalent among the people; and by a proper example in his own person, to which were added several sumptuary edicts, brought the fashions to a more reasonable standard.[1] In the succeeding reigns, these restrictions were by degrees obliterated, the love of pomp again predominated, and the same extravagances, reprobated so strongly by Malmesbury, became the subject of complaint to the future historians.[2]

The *shirt* and the *drawers*, to which we may add the *coxalia*, or *trowsers*,[3] do not appear to have undergone the least material alteration during the early part of the Anglo-Norman æra; and, as they have been so fully described in the former part of this work, there is not the least occasion for enlargement in the present place: I shall only add, that the trowsers, posterior to the Conquest, ceased to form a part of the gentleman's habit, and were confined to the rustics and lower classes of the people; indeed, I believe, that they were the only interior garment that the Norman rustics wore beneath the tunic; for I do not find any just reason to conclude that shirts formed any part of their dress. Whenever they are drawn without the tunic, from the waist upwards they appear to be quite naked.

The Anglo-Saxons, as we have seen in the former part of this work, had two sorts of tunics, which were distinguished from each other by their length; both of these garments were in common use among the Normans, and without any great variation being made in the general form of either.

The Short Tunic of the Normans, as we find it usually represented in their manuscript delineations, was somewhat longer than that of the Saxons; and in the twelfth century it reached to the middle of the legs: at the same time it was also richly adorned with broad borders and collars, superbly ornamented with embroideries of gold, and of silver; to which were even added the embellishment of precious stones. It will easily be conceived, that these remarks refer only to the garments of the nobility and personages of distinction. The tunics of the

[1] Orderici Vitalis Eccl. Hist. [2] Ibid.

[3] Perhaps the modern word *pantaloons* may be thought preferable to *trowsers*. [The Norman name was "*chaussees*."—Ed.]

Norman rustics and slaves do not appear to have differed in the least from those of the Saxons.

The LONG TUNIC was a garment never worn by the lower order of people, though I have observed, that, under the government of the Normans, it appears to have been more generally adopted by persons of rank than at any period prior to the conquest. This garment was also lengthened by the Normans; for which innovation, among others of like kind, they are accused of effeminacy, and severely censured by the historians of the time. It is perfectly unnecessary, I presume, to enter into a particular description of the long tunic, after what has been said upon this subject;[1] the reader, without doubt, will form a clear idea of its form and embellishments from the representations referred to in the margin.[2] The Norman monarchs and the nobility frequently wore two of these garments at one time; and both of them were nearly of the same length:[3] the inner tunic was probably made of linen, and appears to be perfectly correspondent with the *interula*, mentioned by Orderic Vitalis as worn in his time, and which, he tells us, was so long, that it trailed upon the ground; its sleeves were also of length and breadth sufficient to cover the whole hand.[4] The association of the long tunic with the mantle that reached to the heels, according to Fitz Stephen, originated from Germany: we need not therefore wonder that it was a custom adopted by the ancient Saxons.[5]

At the conclusion of the eleventh, or at the commencement of the twelfth, century, the men as well as the women wore the sleeves of their tunics enormously long, which were often richly ornamented with broad embroidered borders; an instance of which may be seen upon the thirty-fourth plate: this ridiculous fashion does not however appear to have been of long continuance.

A Saxon nobleman, towards the conclusion of the eleventh century, presented to the abbey of Ely a tunic, which was composed of red and purple threads interwoven in the shape of rings, and surrounded on every part from the shoulders with embroideries of gold.[6] We may hence form some idea of the richness of this part of the Saxon and Norman habit.

1 Pages 5 and 6. 2 See plates XXXI. XXXII. XXXIII. XXXIV. XXXV. &c.

3 As may be seen, plates XXXIII. and XXXIV; which are early instances of this fact.

4 Orderic Vitalis, Eccl. Hist. lib. VIII page 682.

5 Tunicam et pallium, ab humeris more Alemannorum dependens, ad talos demissum, &c. Stephanide in vitâ S. T. Cantuariensis, p. 60.

6 Tunicam ex rubeâ et purpurâ per gyrum, et ab humeris aurifriso undique circumdatam. Hist. Eliensis, lib. II. cap. 31.

The short tunic of the Normans is represented at the bottom of the thirty-second plate.

THE SUPER-TUNIC, OR SURCOAT.

I AM by no means certain whether this garment ought to be considered as originating from the *surcoat* of the Saxons, spoken of in a former part of this work,[1] or given as a new one introduced by the Normans into this country. The reader will find a perfect representation of the Norman surcoat, as it appeared towards the close of the twelfth century, upon the forty-second plate of this work:[2] it is without sleeves, and, in this example, of equal length with the tunic; the sleeves of which, being of a different colour from the surcoat, are the only distinguishing marks of that garment. The figure referred to holds the gown, a part of dress that appears to have been purely Norman, in his hand; this garment was worn over the super-tunic, which it entirely concealed, as we see in the middle figure upon the same plate, where the skirts of the tunic are represented longer than the super-tunic, or the gown. I am inclined to think, that the super-tunic, or surcoat, was a garment chiefly, if not entirely, confined to the winter.

THE GOWN.

THIS garment was very commonly worn towards the conclusion of the twelfth century; though I do not recollect to have met with it in a much earlier period: it bears great resemblance to the tunic, but it was much looser; and the sleeves, which were long and large, appear to have been contrived in such a manner that the arms might either be inserted in them, or left at liberty,[3] as we see they are in the middle figure upon the forty-second plate: the gown had also a large hood belonging to it, which occasionally was drawn up over the head to defend it from the weather; at other times the hood was thrown back upon the shoulders, as we find it represented upon the same figure.

The gowns of the succeeding centuries, as we shall find hereafter, were made of various precious materials, and lined with furs: they then became marks of

[1] Page 6.

[2] See the figure to the left.

[3] The official gown of the chief magistrate of the city of London is made much in the same manner to this day.

distinction; but, how far they were so at this early period, I dare not take upon me to determine, they are painted, in the ancient manuscripts, of various colours; and it is abundantly evident, that they were not common among the lower classes of the people.

THE MANTLE, OR CLOAK.

THE Normans can lay no claim to the introduction of this garment into England: we have already seen that it formed a very material part of the Saxon dress; but, though it was neither invented nor introduced by the Normans, yet it underwent so many changes and innovations soon after their arrival, that, in several instances, it may be considered as a new kind of habit.

The regal mantles of the Normans, and those worn by the nobility, were not at all times of equal length: in some instances we meet with them so long that they would trail upon the ground;[1] in others they do not appear to have descended below the middle of the legs:[2] they are distinguished by the epithets of *larger* and *smaller* mantles in the writings of the ancient authors.[3] The Norman mantles, like those of the Saxons, were sometimes fastened upon the middle of the breast, and hung equally over both shoulders;[4] at other times they covered the left side only, and were fastened upon the right shoulder, leaving the whole of the right arm at perfect liberty; and, again, we meet with them thrown over both shoulders without any fastening at all.[5]

The hoods, which we frequently find added to the mantles, I take to be perfectly Norman: like the hoods of the gown mentioned in the preceding article, they were, as occasion required, drawn up over the head, or thrown back upon the shoulders; an example of the former we find in the figure elevating his right hand, upon the thirty-second plate of this work.

The hooded cloaks, or mantles, are usually represented sufficiently long and large, not only to cover the whole of the shoulders, but great part of the back also. The hooded mantle, was, I apprehend, chiefly worn for warmth; and, agreeable to this idea, we frequently find the rustics, in the paintings which

[1] See plates XXXII. XXXIV; and the figure of Henry II. plate XXXV.

[2] See plates XXXI. XXXII; and the figure of Henry I. plate XXXV.

[3] Pallia majora et minora.—Du Cange in voce *Pallium*.

[4] See plates XXXIII. XXXIV.

[5] See the middle figure, plate XXXI.

ornament the old Calendars, clad in these garments during the winter months; and particularly the shepherds, whose occupations required their attendance in the fields by night. The figure to the left, leaning upon his staff, in the thirtieth plate, is designed to represent a shepherd: in this instance, the hood is thrown back upon his shoulders; but, when it was drawn up, it covered the whole of the head except the face, as we see in the middle figure of the same plate, where it rises up in two points bearing some resemblance to horns: this figure is also in the manuscript intended for a shepherd.

The hooded mantles of the rustics were probably made of thick and warm materials, and not unfrequently of leather with the shaggy part of the skin turned outwards.

A cloak or mantle of the same kind, and probably of the same form, but made of richer materials, and frequently lined with furs, was worn by the Norman nobility of the twelfth century:[1] this garment was, I presume, the *capa*, or *cappa*, frequently mentioned by the Norman writers, if not the *reno*, or *rheno*, of Orderic Vitalis, and similar to the short mantle of Anjou, said to have been introduced by Henry the Second, who was from that circumstance surnamed *court* or *short mantle*. The following curious anecdote, recorded by Fitz Stephen, will, I doubt not, in some measure justify my opinion concerning the identity of the ancient *capa*, and the *hooded mantle:* "One day, as Henry the Second, and Thomas Becket, who was at that time his favourite and Chancellor of England, were riding through the streets of London in the depth of winter, the king saw a poor old man at a distance, clad in a mean and threadbare garment;[2] he pointed him out to the chancellor, saying, how poor, how feeble, and how naked that man is! would it not be a great act of charity to bestow upon him a thick and warm mantle?[3] Yes, certainly, replied the chancellor; and added, that it was highly honourable for a monarch to commiserate the sufferings of the miserable. In the mean time, they came up to the pauper; and the king, stopping his horse, requested to know whether he would not gladly accept of a new mantle. The poor wretch, perfectly ignorant that it was the king who spake to him, supposed the question to have been put to him merely as a joke, and returned no answer; the king, then, addressing himself to Becket, said, it is now in thy power to perform this great act

1 See plate XXXII, the figure with his right hand elevated.

2 Veste tritâ et tenui.—W. Stephanide in vitâ S. Tho. Cantuariensis, edit. à Sparkes, p. 16.

3 Crassam et calidam capam.—Ibid.

of charity; and laid hold upon the *hood*[1] of his mantle to take it from him; but, as it was quite new, made of the finest scarlet, and lined with furs,[2] the chancellor on his part endeavoured to retain it. At length, however, when he perceived the king to be in earnest, he permitted him, though reluctantly, to take the mantle, which he instantly gave to the poor old man. The contest between the king and the chancellor occasioned no small tumult among their attendants, who were at a distance behind; but, when they came up, the king related the circumstance to them, and they made themselves exceedingly merry at the expence of the chancellor, who had lost his hooded mantle; and the poor man departed full of joy, giving God thanks for his good fortune."

The Reno, or Rheno, was a garment made of the most precious furs; and, consequently, it could not have been purchased but by persons of great wealth. Orderic Vitalis, an ancient writer of good authority, places the *reno* among the royal habiliments,[3] and clearly distinguishes it from the *chlamis*, or *long mantle*; an ancient author cited by Du Cange, informs us, that the *reno* covered both the sides of the body and the shoulders; and another writer expressly says, that it descended as low as the navel:[4] it must, therefore, have been a garment as much calculated for warmth as for ornament, and probably appropriated to the winter only,—especially if it had a hood like the *capa*, which might occasionally be drawn up over the head.

The mantles, worn by the Norman monarchs and the principal nobility, were made of silk, of linen,[5] and of the finest cloths that could be procured, embroidered often with silver and with gold, and lined with the most costly furs: they were also in many instances ornamented with fringes, and decorated with pearls.[6]

We may form some idea of the richness of the mantles, used in the twelfth century, from the two following extracts: "Robert Bloet, second bishop of Lincoln, made a present to king Henry the First of a mantle[7] of exquisitely fine cloth,

[1] *Capicium.*—Ibid. [2] Capam—novam de scarlattâ et grysio, &c.—Ibid.

[3] Regalia ornamenta, chlamydem sericamque interulam, et *renonam* de preciosis pellibus perigrinorum murium.—Ord. Vital. Eccl. Hist. lib. IV. p. 535.

[4] Reno, vel rheno, pellicium vestis ex pellibus confecta, quæ humeros et latera tegebat; and afterwards, rheno est pellicium vel vestis facta ex pellibus pendensque ad umbilicum.—Du Cange, Gloss. in voce.

[5] Palleas lineas, serico coöpertas—Palleas lineas sine serico.—Ibid. in voce *Pallium.*

[6] Pallium unum cum friso et margaritis.—Ibid.

[7] Pallium peregrinis sabellinarum pellibus nigris admodum, atque interjectâ canitie respersis, et exquisitissimo panno consertum.—Anglia Sacra, Vol. II. p. 417

lined with black sables with white spots, which cost one hundred pounds of the money of that time;"[1] and, "Richard the First possessed a mantle still more splendid, and probably more expensive, which is said to have been striped in strait lines adorned with half-moons of solid silver, and nearly covered with shining orbs, in imitation of the system of the heavenly bodies."[2]

The mantle of the nobleman upon the thirty-second plate, is richly ornamented with an embroidered border of gold; and that of the monarch, on the thirty-fourth plate, is lined with furs, and appears to be the resemblance of a very costly garment.

Exclusive of the hoods connected with the gowns and mantles, the Normans had a variety of *coverings* for the *head;* and most of them, I believe, were included under the general name *pileus* by the authors of the twelfth and thirteenth centuries, who usually wrote in Latin. *Pileus* literally signifies a hat, a cap, or a bonnet; and it may be equally applicable to them all. Two examples are given upon the forty-second plate, in which the pileus resembles a modern nightcap. At the bottom of the same plate it appears in a different form: it is there tied beneath the chin, and may properly enough be called a *bonnet:* it is by no means unlike a cone, as we see it worn by the figure, to the right, upon the same plate; and, in some instances, it retained the form of the ancient Saxon hat,[3] while, in others, it bore no small resemblance to the round hat of the present day.

The *pileus,* or hat, was worn by the laity only; for, we find that it was prohibited to the clergy, and to the monks especially,—the capa or hooded cloak being the only covering for the head that they were permitted to wear; but upon this subject it will be necessary to speak more fully in a subsequent part of the work.

The Normans had also a cap, which does not seem to deserve the name of a hat, distinct from any of those above-mentioned: it fitted close to the head, and was tied under the chin; its use was principally to confine the hair; and it was worn by such persons as we find engaged in the sports of the chase, or rural exercises, and by messengers; to all of whom the hair, blowing about by the wind, would be exceedingly troublesome, especially when they were passing through the woods and

[1] Equal in value to £1500. of present money.

[2] Vinisaub.—Iter Hierosol. lib. II. cap. 36, p. 325.

[3] See plate LV.

forests.[1] In some instances this cap was worn by the light-armed military instead of the helmet; but I do not by any means conceive that this practice was universal.

The hats, or bonnets, it is said, were generally made of cloth:[2] those belonging to the lower class of people were probably made of leather, and perhaps of felt; for, felt hats certainly were in use among the Anglo-Saxons;[3] but the hats of the kings, the earls, and the barons, especially those that they wore at public solemnities, were made of the finest cloth, lined with most costly furs, and adorned with pearls and precious stones. The Jews at this period, it is said, were obliged to wear square caps, of a yellow colour, for distinction-sake.[4]

In speaking concerning the HEAD-DRESSES of the Anglo-Normans, I wish the expression to be understood in a limited sense, and to refer simply to the modes adopted by that people of adjusting the hair, exclusive of any extraneous ornaments or coverings for the head. It has been premised already, that the Saxons and the Danes considered the luxuriancy of their locks as an important personal adornment; nor were they easily prevailed upon to retrench them, though instigated thereto by the repeated admonitions of the clergy:[5] and in the beginning of the present chapter it was observed, that the Normans were equally tenacious of their hair, and prided themselves equally in the length and beauty of it.[6]

In the ostentatious reign of William Rufus, the men in general permitted their hair to grow to such an extravagant length, that they appeared like women; their flowing tresses they also curled and plaited with no small degree of attention, which excited the indignation of William the Monk of Malmesbury, as we have seen above:[7] that author severely reproached his countrymen for their effeminacy; nor was he by any means singular in the condemnation of this unmanly custom. Early in the reign of Henry the First, the successor of Rufus, a Norman bishop, whose name was Serlo, acquired great honour by a sermon preached before that monarch, in which he inveighed with great fervency against the popular vices of the time, and especially against the detestable fashion, as it was then called, of wearing long hair.[8] He concluded his discourse with a solemn address to the king, beseeching him to set

[1] See two examples of this cap, plate LIII; and a third, plate LII, where the figure kneeling is a messenger, with the badge or arms of his master hanging at his girdle.

[2] Dr. Henry, Hist. Brit. Vol. III.

[3] See page 38.

[4] Du Cange, Gloss. tom. VIII. p. 483.

[5] See pages 10. and 37.

[6] Page 86.

[7] Ibid.

[8] Omnes (says he) femineo more criniti estis, quod non decet vos, qui ad similitudinem Dei facti estis, et virili robore perfrui debetis. Viros quippe crinitos esse quàm incongruum et detestabile sit.—Orderic Vital. Eccl. Hist. lib. XI. p. 816.

an example to his subjects, that from him they might learn to dress themselves with decency:[1] the remonstrances of the orator had so great an effect upon the king and his courtiers, that they consented to part with their flowing locks; and the prudent prelate, not willing to give them an opportunity of changing their resolution, instantly drew out a pair of shears from his sleeve,[2] and performed the operation upon the major part of them with his own hand, beginning first with the sovereign himself: the king's attendants and the servants of his household followed his example, and, by virtue of a royal edict, the people in general were prevailed upon to curtail their hair; and those precious ringlets, adds my author, which formerly had been their pride, became the objects of their aversion, and were trodden under their feet.

The prevalency of fashion, however, cannot be easily overcome; for, though the prohibitory edicts of King Henry against the wearing of long hair produced a temporary reform: they certainly were not sufficiently coercive to eradicate from the minds of the people the predilection they had imbibed in its favour. In less than twenty-five years after the event above related, the cultivation of the hair was revived; and at that period[3] it received a temporary check from a circumstance which may appear to the modern world exceedingly trifling (the fact is recorded by Malmesbury, an historian of good authority; and he assures us, that it happened in his life-time:) "A young provincial soldier," says he, "who had very long and beautiful hair, dreamed that a person came to his bed-side, and strangled him with his own luxuriant ringlets; the vision was so strongly impressed upon his mind when he awoke in the morning, that he trimmed his locks to a decent length. His companions followed his example; and it became a second time a fashion throughout the kingdom to curtail the hair. But this reformation," adds the author, "was of very short duration; for, scarcely had one solitary year elapsed, before the people returned to their former wickedness; and such especially, as would be thought courtiers, permitted their hair to grow to a shameful length, so that they resembled women rather than men; and those, to whom nature had denied abundance of hair, supplied the deficiency by artificial coverings."[4]

Towards the conclusion of the twelfth century, the men curled their hair with *crisping-irons;* they also bound it up with *fillets,* or *ribbands;* and appeared abroad without *hats,* that the beauty of its adornments might not be concealed.[5] In the

[1] His words are rather remarkable—Unde, gloriose Rex, obsecro te, ut exemplum subjectis præbeas laudabile, et imprimis videant in te, qualitèr debeant præparare se.—Orderic Vital. Eccl. Hist. lib. XI.

[2] De manticâ forcipes extraxit.—Ibid.

[3] A. D. 1129.

[4] Et, ubi crines deficiunt, involucra quædam innodabant. Will. Malmesb. Hist. Novell. lib. I. p. 99.

[5] Crispant crines calamistro; caput velant vittâ, sine pileo, &c. Orderic Vitalis, lib. VIII. p. 682.

early drawings of the twelfth century, the appearance of the hair is by no means ungraceful: it is parted from the front of the forehead to the crown, and flows on both sides of the face upon the shoulders; but not of sufficient length to justify the severe reflections of the historians. Towards the conclusion of the same century, we find the hair more decorated with curls, and extended farther from the face, though not materially lengthened.

It is an opinion generally adopted by the modern historians, that the custom of shaving the beard, excepting only so much of it as grew upon the upper lip, was universally adopted by the Anglo-Saxons of the eleventh century; and that the Normans, at the time of the Conquest, shaved the beard entirely without any exception. The great seal of Edward the Confessor, where that monarch appears with a large beard, exclusive of the mustachoes, militates against the universality of the custom among the Saxons;[1] and the figure of William the Conqueror, upon his seal represented with a short beard and mustachoes, may be thought equally decisive respecting the Normans.[2] The assertion of Malmesbury upon this subject, which has been indiscriminately adopted by the succeeding authors, appears to me to have been taken in too general a point of view, and, perhaps, in both instances, ought to be restricted to the military: The spies of Harold, he tells us, were admitted into the Conqueror's camp; and, upon their return, declared that they had seen "an army of priests rather than soldiers, because their beards were shaved entirely, contrary to the usage of the Saxons, who permitted their mustachoes to grow upon the upper lip."[3] We can hardly credit that the spies were permitted to see the whole of the Norman army: it is more probable that they saw no more than the archers, who undoubtedly formed a large part of it, and might be shaved for the conveniency of drawing their bows in time of battle.[4] William the Conqueror compelled the Saxons to shave their beards entirely; but it is equally certain, that the

[1] See plate XXVII; and Malmesbury, describing the person of the Confessor, speaks of his *barbâ et capillis cygneus*, lib. II.

[2] In Speed's Chronicle, a representation of the great seal of the Conqueror is preserved, which has been copied for Sanford's Genealogy.

[3] Penè omnes in exercitu illo Presbyteros videri, quòd totam faciem cum utroque labro rasam haberent. Angli enim superius labrum pilis incessantèr fructicantibus intonsum dimittunt. Malmesb. de Gest. Reg. Anglorum, lib. III. p. 56, second column.

[4] [It was not merely the absence of mustachoes or beard that made the spies of Harold describe the Normans as an army of priests.—The words of Wace are "tous rez et tondus," and the Bayeux Tapestry with which this metrical chronicle exactly tallies, illustrates his words by exhibiting the Normans with the *backs* of their heads shaved, a Poitevan fashion which they had adopted, according to Glaber Rodolphus, and which naturally reminded the spies of the clerical tonsure.—Ed.]

edict was considered as a wanton act of cruelty,[1] and strenuously opposed by many who in other cases readily adopted the Norman fashions, and perhaps would not have refused obedience to this, had it really been one of them, and universally practised. The manuscript drawings of the Saxons, and those of the Normans coëval with the time alluded to, will abundantly prove, that the beard was regarded as a great personal ornament, both prior and posterior to the Conquest.

The mandate of the Conqueror appears to me to have been a contemptuous mark of distinction, and introduced by him for some political purpose, which indeed has not been properly explained by the writers of that æra: it was therefore justly considered by the people at large as an infringement upon their native liberties ; and that may well account for numbers of them leaving the kingdom, rather than comply with the disgraceful requisition. I do not, however, believe that the edict continued long in force, or that it was ever universally obeyed.

Early in the reign of Henry the First, it was customary with the English people to wear long beards ; at that period we find them reprobated by the clergy ;[2] but, when the king shortened his own hair and caused his beard to be shaved, we may rest assured that his courtiers followed his example ; and fashion, in process of time, reconciled the very custom which force had made so odious. Matthew Paris, it is true, and other historians inform us that, in the reign of Richard the First, a citizen of London, whose name was William, let his beard grow to a great length ; for which reason he received the cognomen *cum barbâ* ;[3] but this seems to have been done as an insult upon the monarch and his courtiers, who were all of them close shaved, rather than to set at defiance a law then existing, by which the wearing of beards was interdicted ; and, indeed, no such law is mentioned by the historians. This circumstance, however, seems to prove that beards were less worn at that period than they had been prior to it, or than they were in the succeeding century.

Gloves were by no means generally worn by the Normans during the eleventh and twelfth centuries ; on the contrary, they appear to have been confined to persons of the most exalted rank : they are mentioned as part of the regal habit of Henry the Second, when his body was laid in state after his decease ;[4] and we find them ornamented with jewels upon the hands of Richard the First, as his

[1] Mat. Paris, in vitâ Abb. Albani, p. 46.

[2] Serlo, in his sermon referred to above, page 94, says, in barbâ prolixâ hircis assimilantur ; and Orderic Vitalis compares the men of his time, because of their long beards, to "*stinking goats.*" Ord. Vit. Ecc. Hist. lib. VIII. p. 682 ; and lib XI. p. 815.

[3] Mat. Paris, in vitâ Ricardi Primi, &c.

[4] Ibid. p. 151.

portraiture is given from his monument by Montfaucon.[1] Archbishops, bishops, and other dignified clergy, are said to have used gloves; but, I apprehend, upon occasions of great solemnity, and more for ornament than for comfort or conveniency.

STOCKINGS, or rather *hose*, which appellation is most agreeable to the ancient idiom, formed a part of the Saxon habit; and of course have been introduced already to the reader.[2] It has been observed, that the hose of the Saxons were of two kinds; the one only covered the lower part of the legs from the bottom of the calf downwards, and the other extended beyond the skirts of the short tunic: both these kinds of hose were worn by the Normans, and without any great appearance of variation.

The stockings, worn by the Norman nobility, must have been a very expensive part of their habit, if we may be allowed to draw any inference from the example of William Rufus, who disdained to wear a pair of less value than a *mark*, which was nearly equal in value to ten pounds of the present money. His chamberlain, says Malmesbury, brought him one morning a new pair of stockings;[3] but, when he was told that they cost only three shillings, he was exceedingly angry,[4] and commanded the officer to purchase a pair for him worth a mark. The chamberlain, adds the historian, brought him a pair inferior in quality to the former, and declaring that they cost a mark, the king was perfectly satisfied with them.

The stockings of the twelfth century were probably made of cloth. In some instances, however, it is certain they were variegated with stripes.[5]

The leg-bandages, so frequently found in the Saxon delineations, are rarely to be met with in the drawings of the Normans: hence we may naturally conclude, that the use of them had in great measure subsided after the Conquest. The rustic, to the left, upon the thirtieth plate of this work, exhibits a very

[1] Monarchie Françoise, tom. II. [The effigy of Richard as well as those of the other English sovereigns at Fontevraud, are very incorrectly engraved in Montfaucon's book; a splendid and accurate print of the effigies will be found in Stothard's Sepulchral Monuments.—Ed.] Fitz Stephen particularly mentiones *gloves* as part of the pontifical habit of Thomas Becket at the time of his interment. Stephanide, in vitâ S. Tho. Cant. p. 89.

[2] Page 39. See also page 12.

[3] Novas caligas. Will. Malmesb. de Gest. Reg. Angl. lib. IV. cap. 1.

[4] I might have said abusive: the words of the historian are—indignabundus et fremens, fili, ait, meretricis! ex quo habet rex caligas tam exilis pretii? Vade, et asser mihi emptas marcâ argenti.—Ibid.

[5] See the middle figure, plate XXX; the figure to the left, plate XXXI; and the figure to the left, plate XXXII.

singular species of leg-bandages; something of the same kind, however, I have seen worn by the ploughmen of the present day, especially in wet weather: they are usually made of hay-bands, or of straw twisted like hay-bands, and wound round the legs from the ancles upwards.

Boots were much used by the Normans; for, they are frequently mentioned by the ancient historians: they do not appear to have been confined to any particular classes of people, but were worn by persons of all ranks and conditions, as well of the clergy as of the laity, especially when they rode on horseback. The boots, as they usually occur in the Norman drawings, are very short, rarely reaching higher than the middle of the legs.[1] In some instances, we meet with them enriched with embroidery.[2]

The soldiers also of the eleventh century are often depicted with short boots,[3] which were discontinued in the century immediately succeeding when the mail was fitted to the legs and covered them entirely, so that boots became useless.

We are assured by the early Norman historians, that the cognomen *Curtâ Ocreâ*, or *Short-boots*,[4] was given to Robert, the Conqueror's eldest son; but they are entirely silent respecting the reason for such an appellation being particularly applied to him. It could not have arisen from his having introduced the custom of wearing short boots into this country; for, they were certainly in use among the Saxons long before his birth: to hazard a conjecture of my own, I should rather say he was the first among the Normans that wore short boots, and derived the cognomen by way of contempt from his own countrymen, for having so far complied with the manners of the Anglo-Saxons. It was not long, however, supposing this to be the case, before his example was generally followed. The short boots of the Normans appear, at times, to fit quite close to the legs; in other instances they are represented more loose and open; and, though the materials of which they were composed are not particularised by the ancient writers, we may reasonably suppose them to have been made of leather; at least it is certain that about this time a sort of leather boots, called *Bazans*,[5] were in fashion; but, as these

[1] See the middle figure, plate XXX; and the figure to the left, plate XXXII.

[2] See the figure to the right, plate XXXI. [These are not boots but a sort of short stockings or socks worn *over* the chausses and *with* shoes.—Ed.]

[3] See plate XLIII.

[4] Some of the old English writers call him *curt-hose;* but Malmesbury names him Robelinus *Curtâ Ocreâ*, lib. V. p. 86.

[5] Ocreis de cute quam vulgus *bazan* appellant. Matt. Paris, in vitâ Guarini Abbat. p. 100.

appear to have been chiefly confined to the clergy, they will be more fully spoken of at a future period.

The *ocreæ restratæ*, or picked-pointed boots, were in general use in the reign of Rufus: they were, however, severely condemned by the writers of that age; and we find them strictly prohibited to the clergy.[1]

The Shoes.—Among the various innovations made in dress by the Normans during the twelfth century, none met with more marked and more deserved disapprobation than that of lengthening the toes of the shoes, and bringing them forward to a sharp point. In the reign of Rufus this custom was first introduced;[2] and, according to Orderic Vitalis, by a man who had distorted feet, in order to conceal the deformity; but, adds he, the fashion was no sooner broached, than all those who were fond of novelty thought proper to follow it; and the shoes were made by the shoemakers in the form of a scorpion's tail. These shoes were called *pigaciæ*, and adopted by persons of every class both rich and poor.[3] Soon after, a courtier, whose name was Robert,[4] improved upon the first idea by filling the vacant part of the shoe with tow, and twisting it round in the form of a ram's horn: this ridiculous fashion excited much admiration. It was followed by the greater part of the nobility: and the author, for his happy invention, was honoured with the cognomen *Cornardus*, or horned.[5] The long-pointed shoes were vehemently inveighed against by the clergy, and strictly forbidden to be worn by the religious orders. So far as one can judge from the illuminations of the twelfth century, the fashion of wearing long-pointed shoes did not long maintain its ground. It was, however, afterwards revived, and even carried to a more preposterous extent.

The *sotulares*, or *subtalares*, of the Saxons were certainly a species of slippers, distinct from the shoes commonly worn by that people;[6] but in the more modern times they appear to have been confounded with each other. Orderic Vitalis mentions shoes of Cordivan:[7] in general, I suppose, they were made of leather; and in some instances, we find them curiously ornamented.[8]

1 Matt. Paris, in vitâ Guarini Abbat. p. 175.

2 Tunc (that is, in the reign of Rufus) usus calceorum cum arcuatis aculeis inventus. Will. Malmesb. lib. IV. c. 1.

3 Unde sutores in calceamentis quasi caudas scorpionum, quas vulgò *pigacias* appellant, faciunt. Ord. Vit. Eccl Hist. lib. VIII. p. 682.

4 The author speaks of him with much contempt: Robertus quidam nebulo in curiâ Rufi Regis, &c. Ibid.

5 Ibid.

6 See p. 44.

7 Sotulares Corduanos, Eccl. Hist. lib. V. p. 596.

8 See the middle figure, plate XXXII.

The Girdles of the Normans differed little from those of the Saxons; especially during the twelfth century: they were probably formed of the same materials; and we are well assured, that such of them as belonged to the kings, earls, and great barons, were not only embroidered with gold, but also adorned with precious stones.

The Apron. I have little to say at present upon this part of the Norman habit. Towards the conclusion of the twelfth century we find the apron was in use; and probably it had been long before, though it does not occur in any drawings that I have seen prior to that period: the reader will find an accurate representation of the apron upon the fifty-first plate. It is fastened round the middle, and part of it passes over the shoulders, where it is attached under the hood like a stomacher.

CHAP. III.

THE HABITS OF THE NORMANS.—THE SURCOAT.—A NEW GARMENT.—THE ALTERATIONS MADE IN THE OTHER PARTS OF THE SAXON DRESS BY THE NORMAN LADIES.—THE UNDER-GARMENT.—THE GOWN.—THE SURCOAT.—THE GIRDLE.—THE MANTLE.—THE COVERCHIEF AND OTHER DECORATIONS FOR THE HEAD.—THE HAIR-DRESS.—THE STOCKINGS.—THE SHOES, &c.

I KNOW not well how to account for the inconsistency of the ancient Norman writers, who, at the time they are most severe in their censures upon the habits of the men,[1] pass over those of the women without any decided marks of disapprobation. Perhaps we ought to attribute their silence to their gallantry, and imitate so good an example by placing the foibles of the fair sex in obscurity. But, whatever motives restrained the pen of the historians upon so delicate a subject, the same impulse was not sufficiently efficacious with the illuminators of the twelfth century to prevent the pencil from explaining what the pen had concealed; and from this source of information it appears, to a demonstration, that the ladies had their share in the introductions of new fashions—fashions—dare I say it? equally preposterous, and equally ungraceful as those so severely condemned by the Monastic authors!

In the twelfth century we find only one garment that can at any rate be considered as additional to those of the Saxon ladies already described,[2] which is the *surcoat*. The gown, the mantle, and the coverchief, underwent great alterations during this period. It will, therefore, be best to speak of them separately, and point out how far they differed from the same parts of the Saxon dress: but previously it may be thought necessary to say a few words concerning the tunic, or, as I have called it before, the *under-garment*.

The UNDER-GARMENT was the only part of the Saxon habit that retained its general form throughout the whole of the twelfth century: in some few instances it appears rather longer in the Norman than in the Saxon Æra, and, in others, more richly ornamented with embroidered borders.[3]

The GOWN formed an indispensable part of the ladies' dress, posterior to the

[1] See the former chapter.

[2] Pages 13 and 46.—[Why should the surcoat be considered additional.—It was surely the same thing as the super-tunic for which the Norman name is a literal translation.—ED.]

[3] See the lady holding a sceptre, plate XL.

Conquest. It was worn by the Norman as well as the Saxon ladies immediately over the under-garment, or tunic; every part of which it frequently concealed, excepting the sleeves, which were generally longer than those of the gown, and reached to the wrist. At the time of the Conquest, it is probable that the gowns of the Norman women varied little in form from those that had been in use at the commencement of the eleventh century: the first material alteration, observable in this garment, is in its sleeves; and they appear in the drawings, towards the conclusion of the above mentioned century, more wide, more open, and more richly adorned with ornamental borders of embroidery, than we find them at the commencement of it.[1] The sleeves are represented still wider, and terminating in a kind of pocket, by the figure to the left, upon the thirty-sixth plate; and again by two figures upon the thirty-ninth plate, where it is to be observed, that the pursey parts of the sleeves, belonging to the figure on the right, are of a different colour from the gown, and seem to have been separate parts of the dress: this is, however, a singular instance of the kind. The *pocketing sleeves*, if I may be allowed the term, were carried to a preposterous length by the ladies of quality in the twelfth century, as we may see fully exemplified in the two figures upon the fortieth plate. These figures prove also that the pocketing sleeves did not exclusively belong to the gown. In the front figure they are evidently part of the surcoat; and in the same figure the gown is represented neatly embroidered, and much shorter than usual; while, on the contrary, the gown of the lady bowing her head is sufficiently long to trail upon the ground; and this fashion appears to have been almost universally adopted by the females of the succeeding century.

The SURCOAT.—If this garment did not originate from that part of the Saxon habit, distinguished in a former chapter by the appellation of the *summer dress*,[2] it certainly must be considered as purely Norman, and to this opinion I shall readily subscribe. The earliest representation of the Norman surcoat, that has occurred to me, is given upon the fortieth plate, where it appears extremely short; and the long pocketing sleeves, which in the opposite figure form part of the gown, in this instance certainly belong to the surcoat. We shall have occasion to speak more fully upon this subject hereafter; for, in the succeeding centuries the surcoat came into general use; and we often find it with a long train descending to the ground.

The *pocketing sleeves*, whether applied to the gown or to the surcoat, were certainly very ungraceful; and nothing but custom could reconcile so vitiated a taste. To the honour, however, of the ladies of this country, the fashion does not appear

[1] See plate XXXVI. [2] Page 16.

to have originated with them; for in a curious illuminated manuscript of the Gospels, which, from the writing and the style of the drawings, appears to have been made in Italy, and as early at least as the tenth century,[1] we meet with a figure of the Virgin Mary; and the sleeves of her gown correspond exactly with those of the lady bowing her head, upon the thirty-eighth plate. From Italy, it is probable, the fashion of wearing long sleeves was imported through France into Normandy, and brought by the Norman ladies into this country, where, in the profligate reign of Rufus, it appears at first to have taken root, and arrived at full maturity, towards the middle of the twelfth century; after which period, like most other fashions that have nothing more than novelty to recommend them, it died away. The ladies, as I observed above, escaped, it is true, the lash of historic censure; but their long sleeves, and the trains of their gowns and surcoats trailing upon the ground, were held up to ridicule by the illuminators of the twelfth century: a remarkable instance of this kind occurs upon the thirty-eighth plate. The figure to the left, which composes part of the ornamental border, is intended in the original manuscript to represent the Devil; and the artist has thought proper to dress his infernal majesty in a lady's surcoat, with one sleeve short and wide, and the other so enormously long, that it is absolutely necessary for it to be tied in a knot to prevent its trailing upon the ground. The surcoat itself is caricatured in a similar manner, insomuch that it would be impossible for the wearer to step forward, if the objection were not removed by the skirts being bound up in a knot to shorten them. Another curious circumstance attends the body-part of the surcoat, which in this instance, and singular indeed it is, resembles the *bodice*, or *stays*, of the more modern times: it is laced in the front from the top to the waist; and the lace itself, with the tag at the end of it, hangs carelessly down from the bottom of the interlacing. This fashion was certainly not common at the present period; and, from its being appropriated to the prince of darkness by the satyrical artist, we may naturally conclude, that in his day it was considered as indelicate or improper to be followed by the ladies.

The GIRDLE, which constantly formed part of the female dress among the Saxon ladies, appears in several instances to have been dispensed with by the Normans; or at least to have been worn beneath the outer garment: the girdles appropriated to queens, princesses, and other ladies of high rank, are spoken of as being richly adorned with gold, pearls, and precious stones. In this state, however, they do not appear in the drawings so early as the twelfth century. The girdles

[1] This MS. is preserved in the Harleian Library at the British Museum, and marked 2821.

belonging to the girls and young women unmarried seem to have been a simple cordon, which hangs down in the front: an example of which is given upon the forty-first plate.

The Mantle. This garment was subject to less change than any other of the external parts of the dress appertaining to the Saxon ladies before the Norman conquest: posterior to that event it was varied continually, not only respecting its length and its breadth, but also in its general form; so that we rarely find that it retained the same appearance for the space of half a century. It seems by the middle figure, upon the thirty-sixth plate, to have been of an oval form, and put over the head upon the shoulders; a perforation being made in it near the middle for that purpose. In the figure to the left, upon the same plate, it is simply thrown over both shoulders, and fastened upon the breast with an embroidered collar. A mantle nearly of the same kind is appropriated to the queen upon the thirty-seventh plate. The corners of the mantle are square in the figure to the right upon the fortieth plate. In the figure to the right, upon the forty-first plate, it appears to have been thrown over one shoulder only, so as to cover but one half of the body. In the middle figure of the same plate it is extended farther to the right shoulder, which, however, it does not cover; and it is fastened upon the breast by a double cordon: there is also a hood belonging to this mantle, which is thrown back in the present instance, but which might occasionally be drawn up over the head so as to cover every part of it, the face excepted. The hooded mantle, appropriated perhaps to the winter, was in common use towards the conclusion of the twelfth century.

The mantles of the women of quality at this period were made of silk and other valuable materials, and embroidered with variety of figures, especially at the borders;[1] and not unfrequently lined with costly furs of various kinds.

The Coverchief, or *veil*, formed, as we have seen, an indispensable part of the female habit before the Conquest; in the subsequent centuries, it not only underwent a great variety of alterations, but was often totally thrown aside. In some instances, and even prior to the commencement of the twelfth century, the coverchief is represented open in the front, so as to disclose the neck, and exhibit to the eye the richly embroidered collars of the gowns and mantles.[2] At other times it bears a closer resemblance to the coverchief of the Saxons, and conceals the neck, together with the upper part of the breast.[3] It is represented by the

[1] See plates XXXVI, XXXVII, and XL.

[2] See the middle figure, and the figure to the left, plate XXXVI.

[3] See the queen, plate XXXVII; and the middle figure, plate XXXVIII.

middle figure, upon the thirty-ninth plate, as hanging very low down on the left side of the head, while on the right it is thrown back over the shoulder. In the figure to the left hand, upon the same plate, one end of it is wrapped round the neck, and the other falls upon the right breast; but, on the opposite figure, one end of it is thrown across the breast and over the left shoulder so as to cover the other end completely: it is also gathered into two folds upon the top of the head, and confined by a diadem, or broad circle of gold. Part of it is wrapped about the neck like the *wimple*, or muffler; as we find in the figure, holding a sceptre, upon the fortieth plate; and probably the wimple, which in the succeeding century became a distinct part of the female habit, took its origin from this method of wearing the coverchief: indeed, as it is represented by the opposite figure upon the same plate, it has much the appearance of being separated from it. The coverchief in this instance which is a very singular one, falls on either side of the face, descending to a great length; insomuch, that on the right side it is bound in a knot to prevent its reaching to the ground.

Towards the conclusion of the twelfth century, the form of the coverchief was totally changed: it became much smaller, and was tied under the chin like the *cap*, or *bonnet*, of the modern day.[1] But, as we have observed above, it was by no means uncommon for the women at this period to appear without the coverchief.

When the hair is exposed to view, we find it constantly parted from the front of the head, and turned on either side of the face upon the shoulders. In the figure to the right, upon the thirty-sixth plate, two large locks of hair are brought forward, and fall loosely upon the breast without any additional embellishment; but it is very rare that we find the head-dress thus represented, and therefore may justly conclude that it was not commonly adopted. The figure bowing, upon the thirty-eighth plate, exhibits a very curious mode of decorating the hair: it is parted from the forehead, and falls at the back in two large masses, which are bound about with fillets or ribbands in the form of two tails, reaching nearly to the ground, and both of them ending with three small curls; and this kind of head-dress occurs more than once in the manuscript from which the present figure is selected.

Towards the conclusion of the twelfth century, the hair of persons arrived to the age of maturity was usually inclosed within a net, or cawl, in the manner it is represented at the bottom of the forty-first plate; over which the cap or coverchief was placed, and bound under the chin, as we find it exhibited by two women of

[1] See the two women-figures, plate XLI.

distinction upon the same plate. It was certainly indecorous for women of character at this time to appear with the cawls upon the hair without the coverchief, because, wherever we find them so depicted, they are constantly the representatives of common prostitutes.

The girls of the twelfth century wore their hair without any covering: it was parted from the forehead, and curled with great precision, as we find it delineated upon the forty-first plate.[1]

It is not possible to determine how the hair was dressed and decorated beneath the larger coverchief, but probably not without some degree of attention; for, whenever any part of it is accidentally discovered, it appears exceedingly neat and formal.

There were several ornamental decorations for the head in use among the Anglo-Norman ladies as early as the twelfth century. The richest and most splendid of them all was the Crown, appropriated only to the queen: it was worn over the coverchief, as we see it represented upon the thirty-seventh plate. The half Bend or Circle of gold: this ornament was also frequently used by the Saxon women; but at the same time it was so completely concealed by the coverchief, that we meet with no representations of it in the drawings executed before the Conquest.[2] The manner in which it appeared at the close of the eleventh century may be seen upon the thirty-eighth plate: the circular ornaments, with which the front of it is decorated, are probably intended for pearls or precious stones. The Diadem, or complete circle, which, like the crown, was worn upon the coverchief, as we see it depicted upon the thirty-ninth and fortieth plates: this ornament was generally made of gold, but not always: for, it is of a bright red colour in the figure bowing her head, upon the fortieth plate.[3]—To these may be added a kind of Tiara, which adorns the head of the lady to the right, upon the forty-first plate: this ornament, from the general appearance of it, seems to have been covered with linen, and probably it was attached to the coverchief.

The Stockings. If this part of the dress, appertaining to the Norman ladies, in reality underwent any material variation posterior to the Conquest, the variation cannot be traced; for the modesty of the ladies, who at that time adopted long garments, precludes the possibility of information.

The Shoes, in use during the eleventh and twelfth centuries, differed so little from those of the Anglo-Saxon ladies, spoken of in the former part of this work, that no particular description of them needs be made at present.

[1] [The MS. from which all the figures on this plate are taken is of the *thirteenth* century.—Ed.]

[2] See pages 18 and 74.

[3] [Red was occasionally used by the ancient illuminators as a substitute for gold.—Ed.]

CHAP. IV.

THE MILITARY HABITS OF THE ANGLO-NORMANS FROM THE CONQUEST TO THE CONCLUSION OF THE TWELFTH CENTURY.—THE MAIL ARMOUR.—THE MILITARY SURCOAT.—THE HELMETS.—THE SHIELDS.—THE SPEARS, SWORDS, AND OTHER IMPLEMENTS OF WAR.

IT has already been proved from incontestable authority, that a species of armour for the defence of the body was in use among the Saxon soldiery :[1] it was called in Latin *lorica ;* and the same word occurs in the writings of the Normans, to express the *coat of mail.*

The *mail armour*, however, as we find it in its improved state, posterior to the Conquest, differs so materially from the *lorica* of the Saxons, that we may with great propriety attribute it to the Normans, and proceed to consider it as a new kind of martial habiliment.

THE MAIL ARMOUR.

THE military accoutrements of a warrior in the days of the elder William, were the *hauberk,* the *helmet*, the *shield*, the *spear*, and the *sword.*[2]

The HAUBERK, originally the *coat*, or, perhaps, rather the *tunic* of *mail,* defended the body only: the *hood* was afterwards added, which protected the neck and the head. In this state we find it towards the conclusion of the eleventh century ; at which time the sleeves of the hauberk were loose and wide, and so short that the hands and the wrists were left without protection : it was also open from the hips downwards on both sides, and of course afforded very little safeguard to the thighs ; the legs and the feet at the same time were totally destitute of any kind of armour.[3]

[1] See p. 54 ; where this subject is fully investigated.

[2] We find them thus enumerated in the laws enacted by that monarch—" de releif al Cunte, que al Rei afeist VIII. chivalz selez e enfrenez, les IIII Halbers, e IIII Hammes, e IIII Escuz, e IIII Launces, e IIII Espés."—Leges Gulielmi I. cap. xxii.

[3] See two figures, the one to the right, and the other to the left, plate XLIII. [The latter figure is from a MS. of the commencement of the 13th century.—ED.]

The *coat of mail*, so far as one can judge of it by the earliest paintings, appears to have been composed of rings of metal quilted upon cloth or leather, in such a manner as to conform readily to the shape of the body: an example of which is given upon the forty-third plate in the figure to the right; in other instances, nearly as ancient, it seems to have consisted of small square plates of metal, attached in like manner to an under-garment, as we find it exhibited by the middle figure of the same plate: but, in the figure to the left, the coat of mail assumes its more usual appearance, and is evidently made of small rings, or chains of metal inserted one within the other, so as to be perfectly pliable; and at the same time so completely connected together as to form a habit of itself, independent of any other assistance.

Soon after the Conquest, the ancient *lorica*, or *coat of mail*, being found, I presume, inadequate to the purposes required from a defensive armour, other parts were added, which covered not only the thighs and the legs, but the feet also; and, at the same time, the sleeves of the coat itself were made to fit the arm with more precision, and so far lengthened as to secure the hand completely.[1] In this state we find it represented by the middle figure, upon the forty-third plate; and more perfectly by the three monumental figures, upon the three succeeding plates.

In the three figures, upon the forty-third plate, the *chaperon*, or *hood* of *mail*, which covers the neck and head, appears to be attached to the coat of mail, or rather to be a component part of it; and, perhaps, in ancient times it might occasionally be so; but, on the other hand, it is equally certain, that a far greater variety of instances may be produced in which the chaperon decidedly formed a separate part of the military habit. The coat of mail, in the example produced at the bottom of the forty-fourth plate, which is taken from a manuscript written and illuminated towards the conclusion of the eleventh century, appears without the chaperon.

In the time of action, the chaperon was drawn up over the head, and frequently supplied the place of an helmet. It was also occasionally thrown back upon the shoulders to give the warrior air; as we find it represented by the monumental figure of one of the Knights Templars, upon the forty-fourth plate.

The *ringed armour* of the ancient Saxons, and the *mail armour* of the Normans, as we find it depicted immediately posterior to the Conquest, bore great

[1] The part which covers the thighs, the legs, and the feet, was called *chausses*, or *breeches of mail*; and the part which covered the hands, the *gauntlets*, or *gloves of mail*, as we shall see more fully exemplified hereafter

analogy to each other.[1] It also seems clear that the Saxons had some faint idea of *plated armour*, derived probably from the Romans, but never carried by them to any great degree of perfection.[2] In the twelfth century the *mail* formed a complete defensive armour, and invested every part of the warrior, his face excepted; so that he may literally be said to have been armed *cap-à-pie*. The plated mail, in the form of small diamonds, appears to have been the first species of defensive armour completed by the Normans; and a curious specimen of it in its most perfect state is given upon the forty-third plate.[3] It disappeared, however, about the middle of the twelfth century, and was superseded by the *chain mail*, which was then introduced with additional improvements, and universally adopted. The monuments of the twelfth century, many of which are now in existence, convey a perfect idea of the chain mail: and from this source of information I have collected three curious specimens, which, I presume, will be deemed sufficient. The first is given upon the forty-fourth plate: the original of this figure is carved in stone, and may be found among the ancient monuments in the Temple church, at London. Tradition attributes it to Robert de Ros, who certainly was buried there;[4] and the armorial bearings upon the shield seem to justify that opinion. The two following plates are taken from monumental effigies existent in the church at Danbury, in Essex: they are probably something more ancient than the Knight Templar just mentioned, and, without doubt, belonged to the family of St. Clere, for in the twelfth century this family resided at Danbury Place.[5] These valuable reliques of ancient sculpture are carved in wood, a circumstance by no means uncommon; and, considering the little care that has been

[1] See pages 50 and 51, and plate XIV.

[2] See plates XXII. and XXIII. [Plate XXII. exhibits a figure of St. Michael in what Sir S. Meyrick has denominated *tegulated* armour, *i. e.* small overlapping pieces of metal of a tile form; a mere variety of the lorica squamata: but the warriors on plate XXIII. are not armed in *metal*, but in *leather*. Vide page 51, notes 1 and 2.—Ed.]

[3] See the middle figure, which is taken from a curious MS. of the twelfth century, in the possession of F. Douce, Esq. The resemblance this figure bears to the generality of the soldiers, represented upon the famous tapestry at Bayeux, imperfectly copied in the Monarchie François of Pere Montfaucon, would naturally lead one to conclude that both the tapestry and the MS. were nearly of the same date. [Sir S. Meyrick has designated this species of armour "mascled," and the Heraldic bearing, termed a mascle, being a metal plate of the lozenge form, with a hole in the centre, is supposed with much probability to have been assumed from the hauberk of this period.—Ed.]

[4] Mr. Gough, in the first volume of his *Sepulchral Monuments*, has given all the figures of the Knights Templars, that are remaining in the Temple Church, upon a large scale. [I believe nearly all these effigies belong to the thirteenth century. Vide Stothard's work for an accurate representation. —Ed.]

[5] See Morant's History of Essex. Camden, in Essex, with Mr. Gough's additions.

taken for their preservation, it is really wonderful to find them so perfect as they now remain. I have spoken warmly in commendation of these admirable monuments in a former publication;[1] and I hope the engravings, however they may fall short of the perfection of the originals, will at least convey some idea of the ease and elegancy with which they are executed: at the same time I must confess myself perfectly at a loss to account for the peculiar excellency of these figures, when compared with others of the same æra, or set in competition with the drawings and paintings of the time. which were greatly deficient both in taste and correctness.

THE MILITARY SURCOAT.

This garment was certainly introduced by the Normans; and indeed it does not appear to have been generally adopted before the middle of the twelfth century: it was made apparently of cloth, without sleeves, and reached below the knees; it was also open in the front from the girdle to the bottom, and fitted to the neck so closely, that the top part of it is usually hid by the chaperon, or hood of mail. I am by no means well acquainted with the utility of the surcoat at the time of its first introduction. It the twelfth century it does not appear to have been marked with the *arms* or *insignia* of the wearer, which was usually the case in the succeeding centuries, when it may properly be considered as a badge of distinction.[2]

There are three representations given of the military surcoat, as it appeared in the twelfth[3] century, upon the forty-fourth, forty-fifth, and forty-sixth plates; which will, I trust, convey a clear idea of its form, and the manner in which it was worn upon the mail, and preclude the necessity of any farther description.

[1] See the hoꞃꝺa Anᵹel-cẏnnan, or Manners and Customs of the English, vol. I. [These also are effigies of the thirtenth century.—Ed.]

[2] I apprehend that the *military surcoat,* prior even to its being embroidered with the armorial bearings of the wearer, was a garment used for distinction sake, and worn only by the principal officers in the army; and indeed the frequent appearance of the *mail* without the *surcoat,* in the drawings of the eleventh and twelfth centuries, may be thought to strengthen this opinion; nor need we wonder in the least that the monumental effigies, which of course were the representatives of distinguished personages, should rarely be divested of this garment. [The received opinion is that the surcoat was first worn over the armour by the early crusaders to veil the iron from the heat of the Syrian sun, as well as to distinguish the many different leaders in those expeditions. King John is the first English monarch who is represented in a surcoat. A. D. 1199.—Ed.]

[3] [Thirteenth.—Ed.]

THE HELMETS.

THE conical helmet of the Saxons, described in a former part of this work,[1] was adopted by the Normans at the time of their establishment in England, with the improvement of a small plate of metal added to the front which descended to the bottom of the nose, and protected the upper part of the face from a cross blow of the sword, and may properly enough be called the NASAL HELMET. There are four specimens of the *nasal helmet* given upon the forty-third plate, one of which is flattened at the top, and apparently ornamented with a circle, or diadem, enriched with precious stones.[2]

The CHAP DE MAILLES, or *mail cap*, succeeded the *nasal helmet*, and was worn over the chaperon, as we find it represented in great perfection upon the forty-fifth and forty-sixth plates.

The FLAT HELMET. I really do not know by what name more appropriate to distinguish the head-piece, given at the bottom of the forty-fourth plate: I mean the head to the left, where the part of the mail, which in other instances forms the chaperon, in the present can be considered as a gorget only; the intermediate space between the gorget and the helmet is filled up with a hood of leather, or some material apparently of equal substance, which covers the greater part of the face and mouth itself entirely. This *head-piece* is copied from one of the monuments existent in the Temple church at London.

The CYLINDRICAL HELMET occurs among the monumental figures in the Temple church. It is flat upon the top, excepting a small ridge extending over the surface; it is rather larger above than at the bottom, from which an appendage passes on both sides of the face beneath the chin, on purpose, I suppose, to keep it firmly upon the head, and a small piece of metal in the front covering only the upper part of the nose.

All these helmets, the *chap de mailles* excepted, were evidently made of metal plates, either of brass or iron; and in some instances they appear to be gilt.[3]

[1] Page 54.

[2] See the figure to the left hand.

[3] The helmet belonging to the middle figure, upon the forty-third plate, in the original MS. is gold. The helmet, on the figure to the left, is enriched with a circle of gold set with precious stones: the lower rim of the helmet, at the top of the same plate, is yellow; and the helmet of the figure to the right is blue.

THE SHIELDS, SWORDS, SPEARS, &c.

THE oval shields so generally used by the Anglo-Saxons were totally laid aside by the Normans, who introduced others of a quite different form, which continued in fashion for several centuries: they were broad and flat at the top, and diminished gradually to the bottom, where they ended in an apex, or point. They were, undoubtedly, of various sizes, but rarely smaller than the one we find represented upon the forty-third plate, which is also bent round the body in a very singular manner;[1] for in general they appear to be flat or nearly so.

The Norman shields were often richly ornamented with gilded borders; and, towards the conclusion of the twelfth century, such of them as belonged to the nobility were usually decorated with the armorial bearings, adopted by the wearer, or appropriated to his family.

The SWORDS of the Normans differed little either in size or in form from those of the Saxons. I shall only observe, that in general they appear to have been rather larger towards the conclusion of the twelfth century.

The SPEARS. If we may judge from the spear-heads represented upon the forty-third plate, and especially from that supported by the middle figure, we shall not hesitate to say that they were considerably increased in size by the Normans: their form also appears to be different from those of the Saxons; and they are rarely represented like them with a jagged part, or barb, at the bottom.

The BOW, as a weapon of war, was certainly introduced by the Normans;[2] and, indeed, the elder William is said to have chiefly owed his victory at Hastings to the skill of his archers.

If the CROSS-BOW was not brought into this country at the time of the Conquest, it is certain that it made its appearance here soon after that period; but, as I have not met with the representation of it in any manuscript delineations so early as the twelfth century, I shall decline entering any farther upon the subject at present.

[1] [This figure is from a MS. of the 13th century as I have already remarked: but the semi-cylindrical shield may be seen on the seals of Richard the First and others of the close of the 12th century.—ED.]

[2] [It would be sufficient, perhaps, to say that the bow had fallen into disuse amongst the Saxons for some time anterior to the Conquest.—ED.]

CHAP. V.

THE ECCLESIASTICAL HABITS OF THE ELEVENTH AND TWELFTH CENTURIES GENERALLY CONSIDERED—INCREASED IN SPLENDOUR, AND ALTERED IN THEIR FORM.—ANECDOTE OF WULFSTAN, BISHOP OF WORCESTER.—THE HABIT OF AN ARCHBISHOP.—THE ADMISSION OF ST. GUTHLAC INTO PRIEST'S ORDERS.—THE HABIT OF AN ABBESS.—THE HABIT OF A LAY PREACHER, AND OF A PILGRIM.

From the middle of the eleventh to the close of the twelfth century, the ecclesiastical habits of this country underwent several material variations: they were not only composed of richer materials than those of the preceding centuries, and more elegantly decorated with embroidery and jewels; but they differed also in their form, as may be seen in the various examples referred to in this chapter.

It is certain, that the habits of the clergy increased in splendour in proportion as the love of finery became prevalent among the people at large. The reign of Rufus is notorious for its luxuries, and for those especially that relate to dress. "*At this time*," says the editor of an old chronicle, "*priests used bushed and breyded hedes, long tayled gowns, and blasyn clothes, shinyng and golden girdelles, and rode with gulit spurres with useing of dyverse other enormities.*"[1] The sumptuary laws of Henry the First are said to contain some few restrictions relative to the habits of the clergy, such as confining the external parts of them to one colour, and reducing their shoes to a decent length, but these restrictions seem to have respected those garments only that were worn by the ecclesiastics when they were not employed in the performance of their religious duties, and may properly enough be called their secular dress; for, their official habits, especially such of them as belonged to the prelates and other dignified clergy, were profusely rich, and decorated with all kinds of expensive ornaments:[2] they were lined with furs, and those also

[1] Fabian's Chron. in the life of Rufus. And this account is confirmed by Malmesbury, who assures us, that neither the preaching nor the authority of Anselm could correct these vices.—De Gest. Reg. Angliæ, lib. IV, cap. i.

[2] The regular habits of the monks, the friars, and the nuns, were governed by the ecclesiastical canons; and, indeed, the only restrictive passage I find in the laws of Henry the First, respecting the clergy, is in the fifth chapter; which is thus expressed: *De habitu et vestitu nihil legimus imperatum divinitùs; quæ ad pompam sunt prohibentur.*—Lambert de Legibus Anglorum.

of the most expensive kind, as we may learn from the following curious anecdote related by William of Malmesbury. This author, speaking of Wulfstan bishop of Worcester, assures us, that he avoided all appearance of pride and ostentation in his dress; and though he was very wealthy, he never used any furs finer than lambs' skins for the lining of his garments. Being blamed for such needless humility by Geoffry bishop of Constans, who told him that "he not only could afford, but even ought, to wear those of sables, of beavers, or of foxes,"[1] he replied, "it may indeed be proper for you politicians, skilful in the affairs of this world, to adorn yourselves with the skins of such cunning animals; but, for me who am a plain man, and not subject to change my opinion, the skins of lambs are quite sufficient." "If," returned his opponent, "the finer furs are unpleasant, you might at least make use of those of cats." "Believe me," answered the facetious prelate, "the Lamb of God is much oftener sung in the church than the cat of God." This witty retort put Geoffry to the blush, and threw the whole company into a violent fit of laughter.

The official habit of an Archbishop, as it appeared towards the close of the twelfth century, is given upon the fiftieth plate of this work: the original delineation is executed with great care, and apparently with equal exactness. The artist designed this curious specimen of his abilities for the portrait of Dunstan archbishop of Canterbury; but, from his total ignorance of the Saxon costume, he has substituted that of his own time, and contented himself with copying faithfully the archbishop's habit as it appeared before him; for, upon comparison, we shall find it differs greatly from the dresses of higher antiquity already given,[2] not only with respect to the richness of its adornments, but also in the form and adjustment of its several parts. The mitre especially, which was flat at the top in the time of the Saxons,[3] approaches, in the present instance, more nearly to the modern form, and is elevated considerably above the head, where it terminates in two points.

The forty-eighth plate is taken from an ancient parchment roll, which contains, in seventeen similar circles, the legendary life of St. Guthlac:[4] this is the eleventh circle; and in it is represented Guthlac's admission into Priest's orders. He appears to be kneeling before the altar, and holds the sacramental cup in both his hands. The prelate, designed by the artist for the portraiture of Hedda, bishop of Winchester, is arrayed in the pontifical habit, and drawn in the act of bestowing his benediction. The figures behind St. Guthlac are, I presume, the *deacon*, the *sub-*

[1] *Sabellinas, vel castorinas, vel vulpinas pelles.*—Guliel. Malmesb. de vitâ S. Wulfstani, p. 259.

[2] See plates XXVI. and XXVII. [3] See the middle figure, plate XXV.

[4] [This MS. is of the early part of the thirteenth century.—Ed.]

deacon, and others of the inferior clergy. The middle figure also of the forty-seventh plate represents a priest in his canonical habit.

The habit of a Monk of the twelfth century is given upon the forty-seventh plate, where the reader is referred to the figure on the right hand holding a book, and pointing: the cowl, or hood, annexed to the external garment, is here represented thrown back upon the shoulders; but the manner in which it appeared, when it was drawn up over the head, may be seen at the bottom of the same plate. The middle figure of the forty-ninth plate exhibits another monk, who was probably of a different order, because we find a manifest difference in the dress of the two figures: the cowls, for instance, are dissimilar in their shape; and the garments of the latter are considerably shorter than those of the former.

The figure to the left, upon the forty-seventh plate, is the representation of an Abbess, as she appeared towards the conclusion of the twelfth century. Her habit is perfectly simple, consisting only of a long white tunic with close sleeves, probably made of linen; and a black surcoat of equal length with the tunic, which she holds up with her left hand for the conveniency of walking. The sleeves of the surcoat are large and loose; and the hood belonging to it is drawn up so as to cover the back part of the head completely.

The figure holding a purse to the left, upon the forty-ninth plate, is habited in a very singular manner, bearing little or no analogy to the ecclesiastical habits appropriated to the present century; but he is called a preacher in the original manuscript, and for that reason I have given him a place in this part of the work. He is reproachfully spoken of by the author as one of the hypocritical deceivers of that time, who preached merely for gain;[1] which is indicated by the full purse that he holds in his hand. This is probably the ancient habit of the *lay-preachers*, a class of men not holden in the highest estimation by the monastic fraternities.

The Pilgrim's habit, represented by the figure to the right upon the forty-ninth plate, is exceedingly curious, being the earliest painting of the kind that I have met with. His tunic is short for the conveniency of travelling; but the sleeves are wide and loose: his mantle is ornamented with a broad welt, or border; it is fastened in the front, and reaches below the tunic; it is composed of skins dressed with the fur part outwards, and has the appearance of being lined: the hood is thrown back, and his head is defended from the weather by a hat, which is

[1] Two bishops are represented in the act of reproving him, and those also that are listening to him; the inscription opposite runs thus: *hoc significat, quòd prelati ecclesiæ debent prohibere falsos prædicatores; et maximè eos, qui pro quæstu predicant.*

however, by no means well fitted to it: he wears the coxalia, or trowsers, which reach to his ancles, and are bound upon his legs by leg-bandages in the manner already described;[1] but his feet are entirely naked, agreeable to the ancient custom of performing penance. A staff was the constant companion of these religious itinerants: the one we see in the present instance is large enough to be rather cumbrous than useful; it is, however, pointed at the top, and appears to be curiously decorated with carved work.

[1] See page 41. [With the exception of the Pilgrim taken from the Cotton MS. Nero C. IV. all the figures on plates 47, 48, and 49, are from MSS. of the early part of the thirteenth century.—Ed.]

END OF THE FIRST VOLUME.

1 2 3

4

5

6

Egyptian Habits.

1 2 3

4 5

Egyptian Habits.

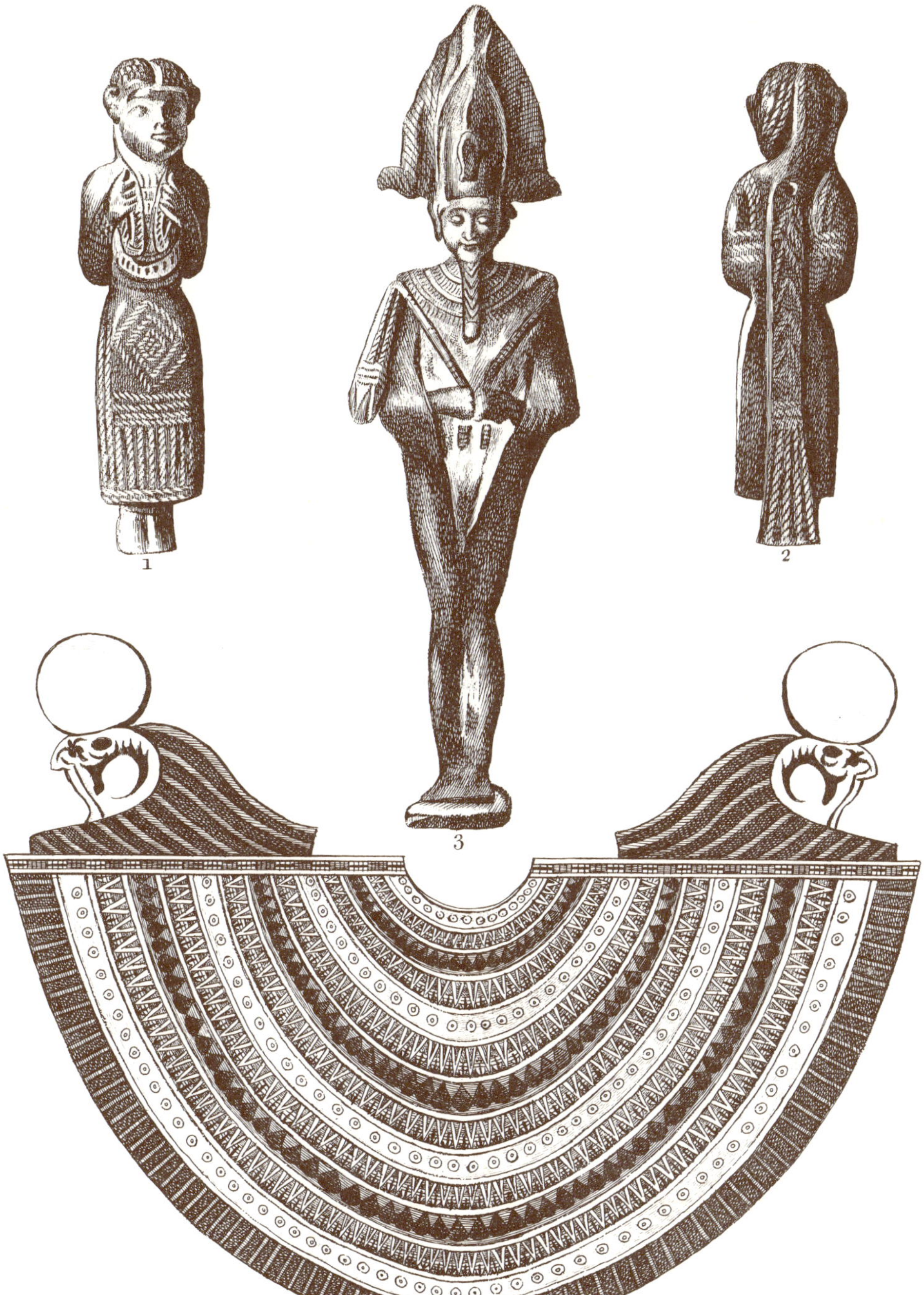

Egyptian Habits.

Egyptian Habits.

1 2 3

4

5

Grecian Armour.

1

2

Grecian Habits.

Pl. 7.

Grecian Armour.

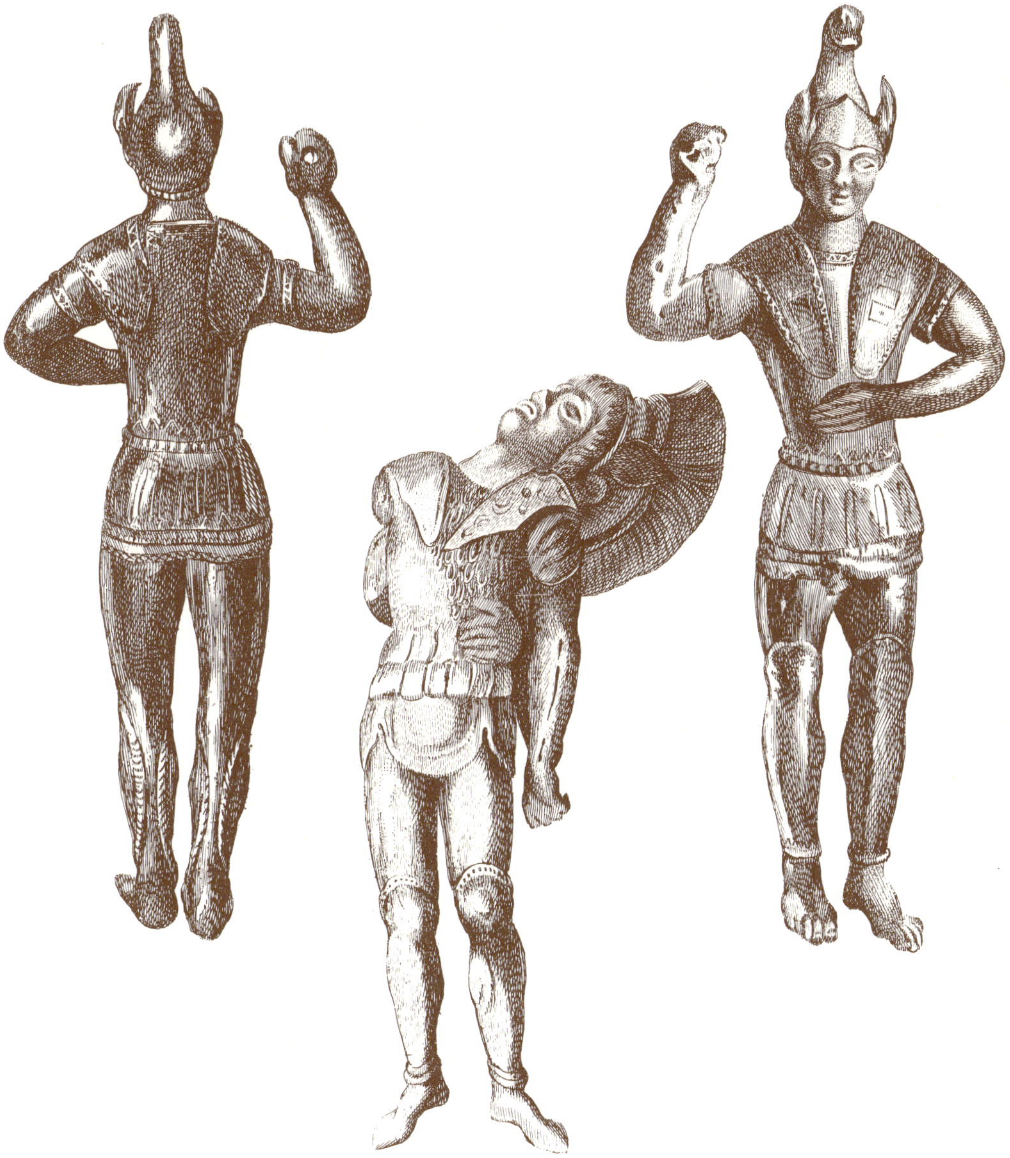

Grecian Armour.

Saxon Rustics,
of the eighth Century.

The Saxon Tunic.
as worn in the eighth Century.

The Anglo-Saxon Monarch
of the eighth Century, in a habit of State.

Pl. IV.

An Anglo Saxon Nobleman,
in his State Dress.

The Saxon Mantles,
as worn in the eighth century.

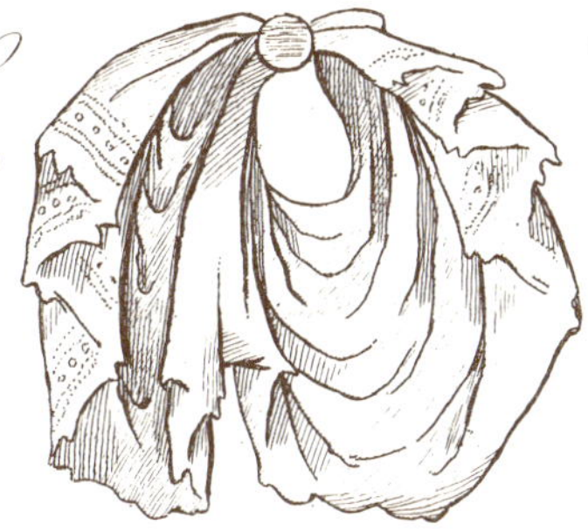

Pl. VI.

The Mantles
of the eighth century continued.

A Personage of Distinction
of the eighth century, in full Dress.

Pl. VIII.

A Monarchal State Habit,
of the eighth Century

Pl.IX.

Dresses of the Anglo Saxon Women.
of the eighth Century.

Pl. X.

The Dresses of the Women,
of the eighth Century continued.

The Summer Dress & Travelling Habit.
of the Ladies of the eighth Century.

Pl. XII.

An Anglo Saxon Lady,
of the eighth Century, in full Dress.

Military Habits,
of the eighth Century.

Pl. XIV.

The Saxon King in his Martial Habit
with his Armour Bearer.

Ecclesiastical Habits.
of the eighth Century.

Pl. XVI.

Aldhelm Bishop of Sherbon.

Pl. XVII.

The Anglo Saxon Monarch,
of the Ninth Century, in his State Habit.

Pl. XVIII.

Dresses of the Ninth & Tenth Centuries.

Pl. XIX.

Personages of Distinction
of the Ninth & Tenth Centuries.

A Lady of the Ninth Century
in full Dress.

Pl. XXI.

Saxon Ladies.
of the ninth & tenth Centuries.

Pl. XXII.

An Ancient Statue,
found in Monmouthshire.

Military Habits.
of the tenth Century.

Danish Habits.

from a curious Saxon Reliquary,
in the Possession of Thoˢ. Astle Esqʳ.

Pl. XXV.

Ecclesiastics

of the tenth & eleventh Centuries

Abbot Elfnoth.

Presenting a book of prayer to the Monastery of St Augustin.

Wulfstan Archbishop of York.

Pl. XXVIII.

Edward the Confessor.
from his great Seal.

Funeral Habits & Saxon Ornaments, &c

1.2.3.4 Crowns & Diadems.

5.6. Royal Helmets......	7.8.9.10 Helmets
11.12. Caps or Hats......	13.14. Arm Bracelets
15. A Signet Ring....	16. A Shoe
17. A Sword and Belt.	18. The double Ax or Bipennis

Pl. XXX.

Norman Rustics,
of the Eleventh Century.

Pl. XXXI.

Anglo-Norman Youths.
of the Eleventh Century.

Pl. XXXII.

Anglo-Norman Habits, of the Eleventh Century.

Pl. XXXIII.

An Anglo-Norman Nobleman,
of the Eleventh Century in his State-Habit.

Pl. XXXIV.

The Regal State Habit,
of the Eleventh Century.

Pl. XXXV.

HENRY I. HENRY II.

from their great Seals.

Pl. XXXVI.

Anglo-Norman Women,
of the Eleventh Century.

An Anglo-Norman Queen.
of the eleventh Century.

Dresses of the Eleventh Century.

Women of the Twelfth Century.

Pl. XL.

Ladies of the Twelfth Century.
in full Dress.
from a curious M.S. in the Possession of
F. Douce Esq.r

Pl.XLI.

Female Dresses,
of the Twelfth Century.

Pl. XLII.

Norman Dresses.
of the Twelfth Century.

Pl. XLIII.

Soldiers,

of the Eleventh & Twelfth Centuries.

Pl. XLIV.

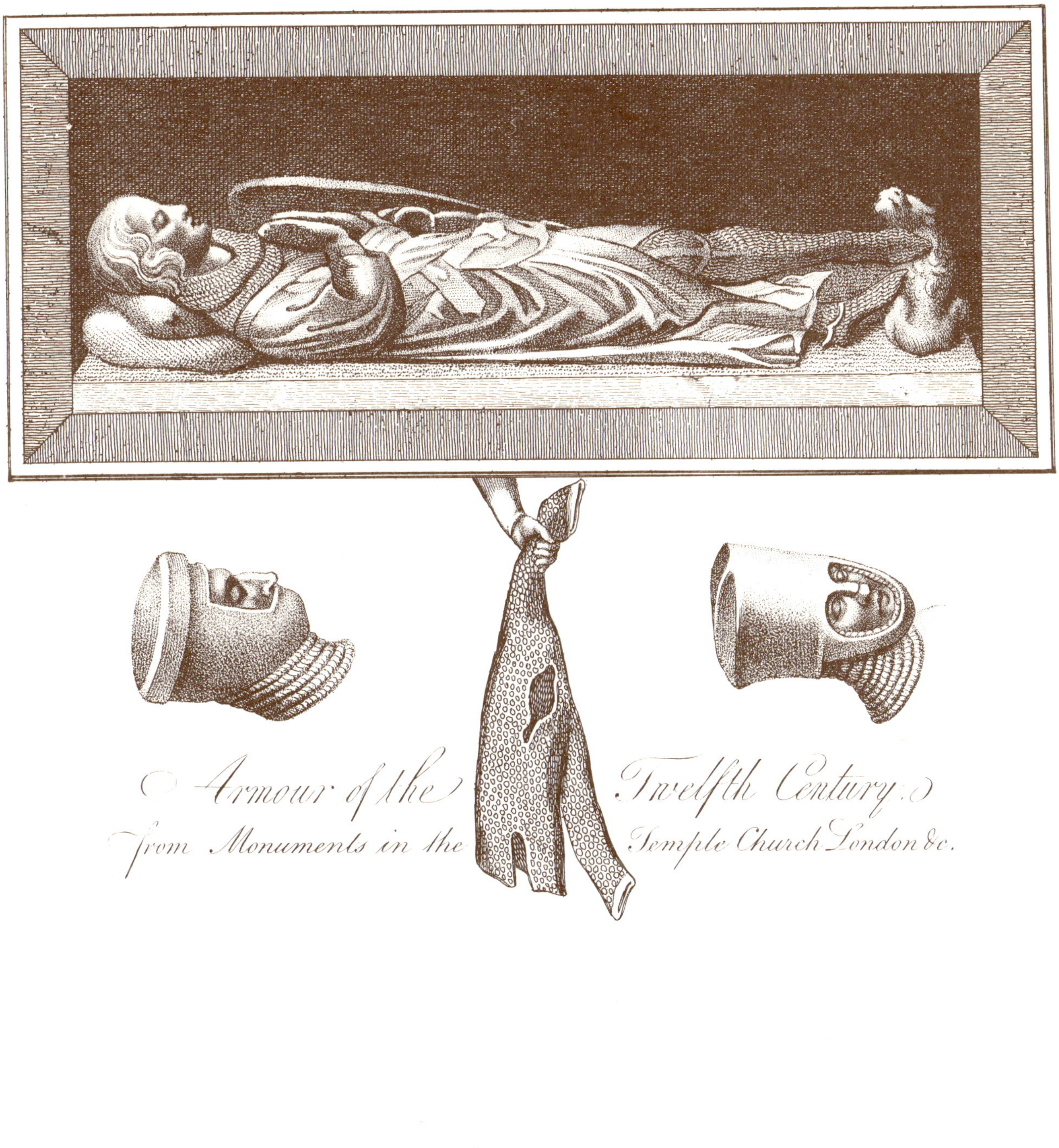

Armour of the Twelfth Century.
from Monuments in the Temple Church London &c.

Pl. XLV.

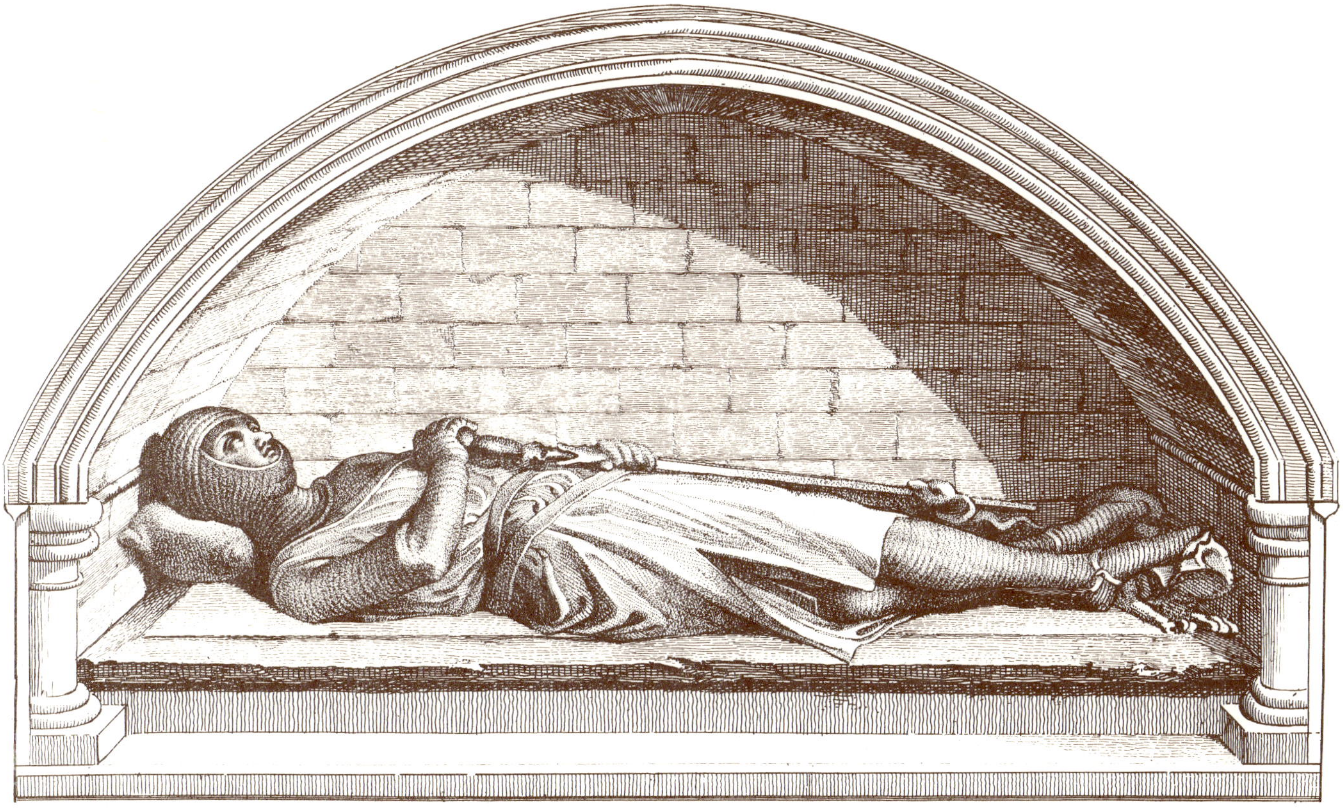

From a Monument of the 12th Century
in Danbury Church Essex.

Pl.XLVI.

In Danbury Church. Essex.

Pl. XLVII.

Monastical Habits
of the twelfth Century.

Ecclesiastical Habits,
of the twelfth Century.

Pl. XLIX.

Ecclesiastical Habits.

of the 12th Century.

Pl. L.

Dunstan Archbishop of Canterbury.
from a M.S. of the 12th Century.

Rustics,
of the 13th Century.

Pl. LII.

Habits of the 13th Century.

Hunting Habits
of the 13 Century.

Habits of the 13th Century.

Pl. LV.

A Physician & his Servant.
from a M.S. of the 13th Centy

Pl. LVI.

A Nobleman of the 13th Century,
in his Habit of State.

A Regal State Habit,
of the 13th Centy

A Coronation Habit,
of the 13th. Cent.y

Pl. LIX.

Henry the Third.

from a M.S of the 13th. Cent.y

Pl.LX.

The Coronation of Edward the First.

Pl. LXI.

Young Women of the 13.th Century.

Ladies of the 13.th Century.

Pl. LXIII.

Ladies of the 13.th Cent.y

A Queen of the 13.th Century.
in her Habit of State.

Pl.LXV.

Military Habits,
of the 13th Centy.

Pl. LXVI.

A Knight of the 13th Century in his Military Habit.

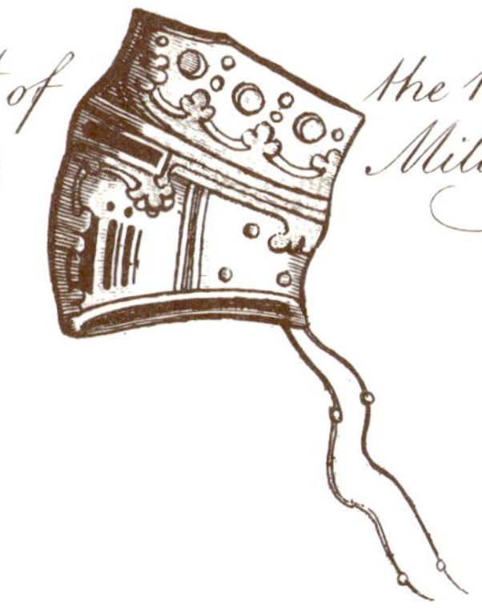

Pl. LXVII.

Ecclesiastical Habits,
of the 13th Century.

An Official Habit of an Archbishop.
in the 13th Cent.y